THE LIFE OF A REAL GIRL

THE LIFE OF A REAL GIRL

JOHANNA GARFIELD

ST. MARTIN'S PRESS
New York

All the characters and events in this book are real, but many names and geographic locations have been changed in order to protect the privacy of those involved.

Design by Amy Bernstein

Library of Congress Cataloging in Publication Data

Garfield, Johanna.
    The life of a real girl.

    1. Garfield, Johanna—Mental health. 2. Garfield, Johanna—Health. 3. Bulimarexia—Patients—United States—Biography. 4. Behavior modification. I. Title.
RC552.B84G37   1986   616.85'2   86-3797
ISBN 0-312-48399-6

First Edition

10 9 8 7 6 5 4 3 2 1

To Hayes, who got me started and stuck with it to the end;
To Ellyn and Dick, for much help along the way;
and especially
To Leslie, for his love, encouragement, and support
throughout.

PROLOGUE: LITANIES

The other day I overheard someone saying solicitously to a friend, "How are you now?" Then—as often when I least expect it—a phrase or sentence will work on me with the force of Proust's madeleine, and I am transported back to the world of Great Oaks, a private mental hospital where I spent two years in my early twenties.

It was the "now" at the end of the ordinary inquiry that did it. Harry Horner, an outpatient at the Oaks at a midway point in his ascent from depressive to manic—his hair a grizzled gray, his manner impetuous, his voice rasping, kindly, sardonic—would drive in every spring and summer evening, park in the driveway below the wards, and chant in a half-humorous, half-mocking tone, "Well, and how are ya now, sonny?" as he gazed up at the patients imprisoned behind crossed-wire fences who gathered for this diversion during the long, painfully beautiful Virginia evenings. He would repeat this over and over, chewing on his shredded cigar with increasing impatience, until someone on the third floor ("Men's, seriously disturbed") would softly reply, "Fine, just fine, and how are ya now, sonny?" the first three words on one note, the "now" about four tones up, the "sonny" in-between, exactly as Harry had done. Harry would repeat the same question and get back the same response five or six times until, satisfied, he would leap into his clattering convertible and speed out the long drive that led to the gate of the extensive grounds. His words were sad and ironic, a mockery of polite interchange in the context of Great Oaks. For how could, or would, anyone be in that strange and terrible world?

Like Harry, a number of patients at the Oaks had certain stock phrases or sentences they would intone almost as a litany; in many cases, these were the only words they would say, and they were spoken with a strange urgency. After a while, these seemingly ordinary utterances, heard over and over, would take on haunting, mystical, almost prophetic second meanings to my ear, just as Harry's had done.

Mary Acosta was hideous and frightening to me when I first saw her. Always accompanied by a student nurse (a sure sign of violent or unreliable behavior on the patient's part), she would wander the grounds haphazardly, her body almost doubled over, her clothes torn, often crying or making ugly, inarticulate, strangled sounds. Her blond hair was stringy and unkempt, her face haggard, with powdery white skin. She had glassy china-blue eyes and an unattractive mole on her cheek. I was told she was forty-five and had been at the Oaks for at least fifteen years. With what I came to recognize as the incredible intuition of the insane, she recognized my fear, and often seemed to single me out maliciously for those rare instances when she attempted human contact. She always said the same thing. A long white arm would suddenly shoot out from her rags and a hand clutch at her victim's arm. Almost choking with the effort, she would croak, "I

viii

want to get well and see my mother; I want to get well and see my mother." Exhausted by this effort, she would wander off again, the nurse following nervously behind. The fact that her mother visited often in no way diminished the pathos of this fifteen-year plea. Clearly, she was not going to get better, and her pathetic cries only seemed to dramatize the hopelessness of her own, and so many others, cases, in the pre-tranquilizer world of the early fifties.

Mary had one other phrase, which I would puzzle over and try to relate to her single sentence. I was convinced that if someone could figure out what the sentences meant to her, she would be cured instantly. This phrase, spoken in the same way—almost as if she had no vocal cords and were forcing the sounds from her diaphragm—was, "That other brown one . . . That other brown one." Did it refer to food? Clothes? Perhaps in some Freudian way to fecal matter? But neither I nor the analysts could decipher the code, and now my children wonder why I sometimes seem startled when, in choosing a cookie, one of them may carelessly say something like, "Oh, give me that other one—that other brown one."

When I first arrived at the Oaks in 1953, I was placed on the second floor, a locked ward inhabited by the less violent and self-destructive women patients. Though my stay on that floor was brief, it was during that time that I first observed Nina—a dark, brooding girl who appeared to be about fourteen, but who I later found was about nineteen. She had been on the floor four years, and her behavior never varied. All day she would pace—the corridor in winter, the fenced-in porch in summer—a secret smile playing about her lips, her arms tightly folded across her chest, dressed in the neat but sadly inappropriate attire of a fifties schoolgirl: plaid skirt, white blouse with Peter Pan collar, sweater, bobby sox, and "saddle shoes." And as she paced, she would bitterly mutter over and over, "Me and my mother in Westchester County; my mother and me in Westchester County." Many times I wondered what domestic tragedy lay behind these words. Or perhaps they were intended as some kind of scathing social commentary on the misguided values of suburban life, which may have driven Nina to her present pass. She never explained, nor did she ever exchange any other words with anyone else, staff or patient. She was still on the second floor when I left the Oaks two years later. I have only to hear someone say, "Oh, we're moving to Westchester County," to evoke the puzzling and tormented image of Nina pacing back and forth, back and forth.

In time, I, like Harry, also drove down that long road and out the gate, though, unlike Harry, I never returned to exchange empty amenities with my former intimates. Yet my memories of the Oaks return with a clarity denied me when I try to remember people and events of much more recent vintage. And I wonder, "How are they now? How are they all now, sonny?"

PART ONE

PART ONE

CHAPTER 1

When I was sixteen, I was starving myself to death. My periods had stopped, and my arms were so skinny that my brother Frank, three and a half years older, said I had "wrists like a bird." At seventeen, I weighed 225 pounds. The dowdy misses dresses my slender mother brought home for me from Lane Bryant were size 44. My favorite ring had to be cut from my finger. Even my feet were fat. I wore 8½ E.

The sequence of events leading to that ultimate grotesquerie went something like this. One day when I was fourteen, I walked into my mother's dressing room in the large Dutch Colonial house I grew up in in Cedarhurst, Long Island—a community known then to those interested in such matters as having the highest per capita income in the United States. My mother—a dark, striking woman who was often said to resemble Delores Del Rio—was putting Maybelline mascara on her lashes in clotty balls that drove me crazy. Suddenly, she looked at me out of the corners of her narrowed eyes, and said, "Jo dear, you're getting a little heavy, don't you think?"

I looked in her full-length mirror and saw a tall girl (five foot six was tall for a fourteen-year-old in the forties) with slightly longer than shoulder-length brown hair worn in a style as close to Lauren Bacall's sultry dip as she could get it, wearing a loose pullover sweater, a pleated skirt with a large plaid pattern that did nothing to modify her hip size, loafers with a penny in each, and bobby sox on what she was sure were the world's most shapeless legs. The skirt, she remembered, was held together with a safety pin where it wouldn't close.

My mother was right, I had to admit it. I weighed 150. Too much even for my height. And I knew I was overeating with Mitzi, my only close friend at school. We had the kind of passionate, twenty-four-hour-a-day, phoning, visiting, giggling friendship only teenagers can keep up. Mitzi—stocky, freckled, with auburn hair, long dark eyelashes that I secretly envied and all the poise I lacked—loved to eat, too. Not to eat with Mitzi was to reject her, maybe even to try to be better than she was. That would be impossible.

Every day we went to the Chateau Pharmacy, the school hangout, to moon over the glamour couple of the school—beautiful Nanette Mermelstein in a fuzzy pink angora sweater, and Bobby Steinberg, football team captain and a top student, too. Guiltily, I'd eat two scoops of coffee ice cream as we sat at the counter and tried to watch their mirrored reflections flirt in the booth behind us. After that, on the way out, I'd buy a Goldenberg's Peanut Chews and Mitzi would buy an Oh Henry to eat on the walk to her house.

"You really ought to take off a few pounds, dear," my mother continued. I was surprised by her persistence.

Though I knew I wasn't the slim, confident daughter she'd have liked, neither did she often criticize my appearance. And suddenly, on that day, I was imbued with a desire to lose weight. I would please my mother, please myself, steel myself to Mitzi's possible resentment. It was almost as though I'd been waiting for just those magic words to trigger what was soon to become an obsession.

I started to diet—sensibly the first time around; counting calories, measuring, being a pest about following the family doctor's small mimeographed sheets (breakfast: a half grapefruit, one boiled egg, a half piece of whole-wheat toast, etc.) to the last ounce. Filled with the fanatic determination of the newly converted, I substituted grapefruit juice for the double cones at the Chateau, apples for the Peanut Chews.

Mitzi didn't reject me. She was surprised but impressed, even a little envious. ("I don't know how you do it, Jo. Well, guess I'll get around to it one of these days," she said. I marveled at her casual self-acceptance.) The diet worked, and I went from 150 in November to 135 in January.

Then something happened—in my case, at least, the first ripple of the tidal wave to follow. When I got closer to my goal, not only did I lose my will to diet, I couldn't even keep off the weight I'd lost. I began to eat with Mitzi again—to eat more than ever.

But I noticed differences in the way Mitzi and I ate. She was enjoying her ice cream; I wasn't. I just had to have it. And we were both gaining weight, but I was gaining more. I was eating a lot at home, too. She wasn't. And

I was alarmed about what was happening to me, more than I'd ever been. Mitzi wasn't.

I went from 135 pounds in January to 165 by June. Camp, which I'd gone to with my brother and cousins every summer since I was three, was out of the question by spring. I refused to go. I was too embarrassed and miserable.

My mother called Sy Kolker, a doctor friend of the family in New York City. A pragmatic man, he said, "Well, if she can't cut the eating down by herself, why don't we try a few weeks in New York Hospital?" Glossing over my mother's shock at such an extreme measure, he reassured her that everything would be all right. "That'll make it easier for her—take it out of her hands," he said. His eyes twinkled. He was delighted to have come up with such a simple solution to the problem. And I was secretly relieved. Yes, I wanted someone to "take it out of my hands."

Nobody seemed to wonder about my emotional state, or question why a supposedly normal teenager would willingly spend her summer losing weight in the depressing milieu of a hospital. Psychiatry was still a hush-hush word in the forties. You had to be crazy, right?

I went into the hospital in early July and left in mid-August. Total loss: fifteen pounds. Reason the loss wasn't more: When I was allowed out of the hospital for a walk, I went straight to the candy store and stocked up on Little Chunky candy bars. I'd wrap them in Kleenex and hide them in the drawer beside my bed, eating them, to my own disgust and self-hatred, when the nurses were out of the room.

I began to feel more and more that I had no control

over what I was doing. I felt some outside power was impelling me, against my will, to buy those Chunkies. It was all ludicrous and terrible, and I felt the nurses, though outwardly friendly, secretly despised me. What was I, a great, hulking girl of fifteen, doing in an expensive hospital surrounded by really sick people? I went home to sit out the rest of the summer and promptly regained the fifteen pounds. But it was the beginning of my sophomore year, and I had to go back to school. By the time school began, I had gained five more pounds. I was 170 now—the most I'd ever weighed. I persuaded Mitzi, who was still overweight, though no longer in my league, to go on a diet with me. Maybe with her support I could succeed. And surely what my father said must be so: All that was needed was a little "will power."

I exerted my will—put everything else out of my head except losing weight. This time it worked. It worked too well. I lost twenty pounds in two months, hit a plateau, and started eating less and less to get results. The lack of control over my eating that had alarmed me was replaced by a new and heady sense of power.

Summer came once again, and I was down to 130. But I still wanted to be thinner. I lost eight more pounds. All I could think about now was not eating. Depleted of strength, I was listless and made no plans. My parents insisted I do something—anything—and sent me on a teen tour of the West with my cousin Toni, nine other girls, and a chaperone.

Toni—daughter of my father's youngest sister—was even closer to me than Mitzi, but because she lived in Philadelphia, I didn't get to see her often. I was delighted at the thought of a trip with her.

My momentary elation at the thought of so much time with Toni was brief. When the trip actually began, my preoccupation with losing weight grew even worse. I looked at the Grand Canyon and worried about whether I'd gain if I ate the yolk of my egg or put salt on the white part. I became obsessed with scales, scouting through every hotel till I found one, miserable if I didn't. My life seemed to depend on where the needle on the scale stopped. If it didn't go down from the day before, I'd punish myself and eat nothing all day. I didn't talk to the other girls; didn't want Toni to talk with them; wanted to be alone with her and with my obsession.

Toni was baffled and upset. She tried to be sympathetic, but at sixteen was hardly equipped to handle what I realized years later was the onset of anorexia. We cut the trip short and came home a week early.

When we got home, I weighed 105. I had no energy, but stuck rigidly to my self-imposed near fast. Even the reliable hard-boiled eggs seemed part of a conspiracy to make me fat again. Still, no one mentioned the possibility of psychological problems.

My mother and father began to nag me to eat, but I wouldn't modify my insane diet. I would sit at the dinner table slowly chewing pieces of grapefruit and would touch nothing else. I went down to 98.

My body at 98 disappointed me. My skin sagged; my formerly full breasts sagged. And my face, high-cheek-boned and narrow to begin with, was cadaverous. I was not, as I had hoped, beautiful, though I preferred this form of bodily ugliness to obesity.

School began again. I was a junior now, and the academic pressure was intense. Formerly a good student, I no longer had any interest in school, nor any energy for handling the work. I felt I was going to fail, but could think of nothing but not eating. I equated Mitzi with overeating, and kept a careful emotional distance from her, though she continued to be my seat partner at the double desks we shared in homeroom.

"Jo, you have to eat. You're ruining your health. We won't have it. Now eat something," my father said one September night at dinner, as he had every night since my return from California. In much the same way as my mother's "Jo, you're getting a little heavy, don't you think so?" had come as a moment of truth two years before, so did my father's oft-repeated plea suddenly strike me with revelatory force. Always before, I had stubbornly refused. Now I was worn out from my struggle with myself and my parents, sick at heart with a terrible fear of what was happening to my life.

I looked at my mother. My urge to please her by losing weight had boomeranged and now she looked ravaged and frightened. My father's face was drawn and tense. I felt a wave of intense regret for the pain I was causing them. But even more, I was suddenly tired of starving myself, sick of the morning and evening rendezvous with the scale. Yes, I would eat that night, I decided. I was thin enough. Why shouldn't I be able to eat normally? Why was I condemned to this punishing regimen? What, after all, had I done to deserve it? I would slowly work myself back to normal portions and still not gain weight, I reassured myself. I took a lamb chop and some peas.

The food tasted good. I hadn't eaten anything besides lettuce, tomato, eggs, and grapefruit for months. I took one bite, then another. My father was delighted, relieved. "Now you're being sensible," he said, and I smiled faintly, trying to repress the frightening thought that I had unleashed a ravening beast. I had chocolate cake—a childhood favorite—for dessert.

And so began the most terrible phase of my roller-coaster history of gains and losses. My weight was soon back to normal, then higher than normal—much higher. In a month I had regained twenty pounds; in two months, forty; in three months, sixty. My narrow face filled out again, the good cheekbones again hidden by the additional pounds.

Now my parents were worried for quite different reasons. My father was silent and disapproving. My mother took more positive action, monitoring my portions at the dinner table and trying to hide any fattening foods before she went to bed at night, but I was soon an expert at finding the key to the burnished highboy where, beside herself with anger and pity, she tried vainly to conceal our cook Nancy's apple pies and chocolate cakes.

Every night when everyone was asleep, I sneaked down to the kitchen and gorged myself on leftovers from the overstuffed icebox. My mother had carried over from her own youthful home, with five sisters and numerous immigrant aunts and uncles in constant transition, a vision of the icebox filled beyond capacity as a natural condition of life. A superabundance of food was always there—often in varying stages of decay. Rotting grapes nestled next to freshly bought apples; mildewed crocks of chocolate pudding covered with waxed paper crowded last night's tempting pot roast. Nancy went along with my mother's policy that until something began to smell, in the "fridge" it remained. To this magnet I was drawn every night, and like an animal on its nightly forays, I'd tear pieces of meat from the leftover ham or roast beef bones with my fingers, not even pausing to cut off the fat. I'd then proceed to the locked cabinet for my "dessert." In an attempt to conceal these raids, I'd sometimes use a long knife to cut off the brown undercrust from the bottom of the cake, and eat that. Bloated, miserable, and filled with self-loathing, I'd crawl up the back steps and into bed, where I'd cry myself to sleep.

The new weight, gained so quickly, padded my body differently than it had the first time around. My anorectic breasts swelled like watermelons, the fat having apparently combined with their normal development to make them huge, even for a fat person. I had to wear special brassieres from lingerie stores specializing in large sizes for the "fuller figure." The bras had extra wide straps to help support the ungainly weight, but still cut cruel red grooves in my shoulders that sometimes turned into sores that wouldn't heal. Because of my oversize breasts, I began to have to wear the tentlike, matronly, half-size dresses my mother bought in New York City. (I wouldn't shop; couldn't bear to see my reflection in the store mirrors.) I cried constantly. But still I ate, driven by some insatiable hunger that I felt was a thing apart from the normal rest of me.

By the beginning of Christmas vacation I weighed 165 again—a gain of 67 pounds in less than three months. When the vacation ended, I was 175. Embarrassed beyond endurance by the grotesque metamorphosis that had taken place in such a short time, I refused to return to school. My mother raged; my father reasoned; but I wouldn't budge. "I'm not going; I can't. Look at me. Don't you understand?" Startled by my desperation and my tears, they retreated. I stayed in bed all that day and the next, listening dully to the soap operas I had enjoyed when I was sick in bed as a child—"Stella Dallas," "Young Widder Brown," "Lorenzo Jones"—and waiting till everyone was in bed to continue my pattern of compulsive midnight eating. I hardly ate at meals, rarely even came down for them, conscious of my parents' scrutiny of every bite I took. And every morning, I lay in bed and refused my mother's pleas to get up.

One morning about a week later, my father knocked on my door and asked to come in. Dad—a tall, handsome, somewhat remote man with black hair slicked back—was a brilliant, self-educated, self-made businessman. He loved music, and by the time he was ten had taught himself to play the violin. He was also critical and a perfectionist. Unlike my mother, with her chronic lateness and her dislike of being tied to the "slavery" of a schedule, he was extremely dependable and punctual. Many evenings he'd call from New York to say "I'll be in on the six-twelve," or "the six-twenty-three." Frank and I liked to take our bikes and act as a surprise welcoming committee at the station. He was always there. If not warm and affectionate, neither was he cold or unkind. He wept copiously in sentimental movies such as *Blossoms in the Dust,* a fact that always surprised me; yet I found it reassuring.

His appearance in my room, however, was unexpected, since we weren't especially close. I often watched other girls with their fathers—girls like Toni whose fathers picked them up and twirled them in the air, so-called

"Daddy's girls"—and puzzled over how different their relationships were from mine. It would never have occurred to me to sit in my father's lap, and I think he would have been astounded if I tried. I felt it had something to do with the kinds of girls they were—prettier, more agreeable, probably less "stubborn" or "contrary" (my father's favorite adjectives for me when I quarreled).

Yet it was puzzling. How was it that though my father often said of women that they were powerful and manipulative—"A pretty woman can twist a man around her little finger," or "Men are helpless when a clever woman makes up her mind," or, drily, "He chased her until she caught up with him"—he had married just such a woman, and clearly admired her.

Still, I was hurt by his comments. Even had I known what I know now—that he was expressing the prevailing masculine wisdom of the times—the acid in his voice would have left no doubt that it was also his own opinion. At any rate, I took the remarks personally and with deadly seriousness. Early on, I had resolved to be different from such women. I would be straightforward, unmanipulative, wear no makeup, be "natural." Yet for all my efforts, I'd felt horsey and awkward around him even before I'd gained weight, and felt he didn't like much about me beyond my successes in school or my alleged promise on the piano.

He often told me and others how capable I was ("Jo can do anything"). Such compliments actually undermined my morale. If he really knew me, how could he say such things? I knew all too well my inadequacies.

Worse yet, if he really believed it, I had fooled him without wanting to and trapped myself into maintaining

13

forever some vague standard of general excellence that—especially now, in my demoralized state—I could never live up to; that, in fact, my weight had excused me from living up to?

Still, it never occurred to me to tell him how I felt. We rarely discussed feelings, and in any case in the past I had been reluctant to lose my one solid claim to his attention over Frank, though Frank had serious problems in school, and lately had been provoking terrible nightly arguments over politics at the dinner table.

I hated these disputes, torn between my admiration for Frank's nerve and some instinctive sense that his defiant, ultra-liberal point of view had at least as much to do with fury at my father as at the government and its inequalities.

But most of all, I resented the fact that night after night during these quarrels I was totally ignored, for I felt—as I often did—that no matter how well behaved I was, how good my grades, how much I practiced, it wasn't nearly as important to my father as Frank's irreverence or his derelictions from duty. Frank's behavior, Frank's opinions, Frank himself, I was convinced, were more important to my father than I was. Whether this was because he was the first child, or a boy, or a combination of both, I didn't know, but I was silently outraged that his bad behavior was always rewarded by more paternal attention than my goodness—undoubtedly a factor in my monstrous weight gain, though of course I wasn't aware of it at the time.

Now, I lay on the bed with the covers pulled up to conceal my massive body and turned my head to the wall. My father sat down on the edge of the bed. "Aren't

14

you going to school today, either, Jo?" he asked, although of course he knew the answer. I nodded my refusal. "You must know that every day you miss will be that much harder to make up. And every day you eat more food, the harder it will be to lose it." As if I hadn't realized that I might miss a year in school, that I might not even graduate with my class if I didn't return. But I felt I had no choice. I had made up my mind to hide from the world until some magic charm—perhaps in the recognizable form of some devastating illness—would release me, miraculously thin again. On my own, I was sure, I could do nothing. I kept my head to the wall, and powerless against my silence, my father left the room.

The weeks went by, and all the time I was unable to control the terrible craving within me. I wept constantly with rage and an overwhelming sense of impotence. To evoke the hoped-for magic, I would walk up and down the street with nothing on beneath a summer raincoat on freezing days, praying I'd get pneumonia and lose weight that way. But I was maddeningly healthy. Often, I didn't brush my teeth, repelled by the swollen visage in the mirror. I refused to leave the house except to hide at the movies, and spent hours in the safe anonymity of the Central Theatre just a block away. Sometimes I'd see the same movie four or five times (I didn't care what movie it was), but never without a huge Hershey bar in my pocket. The midnight binges continued.

One morning late in January my mother came in with a new solution. A friend had told her about Dovecote Hill, a milk farm far out on the island. "It's simply terrific, Jo.

Reggie Fisher went there and lost twenty pounds just like that."

Maybe, I thought, if I could get away from the fatally attractive icebox? Break the pattern? Reluctantly, I agreed to try it.

The place was filled with middle-aged matrons, sad women with soft, flabby flesh on their upper arms—what Toni and I called "Hadassah arms"—and varicose veins in their legs. They went, it seemed to me, like victims to their daily massages and exercise classes. I refused. I found the prissy doilies under the cottage cheese and melba toast, the carefully measured portions, and my exile from the corner movies a painful reminder of the limitations of my present life.

I was drawn to the off-tune piano in the lounge. Though I was said to be musically gifted, the pressure to practice more and more had become unbearable in recent years. A year ago, when my personal problems had become so overwhelming, my father had finally given in, and I was permitted to stop taking lessons. ("You'll regret this in the long run, Jo," he'd said bitterly.)

Now, with nothing else to do, I spent hours at the piano, with the book of Chopin waltzes I had tossed in from home at the last minute. The sad matrons clucked their approval, but I heard one of them whisper, "Such a shame, a talented young girl letting herself go like that." The limpid melancholy of the music only added to my gloom, and after two weeks, I begged my parents to come and get me. Within a week, I had regained the six pounds I'd lost at Dovecote Hill.

One morning after I had been home for almost two months, steadily gaining weight, my mother entered the room again. This time she was neither messianic nor angry. She looked purposeful. "Jo, Sy has suggested that you see a psychiatrist."

"Why? A psychiatrist couldn't tell me anything I don't know," I said scornfully. "Anyway, they don't do any good. Besides, I'm not crazy."

"Jo, please. Things can't go on like this. You've got to try something. Maybe a psychiatrist can help you."

"How can just talking help me?" A psychiatrist could not do magic. A psychiatrist could not make me thin overnight.

"But Sy says," she said, again evoking the doctor-authority who had first recommended I enter New York Hospital, "that if you could find out *why* you're eating so much, maybe you could stop."

"Great theory," I said. "I know why I'm eating. It's simple. I'm eating because I can't stop eating." Nothing requiring a psychiatrist there.

"I mean the . . . the underlying reasons."

"Why would that help?" I said irritably. I didn't want underlying reasons, I wanted results. I wanted to be thin; I wanted to live. With all the pathetic yearning of a seventeen-year-old, I saw life passing me by. I didn't want to explore the past. I wanted a future, and I wanted it now.

"Jo, it's worth a try, isn't it? If you don't like her, you can quit. And she's a specialist in weight problems." Her? I thought of Ingrid Bergman in *Spellbound*. Maybe a specialist would have the answer—the magic charm, the amulet. Finally, I agreed to go.

The doctor's apartment was in the East 80's, and I was driven there one windy March afternoon by Al Riley, our chauffeur and my pal, whose flaming red neck I had as a child considered the height of masculine beauty, and who had been with us for as long as I could remember. I always sat in the front seat with Al if I was the only passenger and usually we talked, but this time I was silent during the ride, embarrassed lest he realize my shameful destination. I remember the doorman's humiliating appraisal as I asked the doctor's floor. "Another fatty," I was sure he was thinking. Then the elevator to four, and a short wait in the cubicle waiting room, with soft pillows, old copies of the *Saturday Evening Post,* and a secretary typing—looking at me also, I was sure, to see how fat I was, or maybe how crazy. Great combination, I thought, fat and crazy.

At last, I was looking into the squinting eyes and thick round glasses of Dr. Trudy Schmidt, famous obesity specialist. Ingrid Bergman beat a hasty retreat. Dr. Schmidt had wiry gray hair worn in a mannish "feather cut," pale, slightly wrinkled skin, and a chunky body dressed in a frumpy and ill-fitting two-piece gray suit. But what drew my horrified attention immediately was the fact that this run-of-the-mill torso and head rested upon two extraordinarily heavy legs, which ended in two equally fat feet shod in stodgy black Oxfords. I was appalled. Her legs bothered me terribly, reminding me that it was quite possible that even if I lost weight all over the rest of me, my legs might stay fat and shapeless. I wondered cynically if Dr. Schmidt, too, had once weighed two hundred (my current weight), or if she had entered her special field because of concern with her own irreducible extremities. No, I decided instantly and arbitrarily, a woman with legs like that could never perform magic for me.

"Sooo . . ." she said, in just the kind of German accent that would be imitated and satirized in hundreds of movies about psychiatry to follow.

I remained standing.

"Sooo," she repeated, "you are Yohanna."

I disliked my full name. I felt it was too exotic for me, too pretentious, especially when the "j" was given the German "y" pronunciation.

"I prefer to be called 'Jo' or 'Jo-Jo.'"

"Oh?" she said curiously. "Yohanna' iss such a pretty name. It iss very popular in my country."

I wondered if this was supposed to be some sort of flattery, the kind that saleswomen in stores gave, who thought they could sell you a dress if they said everybody was buying it that year.

"Well, I don't like it," I said, surprised that she seemed to be questioning me about such a basic matter even before we sat down. Could not liking your name be a sign of incipient madness?

"Okay," she said, the colloquialism seeming strange coming from her lips, "then you are Cho-Cho."

I noticed a wart on her cheek. Ugly, I thought contemptuously. As awful as I considered my own appearance, my standards for beauty in others were high, and of great importance to me in assessing their worth.

"Sooo, where you would like to sit? Here, maybe, on the couch?" But I knew all about psychiatrists' couches. Even in the forties they were something of a joke.

I planted myself in a large armchair facing her and she took out a stenographer's pad and pencil. "Practicing your shorthand in case the psychiatry business falls through?" I said, surprised at my own audacity.

She looked puzzled and seemed unaware of the sarcasm. I realized she didn't understand the expression "falls through" and my heart sank. This would be really heavy going, I thought, wondering if she'd have gotten that pun either.

Being funny—or trying to be—was important to me. In happier days, Toni and I had developed a cult of humor; tried to imitate the zany genius of S. J. Perelman in our letters and memorized the witty dialogue of Noel Coward's *Tonight at 8:30* and *Private Lives*.

While most teenagers of our era had been swooning over Frank Sinatra, we had chosen the verbal, urbane, and decidedly less sexually suggestive image of Coward to worship. From the moment I had come upon Coward's autobiography one rainy afternoon in Toni's living room when I was twelve, I was enchanted. I pored over the pictures of the young Noel in Christmas pantomimes with Gertrude Lawrence and of the older Noel with Lunt and Fontanne. His whole life seemed magical—the expression of all my secret dreams of rising from oblivion to stardom. Why hadn't I grown up in England, where such things could happen, such clever and talented child companions be met? It was, I thought sadly, already too late for me.

Toni, too, was charmed with the book, and since it was out of print, we passed it back and forth from Philadelphia to New York for several years, and haunted record stores for copies of Coward's recordings.

Now I wondered, what could this plodding foreigner, with her limited psychiatric English, do for me, or understand about the charm of Amanda and Elyot?

Yet, dutifully, I continued to go to Dr. Schmidt. Could you quit a psychiatrist because she had fat legs and no sense of humor? These seemed shameful, unmentionable reasons to me. But at home I complained to my parents. "She can't help me. Nobody can but me."

Twice a week I took the 1:30 train to Penn Station from Cedarhurst, and then an intricate and gloomy series of subways to 86th and Lexington, often stopping, after finally emerging into the light, for a *lindsertort* at the German bakery on Lexington. This I would munch angrily on the way to her office, conscious of the irony of stuffing myself on the way to the expert on overweight but, as ever, powerless to stop.

After our first encounter, Dr. Schmidt administered the Rorschach and other psychological tests. So far they had provided the most diverting moments of our time together, but I had almost forgotten them until one day about six weeks later.

When I came in, instead of encouraging me to lie on the couch as she usually did, Dr. Schmidt let me sit in the chair opposite her without an argument. I found her unusually serious expression, which made the corners of her mouth droop unattractively, even more annoying than her usual self-satisfied smile. I could see she had something on her mind.

"Well, what's up? It must be something important," I said, momentarily entertained by the role reversal.

"Up?" she said.

"I mean, what's the matter? Why are you looking so— so lugubrious?" I hoped she'd have to ask what that meant, but she seemed to understand.

"So. You are right. There iss something I must talk to you uff." She paused, as if considering what to say, then went on. "I like to be honest with my patients. There

21

should be no secrets—no games of seek and go hide." I suppressed a laugh but didn't interrupt. "I am going to call your parents later and ask them to come in to see me, yah? That iss all right with you?"

"Why not?" I said. "You don't need my permission."

"I don't want you to think I am talking in back uff you."

"Behind your back," I corrected automatically, bored with her tiresome attempt to establish trust.

"I am going to tell them the results uff the tests I haf given you," she said.

I waited for her to continue. What was she being so damned mysterious about? "Well, what are they?" I said, trying to sound casual, though I was no longer feeling as calm as I had before.

"I must be blunt. You are a sick girl—sicker than you appear. You are good at, how do you say it, covering yourself up"—this time I didn't laugh—"but the tests—especially the one with the ink blots—they show signs of serious disturbance. How you see things, people—it iss not normal."

She went on, and I couldn't believe what she was saying. I was a "borderline schizophrenic" and it was vital that I continue treatment if I were to keep "grips on reality."

I was stunned. I couldn't breathe. I didn't think I was crazy—even "borderline" crazy. But maybe, just maybe . . .

"*You're* crazy," I said, and rushed out of the room.

As if to confirm her diagnosis, I began to develop other obsessions besides food. First came a crippling fear of death. What good was it to be alive since it would all end

22

so soon? I looked at people on the street, in the subway, who were laughing and enjoying life, and felt like screaming at them, It's no use, don't you understand? It's all going to be over. You're all going to die. The darkness of the subway began to frighten and at the same time attract me, and I thought, sometimes, of jumping in front of the oncoming trains.

Waiting in Schmidt's outer office one day, I picked up a copy of *Reader's Digest*. There was an article on how the Russians were working on a drug that would make people live forever. As suddenly as my fear of death had appeared, it disappeared, only to be replaced by an even worse obsession: I would have to become a nun.

"Help me. Don't let it happen. Don't let me enter a nunnery," I begged my mother. Distraught, she called Dr. Schmidt, who told her to be patient, that such "delusional thinking" was not unusual for schizophrenics. The fear of becoming a nun was supplanted, in time, by the last and worst obsession, a fear that I was somehow doomed to become a lesbian. All my good friends were women. And women's faces and bodies interested me far more than men's, since I was constantly comparing myself to them. Wasn't that a sign of lesbianism?

Over none of these obsessions did I have any control. The images were constantly in front of me. Though I knew realistically that Dr. Schmidt couldn't actually make me crazy if I wasn't, still I blamed her relentlessly cheerful but humorless manner, her plodding masculine style, for their appearance. I hadn't had them before I went to her. I had them now. Ergo, it was her fault.

I broke down one day and, crying, tried to explain my despair at the idea of becoming a lesbian to Dr. Schmidt.

She paused briefly, lifted her pencil, smiled, and said calmly, maddeningly, "Und would that be so terrible? Why iss that such a terrible thought to you?"

I was shocked, then furious. "Because I don't *want* to be one, don't you understand?" I sobbed, ashamed to show any emotion in front of her, lest she think she was making progress with me and getting me to "open up."

Still, weight was the primary issue. Her favorite theory was that not only inside every fat person was a thin one waiting to come out, but that inside formerly fat people who got thin "too soon" (this was said with dire and significant glances in my direction) was the fat person ready and likely to overeat again as soon as he or she had to face the vicissitudes of everyday life as a normal, thin person.

"Cho-Cho, you know what I always say: 'Ven you haf understood vy you gained the weight, then you vill be ready to lose it.'"

"Not true," I cried, enraged by her smug assurance. "I'm stuck in a vicious circle now. The fatter I get, the more time I have to eat and be depressed, and the less reason not to. Don't you see? It's so obvious. I have to lose the weight first—at least, try it out. I mean, what could happen? I can't be any worse off than I am. What could be so terrible?"

This basic disagreement was at the core of our conflicts, and neither of us could be convinced by the other. I continued to feel she was deliberately keeping me fat, if for no other reason than to prove her theories were right, and my sense of helplessnesss increased.

If she asked me about my early memories of my parents (Was I angry at them perhaps? Had I gained the weight to get more of their attention? Were there times I had felt deserted, frustrated, ignored?), I was defensive. "Every child feels that way sometimes—maybe even lots of times," I'd snap, temporarily cutting off further discussion. "After all, nobody's parents are perfect. I'm sure theirs weren't either. They do the best they can." And in fact I believed it. I was responsible—not my parents, not my brother, my teachers, my school. But I couldn't fix what was wrong. And neither could she.

When she continued to probe, I confessed grudgingly that I had barely any recollections of my parents from early childhood.

My mother was, in fact, a somewhat shadowy figure to me until I was almost eight. Daily she disappeared, driven by Al, in our black Packard with the tiny blue lantern on top, into that far-off and mysterious city from which people of that era were moving "for the sake of the children." There she shopped for the stylish clothes that were unavailable in the suburbs of those times, or had her singing lessons with Madame Garrigue.

Her voice—a throbbing mezzo-soprano—had in childhood made her the favorite among five daughters (no sons) of her termagant mother, and was still the most important thing in her life. Clearly more important than I was, I sensed early on.

I had a love-hate relationship with that voice. Too often I'd been witness to my mother's tortured "A-a-a-a-a-a-a's" and "E-e-e-e-e-e's," all of the strenuous vocal exercise that resulted, when she performed, in tones of mellow richness. I made fun of the exercises, holding my hands to my chest and screeching in mock-operatic style for my

Aunt Lil and Uncle Perk, who lived nearby. Yet I suffered with her—worried about her voice, about whether she'd been satisfied with her own performance—even as I hated it. Some of my earliest memories are of the embarrassment I felt when, as a part of a group singing "The Star-Spangled Banner" before a concert or theater performance, her voice—clear, pure, and (to me) shockingly loud—soared out into the auditorium and galvanized the attention of the rest of the audience.

I also knew that if she wasn't happy with how she'd sung, she would be moody, irritable, and sad. Even in my mother's lightest songs ("Kiss Me Again" or sometimes, for me and my cousins, "I Chanced Upon a Big Brown Bear") there was, to me, a tragic disturbing note. In arias like "Pace, Pace" or "Vissi d'Arte" she could literally make strong men—and women—weep (my uncles and aunts, my father, the frequent guests in our house). I, too, was often moved in spite of myself. The aunts and uncles worshipped her. Music was all to them, my mother the priestess of the cult. And in the wider world of the Five Towns, where she was often asked to sing at weddings, at fund-raising luncheons and honorary dinners, her voice made her a local celebrity.

I alone seemed to know that she clung to that role center stage with a desperate intensity. Her vivacious public persona didn't fool me for a minute.

Between the shopping and the singing lessons, she was rarely home during the day, and since she had little sense of time to begin with, she frequently returned home hours later than expected. I remember, often, sitting on the cement curb at our street corner in the early gathering dusk of the chill winter evenings waiting fruitlessly for the Packard to round the corner and bring her home.

As for my father, in those early years he was someone I only vaguely recall meeting halfway down the block when he returned from the Cedarhurst station at night. But as we walked back to the house, he always seemed to walk too fast for me to keep up. (Did he want to leave me behind, or was he unaware of me beside him? Either alternative was disturbing.)

I began to tell Schmidt about Hennen. Until my seventh year, the dominant figure in my and my brother's lives was Hennen, a gentle, soft-spoken German nurse. It was fragile Hennen, with her fine brown hair parted in the middle and tied in a knot behind her head, who supported my already chubby body as I struggled to master the small two-wheeler inherited from a cousin; Hennen who sat with me when I was sick; Hennen who accompanied me to school and met me afterwards.

On those rare days when Hennen (a childish mispronunciation of "Helen") went to visit her sister and nieces in Brooklyn, I would become so hysterical at the prospect of a day without her that Hennen would sometimes change her mind and stay home with me. Other times, she'd persuade my mother to let me go with her.

But there were those bleak days when she had to go alone. From the moment I saw the black straw hat, dark print, and black shoes that signified Hennen's day off, I was inconsolable. "Don't go; don't leave me," I'd beg. And as, confused and troubled, her soft, kind eyes moved between my mother and me, my frenzy mounted. "Please, Hennen, please stay. Please, *please.*" Screaming now, I clutched at her feet as she approached the door.

"My God, Jo, what's the matter with you? Don't you think Hennen needs a day off once in a while?" said my mother. But I didn't know, didn't care, about Hennen's needs. I only knew that if she left, she might never return, and while she was gone, my mother might decide to try again one of the enemas she had concluded—in line with child-rearing practices of the day—were occasionally necessary for my well-being. One time, stretched on the bathroom rug, I had found it impossible to hold the water in as long as my mother said I should, and the rank, muddy excrement, humiliating and loathsome, had flowed out and onto the bathroom floor. Her eyes malevolent, my mother muttered, "You did that on purpose, didn't you? Now help clean it up." Choking and sobbing, I acquiesced, conscious of my mother's disgust. Hennen's eyes, I knew, were never malevolent.

When Hennen left for Florida to marry her best friend's widower, I was in the second grade. I fell into a real childhood depression, the prototype for all my subsequent feelings of desertion. I hung around the house, shadowing my mother when she was home from room to room, to her intense annoyance. "For God's sake, why don't you make some friends your own age?" she'd snap.

"I don't want to," I'd say, really meaning "I only want Hennen back. Bring Hennen back."

I studied by the hour a photo Hennen had taken of Frank and me for my parents' anniversary, when we were seven and four respectively, reliving in a paroxysm of grief her helping me put on the brown velvet dress with a lace collar, the white socks, and patent leather shoes she had persuaded my mother to buy me despite my mother's protests that they were "in bad taste. Much too shiny."

By studying the picture, the chubby serene girl and the serious boy, I almost hoped to enter it, and with it recapture the bliss of Hennen's presence, the paradise lost of her love. How calm and happy I looked there, secure in the deceptive belief that Hennen would never leave.

All this I finally, unwillingly, sketched in for Dr. Schmidt as she sat busily taking notes. "Ach, so you must have felt very abandoned then, ya?"

Of course I felt abandoned, you idiot, I thought. Isn't that what I've been saying? Was that supposed to be some kind of revelation? I had realized for years that Hennen's departure had been a devastating event. What I said was, "You don't exactly have to be a latter-day Freud to figure that one out, do you?"

Dr. Schmidt did not respond to the attack. "Und who took her place?" she asked, her pencil raised.

"Nobody, really, just a series of nursemaids," I said, remembering Barbara, who had arrived about two years after Hennen left. Barbara was a pretty, peppy brunette from Syracuse who, I had quickly decided, looked exactly like Loretta Young, one of my many movie star ideals of beauty. I liked her at once.

A few months after Barbara's arrival, my mother, aware of this attachment and perhaps, subconsciously, jealous of it, once played a trick on me when I got home from school.

"I fired Barbara today," she said casually, as I was put-

29

ting my books down in the kitchen. I looked around at Nancy and Al but their faces were impassive. Somehow she'd gotten them, and even Barbara herself, to play along with the joke, and Barbara had agreed to hide in the basement laundry room (two deep tubs, a mangle, and an ironing board, in those days).

For about ten terrible minutes I wavered between hopeful skepticism and horrified belief. I knew that Barbara's high spirits and refusal to knuckle under to either my mother's domination or her charm had caused many run-ins between them, so the statement wasn't completely unlikely. And with Barbara, there was a deeper cause for my mother's envy. Barbara, too, sang. She had a light, effortless, and untrained "semi-classical" voice, and I made no secret of my preference for her trilling of "I Dreamt I Dwelt in Marble Halls" to my mother's soul-shattering "Music I Heard With You." On the other hand, even at nine I knew that "help" of Barbara's caliber was rare.

"You didn't fire her—not really, Mom. You wouldn't," I pleaded, trying to scrutinize her face for the truth. I realized with a cold chill that I could never recall my mother playing a practical joke like this before.

"Oh, wouldn't I?" my mother said airily. Then, keenly, "Why, you wouldn't really miss her, would you?"

Without answering, I dashed up the narrow back steps to search. "She's getting her clothes tomorrow," was my mother's ready explanation for Barbara's still-full closet, when, my heart pounding wildly, I almost fell down the stairs to see if she'd been teasing after all.

"But she wouldn't have left without saying good-bye," I said. Could I have meant so little to her after all?

"Or without leaving me a note. She had to have left a note."

Only after I'd searched the rest of the upper floors and the attic did my hysterical tears elicit the truth—and Barbara, contrite, from the basement.

I didn't wonder till later at my mother's motives in planning and carrying out this cruel trick. Although she had accepted my devotion to Hennen—relieved, perhaps, to have her children in good hands while she followed her elusive muse in New York—she often resented my attachment and somewhat blind loyalty to the other help. And she made no secret of her relief when only two months after her "joke," Barbara, too, left to get married.

But Dr. Schmidt's thoughts remained with Hennen. "Sooo, did you begin to eat more after Hennen left?" she asked.

"Wrong again," I said with annoyance. "It's not that simple, don't you understand? No, as a matter of fact, I didn't. I had always been kind of heavy, I've told you that. But I didn't start eating more when Hennen left. *That* started just two years ago. Remember?"

She switched approaches. "Sooo, she wass German und so am I. You are making some connections between us, maybe?"

"About as much as between Adolph Hitler and . . . and Jesus Christ," I retorted, stuck, annoyingly, for a saintlike German to contrast with Hitler. "No, you don't remind me of her at all. Not a bit."

Now it was Schmidt's turn to sigh. We were clearly getting nowhere.

By May I weighed 220. Dr. Schmidt called my parents

in again. This time we all met together. She knew of a psychiatric hospital in Virginia—Great Oaks. Many world-renowned psychiatrists had trained there, and some were still working there. Perhaps they could help me. "Your daughter hass delusions. She iss probably schizophrenic," she said, repeating her earlier diagnosis (always the cautious "borderline" or "probably," I noticed). "She is unable to function. She appears calmer than she iss, but she iss, unfortunately, very sick."

Me in a mental hospital? Inconceivable. I wasn't that far gone. And besides, if I went I might never come out, might get fatter and fatter. It would be too late for magic charms there.

That week, while my parents wavered between Dr. Schmidt's advice and my protests, Dr. Perry, the high-school principal, called. Was I coming back? Because of my previous good record, I would be permitted to return in September as a senior if I went to summer school and made up the junior year work I'd missed.

I was both elated and frightened. I was 225 now. Going to summer school would mean an end to my hiding out, to the hellish but familiar routine of *lindsertorts*, Schmidt, subways, and trains, and a start to exposing my hated body to the questioning stares of new teachers, other students, new people, new places. But, much as I feared those changes, I knew I had to do it. To refuse Dr. Perry's offer, I suspected, was to seal my fate forever.

Dr. Schmidt wasn't easy to convince. In a heated conference with me and my parents, who were in torment over the decision, she stated her case. "Cho-Cho must go to Great Oaks," she insisted. "She iss not responding well to treatment. She iss too dependent, and she eats too much when she iss at home."

"For once, I agree," I said, surprised that she was at last acknowledging the fat as a problem.

She went on, ignoring me and addressing my parents. "She must break the self-destructive pattern she iss in at home, and the only way to do that iss to leave." With pain, I saw my usually confident parents exchange troubled looks (What have we done? It must be our fault), and I resented Dr. Schmidt's presenting it to them—to us—as a veiled threat, the "or else" unspoken but heavy in the air. "Und furthermore, I think she iss in no condition to do school work," she added, protecting herself in advance, I decided, in case I fell apart during the summer. "She would be best off in a hospital."

But I, too, was adamant. "Just let me try," I begged. "What could happen? The worst is that I'd fail, or get even fatter." Then, suddenly inspired, I pulled my trump card. "It'll be second grade all over again if I leave and then have to come back to another class," I said.

The reference was lost on Dr. Schmidt, but I knew from the exchange of glances between my parents that I'd scored a point. When I was seven, the same terrible year Hennen left, I'd begged to transfer from the Jewish Center School—a comfortable, homey place where I was to have been skipped a grade—to Woodmere Academy, where Frank went. "My school's better than yours," he often teased, "and we have French and music." Yet when I made the change, it was decreed by Miss Viola Clark, the principal of Woodmere Academy and a well-known educator of the day, that not only would I not skip, but that in conformity with a new school rule that no child should graduate before eighteen, I would repeat the second grade. "After all, dear, yours is a borderline birthday—December," she said, "and though you did very well on all the tests we gave you, we feel strongly that too many children are pushed ahead too fast. They suffer for it later on, believe me."

I was horrified. I'd been disappointed enough that I wouldn't be skipped. But to repeat second grade? It seemed impossible. I was large for my age and way ahead in my schoolwork. Everyone had told me so, and I knew it from my own observations anyway. Surely a mistake was being made.

Noting my stricken face, Miss Clark added, "You know, Johanna"—I was chilled at hearing the unfamiliar name they had insisted I use at the new school ("Jo-Jo's no name for a nice little girl. What's your real name, dear?")—"there's a lot to be said for being one of the oldest. You can excel, always be ahead. I know you're disappointed, of course, but believe me, you'll thank me for this some day."

I never did. Being "left back" wasn't common then—except for dummies—and to the stigma was added the fact that now Toni and, humiliatingly, all my friends from my former school would be a grade ahead of me. But worst of all, the decision struck a mortal blow at my self-esteem. Surely if I were really smart, if I'd really done well on the standardized tests I'd taken a few weeks before, this wouldn't be happening.

For several weeks, I pleaded with my parents to intervene. ("Those kids can't even read," I cried—and it was true.) But their attempts were half-hearted. My mother called the school a few times, but when Miss Clark held fast, she gave up quickly. Neither she nor my father seemed able to understand why it was so important for me.

Yet they must have sensed something then, for now the mention of second grade decided the issue.

"Okay, Jo. You win," said my father.

Dr. Schmidt sighed and shrugged her shoulders. "Thiss iss a mistake," she said portentously, but I was—at least for the moment—triumphant. I would not go to Great Oaks!

CHAPTER 2

Though Dr. Schmidt had given in, she did insist upon certain conditions. Since I was "too dependent," I was not to live at home. I would live in the city and go to a tutoring school near Columbia. I secretly wondered why Dr. Schmidt considered that an isolated seventeen-year-old would be better off living by herself in an apartment in a strange and unfamiliar area than at home, but I was so relieved to have avoided the hospital that I didn't raise my doubts. Muttering misgivings, Dr. Schmidt left for two months at Cape Cod, and my mother found me a sublet, an efficiency on Riverside Drive and 103rd Street.

When my mother drove off with Al, I was filled with depression. The peeling paint in the apartment was a bright Mediterranean blue, but the color did nothing to cheer me. With the window closed, the room was burning hot; when the window was open, the furious river wind blew acrid soot into every corner and onto every surface of the apartment. It was impossible to keep clean, and I didn't try very hard. And always, there was the consciousness of my weight. How could this have happened to me? Why? I kept no food in the kitchen, afraid I would eat it all at once.

Aside from my tutors, I saw no one, spoke to no one else. The temporary distraction of classes was replaced with an almost intolerable loneliness at the end of the day. Though the Upper West Side neighborhood was safer in those less violent times of the forties, I was scared of the winos and the sweaty men in undershirts who sat on the steps of the Hotel Empire listening to "Mama Yaquero" on their portable radios. But, shielded by my fat and the heavy brown coat I wore like protective armor on even the hottest days, I slipped by them hardly noticed. I sweated terribly in the coat, but since I felt its dark color minimized as well as concealed my size, I never took it off till I reached the apartment. I would come in soaking wet, just in time for the daily phone call from home, and my mother's anguished, anxious, "Are you all right, dear?"

The sound of her voice alone was enough to bring tears to my eyes, but I was determined to make it through the summer. "Yes, I'm all right. I'm fine."

"Are you sure? Do you need anything?"

"No, I'm fine. Really." And I'd hang up quickly, so that she wouldn't hear my voice begin to quiver.

I ate my dinners at a cafeteria on Broadway, always the same meal—scrambled eggs and french fries, an arbitrary combination I had tested for several days at home. I hadn't gained on the combination, though neither did I lose. Lunches were also a ritual: tuna fish on rye and a glass of skimmed milk at a drugstore near the school. There were several movie theaters in the area—the Olympia and the Thalia among them—and I went to one of them every night. Away from the familiar interior of the Central Theatre, and the near-reflex purchase of a quarter-pound Hershey's as I entered, I chewed gum instead.

After two weeks, I went home for the weekend. Our sunlit terrace, the green lawn, the bright, turquoise-tinted crystal gleaming on the glass table (turquoise was my mother's favorite color and her trademark), and my mother's entourage—a strange conglomerate of relatives, musicians, and artists, laughing together—all seemed part of another world.

My mother was modeling one of her dress designer's latest creations—a bold silk turquoise-and-white print with what seemed to me to be ridiculously exaggerated shoulder pads. "Really, Peter, people, don't you think the shoulders are too wide?" she said, regarding herself critically in the mirror with an antique frame that she and Peter had just installed on the wall.

Peter had been her close friend, "couturier"—the only title he'd respond to—and unofficial decorator for the past seven years. She had discovered him when he was eighteen, a penniless "creative genius," according to my milliner aunt, Polly, whom he was helping put flowers on the spring line of hats she was doing for the famous Lily Daché in New York. In a typically impulsive gesture, my mother had invited him to stay for a week and create a new wardrobe for her. The week had turned into a year and a half.

When we first came home from camp and found Peter installed in the guest room, Frank and I had been startled and resentful; but soon, during that period when I was ten, and then eleven, he had become our friend, too. He took us on early-morning bike rides, gave me drawing lessons, and was always happy to talk to me in the attic room he eventually fixed up as his studio when I got home from school. Having made no school friends since the second-grade disaster, I was there often. "Well, Miz Jo, what tragedy befell you-all down in the mangrove swamps today?" he'd ask, as *La Bohème* or *Madame Butterfly*—to both of which he knew the entire scores—played in the background.

Now, Peter moved behind my mother and adjusted her shoulder pads so that they looked even wider. "Clae, dear, they're absolutely to die. They just can't be too wide. You'll knock 'em dead at the dinner." My mother's next performance was to sing "The Star-Spangled Banner" and "Hatikvoh" at the United Jewish Appeal event, a "testimonial" honoring my father for his work as fundraising chairman for the South Shore of Long Island.

"Well, I hope you're right," she said, with a last glance at the mirror.

"Of course I'm right. They're the living end."

I was not so sure. The shoulders were extreme, and fit in with my vague and uncomfortable sense that my family—and especially my mother—was "different." Aside from her singing, which made her a public figure in the community, she sported wild bandanas and wore custom-designed slacks as she rode through town on a bike at a time when a woman's wearing pants was considered only slightly more eccentric than riding a bike.

"Your mother's crazy. Everyone says so," Louise Sonnenberg had said spitefully a few years before. Louise was a neighbor's child with whom dates to play together had been arranged for me when I was younger, though I disliked her tight sausage curls and the prissy good manners my mother sometimes held up to me as a model.

I would beg my mother not to wear the slacks and the brilliantly colored bandanas, to wear clothes like the other mothers, but her contempt for them—and by association, for me—was obvious. "Don't be so conventional," she'd say scornfully. "Be different." And I sensed early on that her need to make a splash far outweighed my weak protests.

She also paid no attention to the scandalized reaction of the neighbors, and of some of my aunts and uncles, to her long-term relationship with Peter. "That man is positively dangerous," my Aunt Lenore, my father's second sister, would snap. "He's a terrible influence on your mother, and why your father keeps lending him money is a complete mystery to me."

Peter's gestures were effeminate; beneath his puffy, pouting face and flowing hair he wore scarves instead of ties, and brightly colored shirts. Neither Frank nor I even knew what was unmentioned in those more innocent times, but certainly part of the family's disapproval was based on their recognition of his homosexuality, and of his unabashed flaunting of it.

In retrospect, I can see how his continued presence in our household might have seemed peculiar, even to those who were less narrow-minded than my aunt. But after our initial surprise, Frank and I took Peter's presence for granted. While he was clearly not like the other domestic "help," he was doing a job—designing my mother's clothes—and that seemed rationale enough for his being with us.

Despite the digs of his relatives, my father, too, seemed to like and accept Peter—impressed by his knowledge of music, entertained by his irreverent wit, which played off well against his own brooding, dry, humor, and undoubtedly also aware, as I was, of his soothing effect on my mother.

Peter finally moved to the city and, with my father's backing, opened his own shop, "Fashions by Pierre." But he and my mother remained in constant touch, and he visited often. On these visits he was increasingly accompanied by witty and handsome male friends who were artists or actors or ran antique shops.

These men fascinated me. I was charmed, dazzled—half in love with them, sadly aware that they could never return my love, though I didn't know exactly why at the time. I assumed it was because I was too young, too ugly, too fat, too clumsy. Yet they seemed to enjoy me, and my readiness to laugh was undoubtedly an asset.

This was the group that surrounded my mother that day—Peter, his friend Martin, my Aunts Polly and Lil, and my mother's voice teacher, Madame Garrigue.

Late that night, I lay in bed reading, waiting until I heard the last door close, and I was sure everyone had gone to bed. Then, responding to the habits of the past year, I got up and headed for the back staircase that led from the hall outside my room to the kitchen.

We had had a large rib roast for dinner, and I knew there would be lots of leftovers. Almost automatically, I descended the staircase, entered the kitchen, and opened the refrigerator. There the roast stood—rare, succulent, tempting. Bones with some meat on them—my favorites. Trancelike, I picked one up and took a bite.

Then, suddenly, I paused. What was I doing? If I ate now, I wouldn't be able to find out in the morning if the scrambled eggs and french fries, the tuna on rye and skimmed milk I'd stuck to for days before had worked. I knew I was capable of eating enough in one night to gain three or four pounds. So though I was hungry—I still had the compulsive eater's habit of eating almost nothing in front of other people, waiting only for a chance to stuff myself in isolation—I put the bone down on the kitchen counter. I threw the unchewed piece of meat into the garbage, then took a knife, cut off the part of the meat where I'd bitten so my teeth marks wouldn't show, and put it back on the platter in the icebox. Then I shut the icebox door and went back to bed.

The scale in the bathroom the next morning revealed that indeed I hadn't gained on the eggs and french fries—the first time in ten months that two weeks had passed without a gain. I didn't come down to the kitchen that midnight to stuff myself either, or on my other visits home, and though I continued to eat a lot, my weight remained at or near 225 all summer.

The first day I returned to school in September was dreadful. I had been fat enough when I left—175. Now I weighed fifty pounds more. Furthermore, Mitzi told me that my prolonged absence, together with vague tales about my enormous size, had given rise to the absurd rumor that I was pregnant—a particularly ironic fantasy in view of my extreme discomfort with boys. But if it were true, I would have been in my eleventh or twelfth month by now, so my return to school quickly squelched that rumor.

To my relief, the teachers and students were kind,

though the shock my altered appearance produced was clearly registered on some of their faces. Still, after the horrors of the first day, when everyone had finally seen me, it was less difficult than I'd thought.

I found I could keep up with the work, and in the administrative confusions of a new year, the make-up tests in the subjects I'd missed during my long absence were first deferred, and then, finally, dropped. "We're sure you did just fine this summer; you always have," said Dr. Perry, eager to be rid of a sticky problem and at the same time to show my father, a school-board member, his magnanimity.

I was excused from athletics so I could continue to see Dr. Schmidt twice a week. Her lack of enthusiasm for my having held the line on my weight and survived the summer annoyed me. "You see, I did better without you around," I said irritably. "At least, I didn't gain weight. When I see you, I always gain."

"Ya, but there are still many problems to resolve," she said, shaking her head woefully. I sighed, stared glumly at the copy of Millet's *Man With a Hoe* that hung on her wall, and tried to remember that coming to see her was much better than having to change into shorts and go to gym.

The months went by and my weight held steady, but I couldn't seem to lose, had almost stopped trying. I still seemed to be hungry all the time—hungry with a fierce, unnatural appetite that made it impossible to stick with any diet for more than a day. A change in this hopeless pattern came from an unexpected source.

One day in January, I went to meet my mother at Peter's apartment on Central Park South, where she was having a fitting for an evening gown she was to wear to the opening of the opera. I had to be in the city often now, both to see Schmidt and to have extensive work done on my teeth. The year of neglect had had devastating results—deep cavities, a gum condition, a few teeth almost beyond repair.

We were to meet my father at Peter's and all go out to dinner later. As the elevator rose to Peter's floor, my heart turned over, for, coming from inside his apartment, to which the elevator opened directly, was a voice—a light, high-pitched voice very like that of my long-time idol, Noel Coward—singing "Someday I'll Find You" to the strains of a delicate piano accompaniment. But I knew Peter didn't have Coward's recording of the scene from *Private Lives* that contained the song. They were collector's items, and Toni and I had haunted the stores to find them.

The door opened and I saw, seated at Peter's piano, a slender man of about thirty wearing a gray corduroy suit and a startlingly red bow tie. He had puckish features— huge, owlish brown eyes, slightly oversize ears, and black hair flecked with gray and cut to within a quarter-inch of his head. There were interesting lines around his mouth and a sad, world-weary expression on his face, all of which I found enormously appealing. I saw in his face a resemblance to Robert Helpmann in *The Red Shoes*, a movie I had seen five times, fascinated both by its visual beauty and its theme of tragic, helpless compulsion.

But it was the song, and his playing and singing of it, that mesmerized me. When he stopped, he languidly turned to me with a half-smile, and I moved toward the piano, my usual shyness temporarily forgotten.

Peter came in from the fitting room. "Jo, this is Larry— Larry Lester. Doesn't he play divinely?"

"Yes," I said. "But Peter, you must have told Larry to play that song, didn't you? You told him how I feel about Noel Coward."

"Don't be ridiculous, dear. Believe me, I don't tell Larry what to play. Nobody does." And he went back to the fitting room, where I could see, through the door, my mother studying the fit of her new dress, an opulent strapless in creamy satin with hand-sewn sequins. She spotted me with her eyes in the mirror and blew me a kiss, not for a second moving her head as she watched one of Peter's assistants pin up her hem, kneeling at her feet almost as though in worship.

"I told Peter you'd be surprised," she said.

Larry was still at the piano, and I remained next to it, trying now to conceal my width by keeping part of me out of sight behind the curve. "Do you know any others?" I said, not wanting to break the spell.

He knew them all—all the Noel Coward songs, even the less well-known ones Toni and I thought we alone possessed. He knew obscure Cole Porters, French cabaret songs, all of Rodgers and Hart.

Everything Larry said seemed charming to me. He shared some of Peter's expressions and mannerisms, but somehow when the same words came from his mouth they seemed infinitely more interesting. He was not, as I had thought, a professional musician. "I decided I just didn't have what it took, Clae," he said to my mother when she asked. He was, instead, starting his own decorating business. "We all have to face reality sooner or later. Let's face it, a Horowitz or Rubinstein I'm not."

45

Yes you are, I thought.

Suddenly he turned to me. "And what about you, dear? I think it's kinda amazing that a sweet young thing like you knows all those old war-horses. How in the world did you ever learn them?" He was looking at me with what I realized was admiration. I was so nonplussed at being the focus of his attention that I couldn't think of a reply.

Peter rescued me. "Jo's a marvel at old song lyrics," he said. "She knows them all. And you should hear her sing and play, Larry. She's really good." I looked at him gratefully.

"Oh, really?" said Larry. "Well, in that case, maybe you'd like to go and hear Ella Fitzgerald at the Three Deuces sometime when you're in the city." I was sure I would.

So it began, and for the next few months I was obsessed with Larry, could think of nothing else, talk of nothing else. This was the weight-losing magic I had been waiting for. I had no desire to eat—lost ten pounds, then twenty, then five more. Every week I went to Larry's apartment on East 57th Street and waited nervously as he showered and changed before our date. What would happen if he asked me into the bedroom? I couldn't picture it, and pushed aside my doubts about his sexual preferences. He was the perfect companion for me—a sexless, undemanding male whose chaste good-night kisses were about all I could handle at the time, though they aroused in me a passionate desire for more.

We went to *South Pacific,* that year's hit, together, and I carefully noticed the happy relationship that developed between the aging planter Lebeque and the tomboyish Nellie Forbush. If she could overcome twenty years and a complete difference in backgrounds, what were eighty pounds and a questionable sexual orientation? Larry, at least, was American, and was only twelve years older than me. Whenever "Some Enchanted Evening" played after that, we gazed soulfully at each other.

Once, Larry visited us on Long Island. He had played and sung "You Go to My Head" with a worldly ardor that made me tremble when my mother, who felt freer with Larry than I did, asked him casually, "Have you ever been madly, passionately, in love? Physically, I mean."

Shocked at her daring, I waited for his answer.

He raised one black eyebrow. "Tried it once and didn't like it. Quite honestly, Clae, as Gary Essendine says in *Present Laughter,* 'I think the whole business is highly overrated.'"

What did he mean, I wondered, love in general, or the physical part of it? I wasn't sure which would be more alarming. But I decided quickly that he was probably just being funny, and, entertained by the neatness of his phrasing, ignored its troubling implications.

I was so infatuated with Larry that I even told Dr. Schmidt about him. She was skeptical. "Sooo . . . And where iss all this leading, Cho-Cho?"

"You would say that," I said furiously. "At least now I'm losing weight—no thanks to you."

"Sooo, we shall see what we shall see," she said. "You are using this man to hide from—how do you say it, to escape—your problems. It will not end well."

Again I hated her for her dire predictions. Everyone else was happy for me—my mother, father, Frank, Mitzi, with whom I had reconciled when I returned to school, and Toni.

The school year ended triumphantly. I wrote the class song, played the piano for the class show, and even achieved a kind of stardom with a throaty, Dinah Shore–inspired rendition of the "St. Louis Blues," which, still humiliated by my weight, I insisted on singing on a darkened stage while my obliging classmates did some kind of highly original hand motions with phosphorescent gloves. Though I refused to come out for the ovation, it was a gratifying, if fleeting, moment of glory.

At graduation I was *cum laude* and received the English and Glee Club prizes. Larry gave me a gold ring with a small pearl, and I realized that some sort of crisis in our relationship was near. Deep down, I suppose I was aware of what a peculiar pair we were—an effete homosexual (or possibly, an asexual) and a fat, frightened girl caught in a strange affair that was no less heartfelt and potentially painful for not being physically consummated. But I refused to think about it. I only wanted to tie Larry to me forever, and to lose, through his magic, more and more weight.

Finally, one summer afternoon, he spoke up. "Jo, you know I'm so fond of you. Would you—I mean, can you imagine yourself married to me?" His extreme composure was, for once, shaken. He looked, in fact, wretched, and I sensed something forced and unnatural in the question. It was as if he were willing himself, forcing himself, to speak.

The proposal was, of course, what I'd thought I wanted, but the moment he said the words I realized that marriage to him was impossible. Though I'd never experienced sex, and was as repelled by what I'd heard about it as I was fascinated, still, at eighteen I wasn't ready to give it up for life. I told Larry I would have to think about it, but I think we both knew, then and there, that it couldn't be.

Yet I couldn't let go of Larry. If he dropped out of my life, so would the magic that had sustained me, that had made me lose the weight. He called less and less, and I longed for him, yearned for his return. Most of all, I feared that without him I'd not only stop losing, but perhaps regain, the weight I'd lost. I had reached a stalemate at 190; the magic was gone.

My cousin Toni came to town, and with my parents we went out to the Blue Angel with Peter and Larry. In the previous months, I had told Toni all about Larry, and she was eager to meet him. Larry and I were awkward together now, but Toni and he hit it off at once. So that night, to my despair at losing Larry was added the anguish of what I saw as his immediate attraction for my cousin, my best friend. The very things she and I alone had shared, then Larry and I—the passion for Coward, for Porter, for nostalgia of the twenties and thirties—they now shared together. I was losing both of them at once.

Jealousy of Toni, combined with my longing for Larry and for what had been and was now over, overcame me. After we dropped off Peter and Larry, I sobbed hysterically all the way home in the car and throughout the night and the next day, ashamed to admit to Toni or my mother what was wrong. I stayed in my room, coming down only for meals.

My mother, alarmed, called Dr. Schmidt, but I refused to see her or talk to her. No, I decided, she couldn't help me; she would only be thinking, even if she didn't say it, "So you see, Cho-Cho, I was right. You must stop looking outside yourself for answers. You are still that fat person in chust a slightly thinner body." The thought was intolerable.

The next morning I went to the telephone and took out a piece of paper I'd tucked under the pad next to it a few months before. On it was scrawled the name and number of a famous diet doctor in New York whom a well-meaning aunt had for several months been encouraging me to see. "He gives you pills that work like a charm to kill your appetite," she had assured me. Her best friend, in fact, had lost forty pounds in "no time at all." High on my friendship with Larry, I had ignored her advice. But now, afraid to test myself on my own, I was ready for a charm, ready for a new form of magic to solve my problems. Calmly, I picked up the phone and made an appointment for the next day.

CHAPTER 3

Dr. Weinstock was jowly, balding, a Camels chain-smoker, and about sixty years old. His eyes reflected hyperthyroidism and he wore thick glasses. But I found his soft, gravelly voice soothing, and sitting across from him at our first meeting, I poured out my despair and feeling of helplessness about my weight. He startled and delighted me by backing me in my desire to leave psychoanalytic therapy and lose weight right away.

"Of course you have to lose weight first. What idiot said you didn't?" He was indignant. "You want to live a little. How can you do that with all that weight on you?" His nurse Jackie had weighed me in at 195 in the outer office. I had dreaded showing my body even to the nurse, and was relieved when all I had to do was strip down to bra, underpants, and slip.

I told him about Dr. Schmidt.

"Schmidt? Never heard of her," he said emphatically. Marvelous. A well-known diet doctor had never even heard of the supposedly world-famous authority on obesity. "Here, give me her number," he said, reaching for a pad. "I'll call her right up and tell her what I think about her crazy theories."

His boldness thrilled me, but I wasn't prepared to precipitate a doctor-to-doctor confrontation just yet. I knew Dr. Schmidt wouldn't approve of this visit and I had no intention of telling her about it.

"No, no, don't bother. I'll tell her about it myself," I said quickly.

I was still enormously fat, but since I'd lost the first thirty-five pounds, my features had begun to reappear. And during the last months of high school, Mitzi had taught me how to use an eyelash curler, eye pencil, and mascara. The transformation, on me, was much like in the ads: my formerly nice but unremarkable brown eyes took on size and brilliance. I had stopped trying to look like Lauren Bacall and discovered a flattering hairstyle, bangs and a pageboy—like a brunette June Allyson, I hoped. With a touch of lipstick, I no longer found the image reflected in the mirror completely repulsive.

"You know," Dr. Weinstock said suddenly, "you're a beautiful girl. Really beautiful. And when I'm through with you, you'll be even more beautiful. I believe in getting results, and believe me, honey, I get 'em.

"I'm going to start you on a thousand-calorie diet," he said. "And I'm going to give you a prescription that'll make it much easier for you to control your appetite." He wrote something on a pad.

"You don't have heart trouble or anything, do you?" he asked casually, barely looking up.

The question, I assumed, was by way of a medical history.

"No. I used to have a low metabolism, though."

"Yeah?" he said. "Well, we can include some thyroid in the medication." He added something quickly to what he had already written.

"I guess, aside from that, I'm pretty healthy."

"Good. Now I want you to take one of these about an hour before lunch and an hour before dinner. If you find you're having trouble sleeping, cut down to one before lunch and we'll talk about it next Thursday. Okay?"

"I'm not sure I want to take anything," I said. Though my original plan had been to do so, I felt so buoyed up by Dr. Weinstock's support that I felt I might not need it. And some innate sense of caution suddenly gripped me. Something about a capsule powerful enough to kill my desire to eat was alarming as well as fascinating.

"What's in them?" I asked.

"Don't worry, they're safe. All my patients take 'em, and there's never been a problem," he said with assurance. "Just an appetite killer—great stuff they call Desoxyn—with a little Phenobarb, to keep you from getting jittery, and of course, since you have the metabolism thing, some thyroid, too."

I had heard of the last two ingredients. The Desoxyn—a derivative, I later found, of Dexedrine—was unfamiliar to me. The term "amphetamine" was almost as unknown in 1948 as its trouble-making potential.

"When you've lost the weight, you quit taking 'em. It's simple as A, B, C," he said. Still, I didn't reach for the slip of paper he was holding out to me.

"Honey, do as you please. I think they'd help you a lot, but it's up to you. Anyway, you and I are going to work great together. I can tell."

I took the prescription and put it in my purse. I'd keep it in reserve, I decided.

The next week flew by. I had no trouble sticking to the diet. I still yearned for Larry, dreamed of him, waited stupidly for a call from him, but I also had a new focus: the diet and the Thursday visit to come. I told my mother only enough to enlist her cooperation in buying special foods. She and my father were delighted to see me in better spirits. They didn't pry.

On Thursday, Jackie took my blood pressure—the one concession to possible "complications"—and weighed me. I had lost four pounds. When I dressed again, she ushered me into Dr. Weinstock's office and handed him my chart.

"Nice going, babe, I'm proud of you," he said. "Jackie, you can go now. And don't come back until I call you."

The door closed and we faced each other across the desk. "Give me your hand," said Dr. Weinstock. I had to draw my chair closer to his desk to do so, but obediently, I obliged. He was staring at me, hard. "Have you been thinking about what I said last week?"

"Which part?" I asked, not sure whether he meant about my weight and the diet, the psychiatrist, or my looks.

"About how pretty you are," he said.

"Well, there's really not much to think about, is there?" I said nervously. "I mean, anyway, I don't really think so, but I'm glad you do." I had been thinking that perhaps the reason he thought me so attractive was that all he ever saw were middle-aged fat women.

"Well, it's true." He stubbed out the wet end of the cigarette he'd had in his mouth, reached into his jacket pocket and drew out another. "Terrible habit," he said, looking up. "How'd you give it up?"

I was flattered that he thought me worldly enough to have cultivated and broken such a grown-up habit at barely eighteen. "It was easy. I never started."

He laughed. "I like you, Jo-Jo. I like your honesty," he said. "You're not a phony like a lotta my patients out there." I felt uneasily that his cavalier attitude toward his other patients didn't reflect very well on him, but I was flattered nonetheless. "I think you should come in to be checked twice a week," he said. "I won't charge you extra. Can you do that?"

"Well, I guess so," I said. "I mean, is that usual?"

"Only in very special cases," he said meaningfully. He let go of my hand and came around the desk. He was taller than he appeared when he was sitting down—about six feet—and thinner, despite a slight paunch.

"Stand up for a minute. I like to look at you."

Again, obediently, I got to my feet. He took my hand in his soft fleshy one and surprised me by pressing it to his somewhat flaccid lips, looking at me with a curiously wistful expression. Suddenly I felt his arms around me, and he was holding me close, the faint smell of tobacco emanating from his clothes.

Strangely, I wasn't shocked. I knew that in theory what he was doing was highly unusual, but I felt so comforted with his arms around me that it didn't seem to matter.

"Do you mind?" he asked, as if to echo my thoughts.

"No."

"Would you give me a kiss?" he asked, his voice trembling.

I didn't answer, and the next thing I knew I felt those soft lips on mine. The sensation was pleasant, and I wasn't surprised when I felt his tongue enter my mouth. I felt passive and peaceful as he pressed against me, the buckle of his belt, the buttons of his jacket, hard against my skirt and sweater.

So this was it, I thought, my first real kiss—what the girls at school had gigglingly described as a "soul kiss"— and I was receiving it from a sixty-year-old diet doctor. But the thought of reporting him, of even mentioning it to my mother or to Schmidt, never occurred to me. I welcomed his kisses, saw nothing really wrong with our odd doctor-patient relationship.

By my third visit, the kisses were an established part of my "check-up"; by the fourth, he was urging me to accompany him to Atlantic City for the weekend. "C'mon, we'll have a great time," he said. "Just the two of us. 'You and me, babe.'" He hummed the line from the song "From This Moment On." "So, what do you say? How about it?"

I was—again—flattered, and not in the least offended. I had heard girls at school talk about being propositioned, but along with the rest of that boy-girl, man-woman world I knew of only by hearsay—a private club from which I had felt automatically excluded because of my weight—had been convinced it would never happen to me. Now it had happened, and I knew instinctively that this was not part of Dr. Weinstock's standard treatment, that all the fat ladies in his waiting room were not being given invitations to Atlantic City as part of their weight-loss plans. But I never seriously considered accepting. "I couldn't do that," I said. "I'm sorry. I just couldn't." I was happy with the kisses but still considered my body ugly, and feared more sexual intimacy.

Dr. Weinstock didn't argue. Perhaps he never really thought I'd agree. Or perhaps he feared that if he pushed too hard I'd become angry and tell someone. In any case, after my rejection of the weekend invitation, he never tried to go farther than those initial hugs and kisses. But along with his moral support they were balm to me, and my long-held conviction of ugliness melted even further, along with the pounds: ten, then fifteen. It was a quiet thing, and when I was away from Dr. Weinstock, I was not obsessed with him as I had been—as I continued to be—with Larry. There was no real passion in my response to his kisses, but I looked forward to them, to the bi-weekly "check-ups." I lost another five pounds, and one unusually hot Indian summer day, I even left the house without my protective brown coat.

I still carried the first prescription in my wallet. Though the doctor had continued to encourage me to try the "medication," some continuing and instinctive reluctance had stopped me from having it filled. Perhaps I feared my potential for going to extremes. But after the easy loss of the first twenty pounds, I reached another impasse, and Dr. Weinstock began to urge his medication upon me once again.

Taking the first capsule didn't seem very momentous at the time, though I do recall clearly, just before putting it in my mouth, having the same sensation I'd felt years before when plunging off a diving board I suspected was much too high for me. But the pill worked with such immediate and astonishing success that I wished I had discovered it years before. Just as Dr. Weinstock had predicted, I wasn't hungry. It was miraculous, marvelous, the very magic I had been looking for—a wonder pill that would set me free from fat forever. At the end of the week I had lost six pounds.

How does an addiction take hold? In a way, I suppose I was addicted from that first pill. But my awareness of my dependence was so gradual that I cannot pinpoint the hour, the week, or even the month when I realized I could no longer face the day without the bolstering compound with which I was drugging my body and mind. It surely began in that winter of my eighteenth year.

By now, I was at Barnard College, commuting daily from home, since I didn't live far enough away to be given a room on campus, and off-campus apartments for freshmen were forbidden then. I made friends, did well in my courses—but slowly, I began to have a sense of unease. I felt a subtle difference in the way I was relating to people as well as to food. How was it that I was suddenly so much less inhibited? Being thinner didn't seem enough of an explanation.

Usually I made new friends or could talk comfortably when I was feeling "up," just before lunch. The hunger pangs I had had to expend so much effort controlling were replaced then with a pleasant, an almost euphoric, burst of nervous energy. It didn't take me long to put the pills together with the "up." Then was it really me who was doing so well? Or me plus something artificial?

I realized that I was more animated at home, too, yet was secretly ashamed to face my parents, who so far hadn't noticed—or at least hadn't commented on—any but the physical changes in me. My mother was delighted that I was finding it so much easier to diet. "See, you had the will power all the time," she said proudly. Apparently, it didn't occur to her to wonder at its source. My father paid the doctor and drugstore bills automatically, glad to see results at last from an investment. Dr. Schmidt sensed something was amiss with my sudden vivacity, but couldn't put her finger on what it was.

"You are feeling much happier now that you are thinner, yah?" she asked.

"Exactly as promised," I said sarcastically. "But you never believed me when I said I would."

Though I reported her confusion with glee to Dr. Weinstock, I secretly began to yearn to tell someone about the chemical that was transforming me both physically and psychologically. But I didn't dare, lest it be taken away and my relationship with Dr. Weinstock revealed. To tell about one, I felt, would be to tell about the other. They were, to me, inextricably linked.

The problem was complicated even more by the fact that I was sure I'd gain back all the weight I was losing with such ease if I stopped taking the capsules. The possibility that I could keep my weight down or even lose more without them didn't enter my mind. I had gained no confidence from the losses that had preceded the medication. The memory of my ten-month binge and the 127 pounds I'd gained was too recent—a nightmarish reality I couldn't bear to think of. What I didn't realize was that I had traded one nightmarish reality for another.

I continued to take the medication, the proportions of which Dr. Weinstock had slowly increased. "Everyone develops some tolerance for a drug they take regularly," he assured me. "Your body's used to it now. We just have to give it a little more oomph." No longer asking questions, I had the new prescription filled.

Summer, and I was down to 160. Bent only on losing more weight and keeping hidden the truth of my secret life with Dr. Weinstock, I worried about staying at home. Too much time at home might lead to discovery. I leaped at my father's suggestion that I take a summer stenography course in Cambridge, Massachusetts. "Learn something practical. Every girl should know how to type," he said. "You can always make a living if you can type." Armed with a prescription from Dr. Weinstock and the assurance of six weeks of anonymity, I left.

The secretaries-to-be were housed in the dorms of Radcliffe College. Once there, I found that I hated the shorthand, hated the typing, disliked the prim, purposeful students in the course, and was too jittery to settle down and do the homework. I began to be obsessed with memories of Larry, with a sense of irretrievable loss. Yet I felt I couldn't disappoint my father. I would fight the depression and justify my stay there by losing weight even faster.

I'd have to take more medication every day to do it, though, I decided. Anyway, I rationalized, maybe a little extra would lend the work and the other girls the same charm with which it had infused my days and my companions at Barnard. But how could I add just a little? I studied the capsules, which were filled with a powdery, pinkish-orange substance, and made a plan.

Boldly, I entered a local drugstore. "I'm in pre-med and I'm running a kind of science experiment for summer school," I lied. "I need some empty capsules for it. Do you think you could let me have a few?" Delighted to be helping a struggling science student, the pharmacist gave me twenty-five. "Is that enough?" he asked. "If you need more, be sure to come back."

"Thanks a lot."

I darted out, amazed at how easy it had been. Back in my room, I carefully emptied one of the full capsules onto a Kleenex, divided the powder into three roughly equivalent piles, and put it into three of the empty capsules. I was, I felt, all set. I could add an extra one-third to every dose I took.

But still I couldn't concentrate. I blamed it on the monotony of the work, and repressed the sneaking suspicion that the medicine might have anything to do with it. After all, what had I to do with shorthand and typing? I stopped going to the stenography course and signed up for a creative writing class at Harvard. I told my parents I could manage both.

My father wrote:

> Dear Jo,
>   Just carrying out orders. Herewith, two checks—
> one for $100, which you can fill in to the proper party
> at Harvard, the other to cover your school
> requirements—books, etc. I hope you're not
> overextending yourself.

Beneath this letter, which had been dictated to his secretary, like almost all the letters I'd ever received from him, was something new, a handwritten note:

*My gosh, I just read this over and it sounds terribly
formal. What I want to say is that I am delighted you
are feeling so ambitious, and that I will miss you a lot.
Take care of yourself—anything you want, just let me
know.*

Affectionately,
Dad

Sadly, I realized that his expressions of caring and affection seemed to rise in direct proportion to my inner distress and outward frenetic activity. When I was younger, and calmer, my academic success had been taken for granted.

I started to go to the writing course. But I found I couldn't concentrate on that either, was incapable of organizing my ideas in any coherent way. I stopped attending that class, too.

Really frightened now, I wrote a long letter to Toni, telling her everything—about Dr. Weinstock, the capsules, my fear of gaining, and of my increasing sense that I was no longer myself—then tore it up and wrote another that only vaguely hinted at something wrong. She wrote back:

Dear Jo,
*I'm so glad you wrote to me, even though age is
rendering you more and more cryptic. It's funny,
though, I had a feeling (one of a series) that there was
something rotten in the state of Massachusetts. Please,
PLEASE send me the letter you were going to, or else
write me a reasonable facsimile thereof. I don't
understand why you don't want to tell me what it's all*

about, but I suppose you have some distorted idea
which approximates the instinct of the wounded stag
who takes himself off into the wilderness to die alone
on a windswept hillside or something. Knowing you,
you're probably harboring the notion that if you were
any kind of a person you should be able to solve your
own problems. I can't say anything else, but please let
me know what's the matter, Jo, or why things have "hit
a new low," or what you're thinking about . . .

I didn't answer the letter.

I was more successful in continuing to deceive my parents, my aunts and uncles, who were following my "before and after" transformation with intense interest. My Aunt Lil wrote, "Our call to you was absolutely the most satisfactory one I've ever made. Your voice was so joyous—I hated to hang up." I recalled grimly that she had called just before dinner, an "up" time.

But for all the contact, all the reaching out, I didn't tell anyone what I really wanted to say—that I was in trouble. Since no grades or reports were given in either course, except to those enrolled, it was easy to maintain the deception at home.

I muddled through the summer, sometimes going to classes, sometimes not, being lively and animated at meals among the conscientious girls who smiled at me vaguely and then went off immediately after dinner to do their homework.

Five more pounds dropped off effortlessly, and I noticed that the boys at Harvard were beginning to look at me with interest. I was still too scared to return their glances. Once, at a dance, I felt something hard against my legs as I danced cheek to cheek with a pimply boy who had been in my writing class. I was horrified. This was nothing like Dr. Weinstock's soft embraces. I tried to pull away. The boy was angry. He followed me as I ran across the park between Harvard and Radcliffe back to the dorms. We struggled on a dimly lit path, and he ripped my dress. "Come back," he begged, "you've got to touch it. You've got to do something." Then, angrily, "You started this, you bitch."

I managed to make it back to the dorm, terrified at the force of the mysterious process I had inadvertently set in motion.

Home again. I dreaded the beginning of school, the return to Schmidt's increasingly skeptical gaze. I wondered how long it would be before she brought up my altered behavior to my parents, who would then undoubtedly tell her that I was seeing Dr. Weinstock and was taking some sort of medication. With her medical background, she would understand at once.

Panic-stricken at the thought of discovery, and at the same time longing for the life of a real girl, I begged my parents to let me transfer to the University of Wisconsin. My brother Frank had planned to go there before he enlisted in the navy during the war. And my Aunt Polly had recently remarried and settled in Wisconsin. It had, I felt, a certain family continuity.

Surprised and pleased by this new spirit of adventure, they acquiesced. Meanwhile, I managed to persuade Dr. Weinstock to agree to an unholy alliance: He would supply me with prescriptions by mail, as needed. I told him, and I meant it, that I intended to reach my goal of 135—a weight that we had agreed was right for my height and frame—soon. "Then I'll stop taking the medication, of course. Okay?"

"Sure, baby. Anything you say. Just write to me and let me know how you're doing." He looked at me sadly. "But you know, I'm really going to miss you."

Dr. Schmidt was not so agreeable. "Ach, Cho-Cho, what you are doing now? You are making a big mistake. Running away. Escaping again." She looked at me keenly, and for once I felt she could read my mind. "Why you are going so far? What you are running away from? You can't run away from yourself."

Cliché, I thought, ignoring the truth of the statement. "I'm not running away *from* anything. I'm running *to*—to Life," I said, aware of how melodramatic that sounded. But I really meant it. I'd resolved to make a new start in Wisconsin. I would finish losing weight and taking the pills, maybe begin to go out with boys like other girls, be a new person—not the formerly fat "Johanna" of my schoolmates at Woodmere Academy, not the frenetic Barnard girl or the scattered secretarial student. I would find myself there. I would "live a little."

CHAPTER 4

I'm terribly sorry, my dear. The rooms in college housing close to school have been taken for months, and the vacancies we had even a week ago from cancellations were all snatched up immediately," said Mrs. Green, a harried employee at the Wisconsin Student Housing Office. "How is it that you waited so long to take care of this?"

No room at the inn—or at any of the inns. The large, rambling houses for out-of-state students that lined the gentle curve of Langdon Street were full. I had been in Madison only a few hours when I learned that this street, rising from the base of the architectural hodge-podge called Bascom Hill—academic heart of the university— was at the core of social life for non-resident Wisconsin students.

"Well, I was just accepted at the end of August," I said. I didn't tell her about my frantic, last-minute decision to leave New York.

"Of course, we can put you up on the other side of town," Mrs. Green said, reaching for a file box. "There are some lovely places out there. Families that have extra rooms and rent them to students. You could take a bus in for classes. And it's much cheaper than the residence halls." She smiled at me brightly.

Family life? Miles from the campus? Impossible. My head was filled with celluloid images of midwestern college life, based on childhood memories of Sonja Henie and Richard Green in *My Lucky Star,* or more recently, June Allyson and Peter Lawford in *Good News.* None of this could come true in a room with board so far away from the campus. "Are you sure there's no space? Maybe someone will move out—get homesick or something."

"Well, things *do* happen sometimes." She smiled distractedly, glancing at some papers she had been working on when I approached her desk. "Of course there is the hotel, if you can manage that for a while. But it's expensive. Check back with me in a few days."

A few days. My heart sank.

I stumbled out into the dazzling weather of Madison in September and headed up Langdon Street toward the Park Hotel a few blocks away. There I would be closer in, though still not part of the college life. My money had given me this option, and briefly, guiltily, I mused on how it might have been otherwise.

My thoughts were interrupted by a tap on the shoulder. Instead of Peter Lawford, there, standing behind me, was a short, dumpy boy with glasses. "Are you looking for a room, too? I saw you at the housing office," he said. "My name's Don. What's yours?"

I wanted no part of Don, a rootless outcast like me, but I didn't know how to get rid of him. He followed me up the street. "Are you going to the hotel?"

"I don't know," I lied.

"Maybe we could be friends—help each other," he said. I heard in his voice echoes of my own despair. "No, leave me alone," I said abruptly, crossing the street. I was shocked at my own cruelty, my snobbery. Don dropped away, and even more upset, I reached into my pocketbook to feel around for the comforting plastic bottle. I closed my shaking hands around it, glanced down, and spotted several half-filled capsules among the full ones. Since Radcliffe, my homemade supplements had increased from thirds to halves. In an increasingly familiar movement, with my hand still concealed in the bag, I pushed off the bottle top. I rolled one of the shiny, half-filled capsules up and into my palm with my forefinger, then dexterously pinched it with my thumb, while I snapped the bottle cap back on with my free fingers. In a swift gesture, I popped it into my mouth and swallowed.

At the hotel, I discovered that I had lost my only identification, the Air Travel Card my father had given me. It crossed my mind that since taking the medication I was losing things in direct correlation to the number of capsules I swallowed. I ignored this discomfiting realization, and with Dexedrine-given bravado, convinced the desk clerk to take a Long Island bank check.

From the hotel room, I called home. "Dad, help me. What should I do?" My mother got on the other line, and at the sound of both of their voices, I began to cry.

"Why don't you call Aunt Polly, dear?" my mother asked.

"Wausau is a hundred and forty miles away," I sobbed. But the truth was, I didn't want to call her. She would, I knew, be in Madison within hours to take over, and I felt I would lose whatever was left of my determination to make a break with the past, away from the family's watchful eye.

My father was calm. This was just the kind of situation he liked—a challenge in which he could use his persuasive powers. But at the same time, I was uncomfortably aware, as I had been at Radcliffe, that without the pills I would have been less distraught, and he less helpful. We were in a very different relationship now than we had been only a year ago. My increasing desperation was giving him a chance to be a hero—my hero. The new arrangement was strangely alluring to me—and, I suspected sometimes, to him.

"Now, Jo, I want you to calm down and go back to the housing office right now."

"They'll be closed. They close at five."

"All right, then just hold out and go there tomorrow. Be there at nine and I'll see what I can do."

I arrived at the housing office before it opened, frightened and vulnerable. I hadn't had a capsule yet. I had made it a rule never to take one before breakfast.

Mrs. Green was startled to see me at the door, but told me to come in. "We'll see what we can do," she said with a sigh. Her phone rang even before she had a chance to take off her jacket. "Yes. She's here. Yes, Mr. Rosengarten, of course we're trying to do whatever we can." I could see she was surprised to hear from a parent. "I don't really understand why she couldn't stay across town for a while," she said, sighing. "Lots of students do." I didn't know what my father was saying, but apparently he had gained her sympathy. "Yes, yes, of course we'll keep on trying."

Almost on cue, I burst into tears. I hadn't slept. A combination of anxiety and, I suspected, too much medication had kept me up almost all night. Mrs. Green was alarmed at my unexpected show of emotion. "Well," she repeated hurriedly, "I'll certainly try, Mr. Rosengarten, you can be sure of that."

She offered me a Kleenex and leafed through her file once more. She took out a card. "The woman who runs this house is very kind. Maybe . . ." She dialed a number, turned away, and spoke in a low voice for a while, then hung up. "Well, there may be a chance. Now you just sit there and be patient till she calls back."

Ten minutes later the phone rang. Mrs. Green picked it up and listened, then smiled. "Well, you're in luck," she said when she put down the receiver. "Two of the girls at Walden House have agreed to turn their double into a triple. You can go over there, talk to them, and move in right away."

I'd been saved. I repressed the nagging memory of my recent panic, of the extra dose of pills I had taken the day before, of the desperate phone call home, and the humiliating scene this morning. Never mind. Everything would be all right now.

Fifteen minutes later, I took my first full capsule of the day, checked out of the hotel, and followed Mrs. Green's directions to 222 Langdon Street. Walden House. A Tudor mansion at the center of the center. A living room with a piano (my father would rejoice), comfortable couches, and girls in bobby sox who could have been bit players from *Good News* sitting on them.

Life at Walden was everything I expected. And I my-self was more than I expected. Less self-conscious, with a figure closer and closer to normal, and hyped up twice daily by my "medication"—to which Weinstock, as a part-ing gift, had added even more "oomph"—I entered a new phase: I was a social success for the first time in my life, popular with boys and girls alike. I was elected vice president of the house (essentially a popularity contest) within two months of my arrival. With the capsules to sus-tain me, I found I could be witty and deceptively open in a way I'd never been before. It was almost as though the pills had opened a long-closed part of my brain and re-leased another me—an energetic, lively, humorous char-acter I found it irresistible to impersonate, but in whose success I could take no satisfaction.

I got straight A's with half the effort expended at Bar-nard or at Woodmere Academy. I was sure the pills were responsible for these, too.

But not everything was going my way. Increasingly, the sight of my sagging breasts alarmed me. The skin, stretched and then re-stretched by my gains and losses, had lost some of its elasticity. I was reminded of my grandmother's aging breasts, and I shuddered. Would I, at nineteen, end up with breasts like hers? In the Field House, where all the new students had to go for a phys-ical, I kept a sheet wound tightly around me. There was not one girl like me. Even the overweight ones had plump, full breasts. Not one had ruined her youthful body as I had.

If you had a handicap that no one knew about, I won-dered, was it better or worse than one that was obvious? Worse, I decided. You got no sympathy, were expected to act the same as everyone else while under the yoke of a disability; in my case, two yokes: a disfigured body and a pseudo-personality—a person I began to think of as the Other Me.

For when I was dressed, boys often whistled at me, heads turned. Though I still wore a "special" bra, with extra wide straps, the new, smaller bras made me look shapely and desirable—even sexy. Nor could I ignore the implied or sometimes spoken admiration of my friends at Walden. "I wish I looked as good in a sweater as you," said Enid, a shrimpy, nervous girl who had attached herself to me from the first day and hounded my footsteps whenever I'd let her.

I thought about the changes in me and made a conscious decision. I would actively squelch the convictions that my newly thin body was not what it appeared to be when I was dressed; that no one would like me if he knew the "real," unmedicated me; that the only way I could deal with the challenge of male admiration was with courage from a pill bottle, and would ride the crest.

In October, at the Quonset hut library built to accommodate the influx of war veterans studying under the G.I. Bill, Enid introduced me to Mike Dworkin. He was a first-year medical student who, I later found out, had a reputation among the girls on Langdon Street for "loving and leaving 'em." He had melting brown eyes, an interest in psychiatry, and a cold-blooded determination to finish medical school "with no strings." ("I can't get involved. My parents won't pay my way through medical school if I do. I explain that to all my girlfriends before I go out with them," he said matter-of-factly on our first date.)

I was startled by his chilling frankness, but decided to

ignore it. And when we kissed, at the top of the steps of the Capitol building, not far from the hotel where I had spent my first terrible night in Madison, I felt an overwhelming physical attraction—for me, a completely novel experience. We couldn't keep away from each other. We studied together at the Quonset hut, holding hands until, unable to bear it, we went to the small storm door enclosure to kiss—deep, long, passionate kisses, true "soul kisses," in which I felt I was pleasantly drowning.

At Walden House, where, like all the houses, a 10:30 weekday, 12:30 weekend curfew was strictly enforced, we kissed good night again, at first gently brushing our lips back and forth against each other's mouths, then, unable to resist, again thrusting our tongues deep inside, rotating them around each other, biting softly, unable to pull away. Sometimes we sat on the living room couch, surrounded by other couples discreetly necking by the forties college rules: one foot of each pair must be flat on the ground. I felt pressing against me the same hardness I had felt with the boy at the Harvard dance, but now it was exciting.

The next step was inevitable. Mike lived on State Street, a block from Langdon, in a furnished room that was not run by the school. Only boys or upper-classmen girls were allowed the privilege of living off campus. "Joey, you have to come with me," he begged. My hesitation had nothing to do with my desires or morals, everything to do with my sense of bodily ugliness and psychological unreality. But I dared not say no. I could no longer imagine my life without Mike. I ignored the memory of his early warnings, his reputation as a heart-breaker, and the picture of an ex-girlfriend, Sally, he still kept on his dresser.

"I want one of you, too," he said casually when I asked him about her.

For the time being, my fears were unfounded. We went to his room and necked into a frenzy—both feet *off* the floor. But though my skirt was off, I was still in a sweater, slip, and underpants. He still hadn't tried to remove my bra. My passion was now cooled by the terrible fear of what would happen when he did. I was sure he would recoil in horror; reject me; maybe, even, expose me to the world. In just a few months, I had become completely dependent upon him, and I was determined to go to any lengths to hold him and avoid the inevitable discovery.

Soon, I was called upon to go to lengths I had never anticipated. A few days after we had established the habit of meeting in Mike's room at lunchtime, he finally felt for the hooks on my bra. I squirmed away, terrified, but he mistook my reluctance for conventional morality.

"Okay, I guess you're right," he said, and I was filled with despair. Now he would drop me. But no, it seemed he had decided to take another tack. To my amazement, I heard the zipper of his pants being pulled down. Although frightened, I was relieved that his focus had shifted. "Here, hold it," he said, as though it were the most ordinary thing in the world. I did; it felt hard and warm, shocking but not unpleasant. "Move your hand up and down," he said. I would do anything, relieved that his attention had shifted away from my breasts.

In a daze, I realized he was pushing my head downwards toward his penis. Why?

"Put it in your mouth," he said quietly.

74

Dumbstruck, I did as I was told until suddenly, when I thought I was about to choke, he pulled it out of my mouth and swiftly, efficiently, manipulated the swollen thing—hardly recognizable as the same one I had handled just a few minutes earlier—until a whitish fluid emerged. He groaned with pleasure.

I couldn't believe I was in this room, witnessing this phenomenon, and having performed this strange and, I was sure, never-before-heard-of act. I was convinced that I would not have been doing it if we had continued to neck in the usual forties order: kissing, petting with a bra, petting without a bra; that my fear of discovery had driven us to this strange perversion. (Months later, when I checked the practice out and found it had a name and was not, after all, quite as unusual as I had thought, it struck me as ironic that I had performed fellatio with a man before I had even had my bra off.)

What I had thought was surely a one-time event now became a habit. Mike met me daily after morning classes at the top of Bascom Hill in the icy cold of a Wisconsin winter, and we went to his room. But I was no longer enjoying our lovemaking. The long, voluptuous kisses had been superceded by Mike's interest in this new activity, and I slowly became depressed and silent. Although I found the act itself not altogether unpleasant, my awareness of why I was participating in it was.

I had gone with Mike for six months now—a record, someone told me, for one of his girlfriends. And I had also lost ten more pounds. I weighed 145. But I noticed that Mike was more distant. I now remembered with terror his original warnings—warnings I was sure he'd forgotten in the heat of our first passionate attachment, warnings I was sure I could have made him forget forever if I were not a fraud. I sensed that he was slipping away and was convinced that this was again the cost of my earlier and current follies.

The end came swiftly. Mike had been increasingly moody. When we walked down the street he no longer held my hand. Some days he didn't show up to pick me up after classes. "Look, Joey, I hope we can be friends. But if you think about it, realistically, where can our relationship go at this point? I mean, do you want to marry me? You don't really want that, do you? I can see you're not ready to sleep with me. I don't blame you. Honest." I turned scarlet, ashamed that he should think me so conventional. But of course, I couldn't explain my problem.

There was, I realized, no way I could hold him. I had to let him go.

CHAPTER 5

Two weeks later I was crying again, in the middle of the vast geology lecture hall where Professor Loudon was explaining conglomerate rocks and their formation. "Y'see this," he said, holding up a rock bulging with the many different stones embedded in it. "All those little fellers in there are different from each other. Every single one! Amazing, ain't it!"

Seeing his enthusiastic face made me feel even worse. What had happened to the lonely but curious child who had spent long afternoons studying breeds of cats in the C volume of Compton's Encyclopedia, who had memorized the lyrics to *Finian's Rainbow, Call Me Mister, Tonight at 8:30*? Would I ever again get excited about something—anything—outside of myself, as Dr. Loudon had?

Meanwhile, the tears, coming from some bottomless well of grief and abandonment too deep for the medicine to reach, flowed more and more rapidly down my face and dripped onto my carefully outlined notes.

The tears had no respect for surroundings. Embarrassingly, shockingly, unexpectedly, just as then, I cried;

77

in Rennebohm's drugstore, at meals in Walden House, and especially in bed at night, when I wished I could go to sleep and never wake up.

Now, surreptitiously, as Dr. Loudon darkened the room to show slides, I reached in my bag for another capsule, thrust it into my mouth, and swallowed it quickly. Though I'd found the medicine could only dull the pain, not eliminate it, I was sure it was the only thing that would get me through this. All thoughts of cutting down, of eventually stopping the pills, were temporarily forgotten. I felt I had no choice.

One day about three weeks after breaking up with Mike, I ran into Midge Marcus, a sultry brunette with a beautiful figure and a face like Ava Gardner's. I'd heard through the grapevine that she was Mike's newest conquest. I knew her vaguely from mixers.

"Oh, Jo-Jo, how are you?" she said, stopping me before I had a chance to cross to the other side of Langdon Street.

"All right," I muttered, lowering my eyes against the stinging warning that more tears were on the way.

"I don't exactly know how to say this," Midge went on, with what seemed to me a patently false attempt at compassionate camaraderie, "but I hope you don't mind about what's happened. I mean, about me and Mike. You were breaking up anyway, weren't you? Everybody said so. Anyway, that's what Mikie told me."

Mikie! I couldn't answer. Head lowered, I walked carefully past her and took a moment's brief satisfaction in the fact that my eyes didn't overflow till I was several steps away. Though I had taken a capsule just an hour before, I immediately took another one. I was using the capsules with such frequency now that I needed more and more prescriptions. Dr. Weinstock's letters grew cautious, though he continued to send the prescriptions.

> *Dear Jo,*
>   *I am beginning to feel that you have been taking the medication for too long. It has been almost two years now and you are close to your ideal weight. . . . Sometimes the medication produces a psychological dependency, though, as I assured you, no physical addiction is possible.*

Curse him! Ashamed, but past caring, I grabbed the life-saving piece of paper he'd enclosed and rushed to Rennebohm's, where the druggist was beginning to regard me with suspicion. "Weren't you in here just a few weeks ago?" he asked.

"Oh, I have plenty left from then," I said, secretly reminding myself to be sure to go to another drugstore the next time. "I just wanted to get this filled before I lost it."

The medicine was expensive, and my father wrote a note of mild protest about my increasingly frequent calls or letters asking for money. I explained away the extra thirty or forty dollars a month the pills cost by saying I needed some clothes, or new books, or school supplies.

My father, of course, had no idea that I was still in touch with Dr. Weinstock, or that I was taking any medication, and the new sweetness of his tone was deeply troubling.

The other news from home saddened me further. My brother Frank, only twenty-two, was engaged to be married, and I felt cut off from what I knew would be a lot of excitement at home. Worse, I felt removed, emotionally and physically, from Frank himself. In spite of my father's seeming preference for him years before, we had been close, and though I had liked Beth, his fiancée, now that he was to be married I found I was intensely jealous. I was losing Frank, too. My sense of abandonment increased.

At the same time, the false optimism and solicitude my letters home inspired remained a painful contrast to what was really going on. I had succeeded in convincing everyone that things were just fine. And as usual, my father had managed to turn the last-minute Barnard withdrawal into a victory.

> *Dear Jo,*
>   *I know that Mother wrote you yesterday, and*
> *perhaps has given you all the information with*
> *reference to our visit with Miss Elliot. I presume you*
> *already know that your place at Barnard is so secure*
> *that you could re-enter any time you chose to do so.*
> *However, we all know that it would not be*
> *particularly wise to make any change except at the*
> *very beginning or end of the semester.*
>   *We were very much interested to hear that she had*
> *always been of the opinion that it was most desirable*
> *for students to vary their college careers rather than*
> *spend their entire college lives in one spot, so you see*
> *what you have done will perhaps turn out to be a good*
> *move. We do hope that you will find Wisconsin*
> *offering what you most desire.*

Then again, an uneasy reference to the money situation:

> *I trust you have enough funds to carry you for a
> little while, but I expect you to write me and let me
> know the name of the bank that you would find
> convenient so that I can establish a contact.*

And shortly after, in another handwritten note, this
time from home:

> *Jo dear—We are so happy that you are at ease now,
> and we have so much respect and admiration for the
> manner in which you handled that first difficult week
> out there, and how you have been holding your own
> ever since. It would have undoubtedly floored most
> anyone who had less fortitude and control.*

The next paragraph was the hardest of all to take.

> *I know I have been complaining a bit about the
> money you have been asking for, but I know you are
> not a spendthrift, and I want you to ask for anything
> at all that you need, and would perhaps be agreeable
> to your asking for something you just want without
> needing it. Good night—it's just midnight here—all
> send their love.*

Slowly, as the weeks went by, my crying decreased, but
I continued the increased dosages: three or four full capsules a day. I was, as Dr. Weinstock had said, close to my
weight goal of 135 now, but every time I got near it, I'd
gain a few pounds in order to justify—to myself and to
Dr. Weinstock—the need for more.

One day in February, about a month after the breakup

with Mike, I heard that there were to be tryouts for Noel Coward's *Fumed Oak*. I knew the play by heart from a recording. And I was thin enough now, I thought, to try out for a part. I popped a capsule and went to the tryouts. I was good and I knew it—one of the few at the auditions who was familiar with Coward, with the touch of Cockney accent required, with the picture of drab, middle-class British life Coward was trying to portray. I felt somehow that if I got a part it would turn me around, would enable me to give up the pills, or cut down. I would get the public recognition—the attention—I so desperately wanted.

I was called back twice, then again. There were three of us left and only two women's parts. I didn't get either. When the director took me aside to explain the decision, his kind comments were cruelly ironic. "Your reading was terrific, but you're just too striking—too attractive a type, physically, for the part. We needed someone plumper, dowdier. Try out again, though," he continued encouragingly. "You certainly have talent. And we'll be casting some more one-acters in about a month." A month. Too long to wait. I had wanted a part now, when I needed it.

"Thanks. I'll think about it," I said. But what I was really thinking about was the reassuring vial of capsules in my pocketbook.

The following weekend, Enid fixed me up again—this time with another medical student named Conrad, a smooth operator with experienced hands. He invited me to the medical school dance, and reluctantly, I agreed to go. Maybe Mike would be there. He would see me, realize he'd made a terrible mistake, drop Midge, and insist on taking me home. This, in spite of the overwhelming evidence that he was lost to me forever.

I never made it to the dance. Conrad, it turned out, was a friend of Mike's and had arranged for us to share our cab down to the hotel, where the dance was being held, with Mike and Midge. My fantasies crumbled in less than the five minutes it took to reach the hotel. Mike treated me with polite (and, I felt, cruel and calculated) indifference, and the sound of his soft voice, speaking to Midge with the same solicitous interest he had shown when we first went out together, was too much for me to take. My equilibrium toppled, my Desoxyn high became a low, and to everyone's astonishment, I burst into tears in the cab. Unable to stop crying, I left Conrad gaping at the hotel door and returned to Walden.

The next weekend, there was an Open House—what some of the girls cynically referred to as a "cattle auction"—at Walden. Boys from all the fraternities and the independent houses came over to meet and size up the second term's new crop of coeds plus any they might have missed in September. I couldn't bring myself to go down. I didn't want to meet anyone new.

Enid came upstairs. "There's a boy here you just have to meet," she said. "Come on. Just come down for a minute. He's from New York, too. You'll like him."

"So far your introductions have left something to be desired," I said, "so how about leaving me alone."

"Come on," she begged. "I told him all about you."

"Oh, all right," I said suddenly. I couldn't bear any more of Enid's wheedling arguments. And in spite of my depression, I was faintly curious. "But just because he's from New York doesn't mean I'm going to like him."

Ross was a tall and gangly boy who bore a vague but strangely comforting facial resemblance to me. We both had angular faces, large brown eyes, wide mouths. And I found his slight New York intonations surprisingly reassuring after all. I think he, too, felt a spark of recognition. "So this is Jo-Jo," he said with a wide grin. "Enid's been telling me all about you—what a paragon you are," he said. His smile took the edge off his sarcasm. "Sings. Plays the piano. Smart. Gets good marks—"

"She walks, she talks, she rolls on her belly like a reptile," I interrupted, in a con man's singsong, and we both laughed.

Do you ever realize it when you've met someone who will become a significant figure in your life? Certainly I didn't, on that bleak day in February. Ross and I continued to talk, and I discovered that he came from the same kind of family as mine, with aunts and uncles who visited often, though he was not as well off. None of the other boys I'd met at Wisconsin, including Mike, had ever mentioned their families except in the most casual way. They were far too busy trying to project smooth, independent images, and might have been hatched full-grown on campus for all they ever spoke of home and hearth.

Then Ross left. I sensed he would be back and had, for the first time, a sense of regret not only that I had again met someone I liked as the false Other Me, but the discomfiting realization that Ross was a person with whom I could probably have talked almost as easily without the pills.

But within days another crisis arose that put such passing regrets out of my mind. Dr. Weinstock wrote:

> Dear Jo-Jo,
>   I am increasingly concerned about the length of time you have been taking the medication. I am quite sure you can do without it now. My conscience won't

*allow me to send you another prescription. Maybe you
should see a doctor out there if you feel you still need
some help in losing those last few pounds. . . .*

"Need some help." So delicately put. Christ, I had been
increasingly hooked for more than a year and a half, and
now, while I was stranded in Madison, Wisconsin, he proposed to cut me off. And after his soft, sixty-year-old
kisses, the invitation to Atlantic City, the promises to *keep
me supplied* with which we had parted.

The letter went on:

*You know I am so fond of you and want only the best
for you.*

Bastard! "Only the best." Didn't he know it was too
late? That if he'd wanted "only the best" he'd never have
told me, "It will just cut your appetite down a little, just
make it a little simpler to lose"?

*Write me about your life there, and don't think you
are imposing on me, as you certainly are not. Your
letters needn't sound so official. I like to hear of your
intimate things. If they are too intimate, don't worry,
they will be destroyed.*

So on top of everything else he wanted a report on my
sex life. Shocked, I dropped the letter in my wastebasket.
But my shock was nothing compared with the panic that
seized me at the thought of having to get along without
the pills.

Within a week I had conceived of a desperate plan. On

85

a sunny, bitter-cold day in early March, I walked toward the university clinic with my coat, as usual, unbuttoned in the twenty-below weather. It was a side benefit of the constant, drug-induced high I was on that I was never cold—that I was, in fact, warmed by the fires of an almost feverish energy. And that day, fear was added to this manic energy. For I was planning a criminal act—my first. But I was also, I reflected drily, taking part of Weinstock's advice. As he suggested, I *was* going to see another doctor.

The hospital was at the outer edges of the campus. This was the terrain of the docile, corn-fed boys and girls from in-state who lived in the neat, square dormitories on campus—a world apart from Langdon Street, with its old, rambling houses and exotic blend of New Yorkers, Californians, blacks, orientals, Indians, and more adventurous native Wisconsinites. Out here, I passed no one I knew, and I was glad.

In the clinic, the receptionist—a slim, white-haired lady with rimless glasses—looked up shrewdly. I was convinced she could read my mind. "Did you have an appointment?"

"Oh, no. I was told you could just come in between three and five and someone would see you."

"Yes, yes. That's all right. What seems to be the problem?"

I was not prepared for questions at this level, and managed only a feeble, "Well, I'd rather discuss it with the doctor, if that's all right?"

"I see." She was not unsympathetic, but her keen glance again unnerved me. "Here. Fill this out."

86

Oh my God. Forms. Records. They'd trace me down, report me to the police, to my parents. But if I didn't fill them out correctly, they'd figure something was wrong when they checked my school records to be sure I was a student entitled to medical care. And perhaps they'd do that right away. I filled out the card, my hands shaking.

"Just wait there. I'll get one of the interns as soon as one of them is free."

Oh God. An intern. He might not even know about Dexedrine, no less its compounds. Or worse yet, he might know all about them. ("Sometimes they produce a psychological dependency . . .") I couldn't decide which would be worse.

Ten minutes later I was in an office, a small cubicle that put me close to the desk. Convenient for my purposes, I noted gratefully. The intern, disconcertingly handsome, was about to sit down, and I braced myself for putting into effect my two-pronged plan—the first part a legal cover for the more important and illegal second part.

He was preoccupied, looking around on his desk for something. There, casually brushed aside by his searching fingers, were three prescription pads—two thick ones and one thinner one on top of the others. He found the slip of paper he was looking for, stuffed it in his pocket, sat down, and turned to me with an apologetic smile. "Sorry. Now, what seems to be the problem?"

"Well," I began, feeling that my face must be bright purple, "you see, I used to be very fat."

He looked puzzled, surprised. "Yes?"

"Well, back in New York, to help me lose weight, I was taking—"

The phone on his desk rang sharply and I came to a dead halt.

"Be with you in a minute," he said kindly, picking up the receiver. He listened for a few seconds, then said, "Okay, I'll be right over. Sorry, Miss—uh"—he looked at the form I had filled out before—"Miss Rosengarten? This is kind of an emergency. I'll be right back, I promise."

He left the office. I realized that chance had given me an incredible opportunity to fulfill my plan. Now all that was needed was the necessary courage. Yet I hesitated. Perhaps he'd notice if one of the pads was missing. Then what? Even if I dashed out with it before he returned, he had my name on the hospital form. And if I took the form with me, he might remember my name anyway. "Miss Rosengarten," he had said.

But I had to take the risk. Trembling, I leaned across the desk, ready to spring back into my chair at the sound of a footstep. But the hall was quiet. With one swift gesture, I grabbed the second pad—the thickest—and, dizzy, replaced the skinny one on top. The stolen pad was in my pocketbook.

Almost immediately, I heard voices down the hall, but I didn't turn my head, afraid, by any extra move, to betray an undue anxiety. I forced a smile as he entered the room. "Everything all right?" I asked, with phony interest. Don't look at the desk, I prayed. Don't. *Don't.*

"Oh, sure—nothing that serious after all. Now, what were you saying?"

I ran through my history of overweight, but he was not a good audience, and didn't react with the pleasing combination of surprise and interest my story usually elicited.

("What? You really weighed two hundred and twenty-five pounds? I can't believe it!") I made a point of emphasizing how much the medicine had helped me, casually mentioning the combination of ingredients to gauge his reaction, but he remained impassive.

"So you see," I wound up, "I still have about five to ten pounds to lose." (The same five to ten pounds I'd been gaining and losing for months to justify continuing to take the capsules.) And I also thought that if I could just get this prescription from him, I'd have pulled it off. I tried to smile brightly, though my knees, fortunately concealed behind his desk, were trembling.

He hesitated, and I felt as though he must surely hear my heart pounding. I knew, of course, exactly what was in the capsules, but I had to have him write it out, because I couldn't recall just how it had appeared on the last form. Fool that I was, I thought, I had had the last one from Weinstock filled just a few weeks back, never suspecting it would be the last. That was why I needed a new sample—a model from which to work.

"You know," he said, as he turned slowly toward the prescription pads, "you really have to watch it with that stuff. It isn't wise to keep taking it too long." He stared at the pads, then looked at me. My legs were shaking so badly now that I had to mash my pocketbook down on them to keep them from affecting my upper body. This would be it—the moment of discovery. His hand moved toward the pads, and again he hesitated. "I'm thinking that maybe we ought to weigh you first," he said. So that was it. He hadn't even noticed the pads. I was aware that I was sweating and hoped it didn't show.

I tried to speak calmly. "Oh no, that's really not necessary. My doctor in New York and I agreed on what I should weigh." I didn't want to be weighed because I didn't want to have to come back to the clinic for a check-up—didn't want to come back ever. "I weigh one forty now, and I'm five foot six. We think I should be about one thirty." Not true. I was all right at 135, as Dr. Weinstock and I had agreed. I tried to keep the note of desperation out of my voice.

"Well," he hesitated, then apparently decided to take me at my word and be rid of me, "I guess if this is the last time, it'll be all right."

"Thanks," I said, trying not to sound too groveling.

"Now what were those proportions again?" he asked. I told him:

> Desoxyn 5 mgs.
> Thyroid ¼ gr.
> Phenobarb. ¼ gr.
> # of caps. 50

It crossed my mind to suggest the addition of a skull and crossbones for decoration, but I repressed the thought. Casually, he wrote the prescription, tore it off, and handed it back to me. "Good luck," he said.

I had been granted a reprieve! I would be able to continue as the Other Me for a little longer—maybe, I realized, much longer. And, reckless now, I opened the container and took a capsule to celebrate.

CHAPTER 6

That night, when I was sure everyone had gone to bed, I crept down to the living room, the prescription and extra pad carefully hidden in my notebook. As usual at that hour, the room was deserted. Only a few lamps were lit for that rare Walden House student who might want to study past 10:30. I sat on the couch where, in happier times, Mike and I had necked. Then I took out the pad of blanks and put the prescription I had planned to use as my master copy underneath the top slip.

Panic-stricken, I saw that the blank prescription paper on the pad was much too thick for tracing. What could I do? Copying seemed too risky. Suppose I missed some small dot or curlicue that would be a giveaway to the pharmacist that the prescription was a forgery? Or suppose, by some terrible coincidence, the pharmacist had just filled a prescription written by that same doctor, and noticed that the handwriting wasn't quite the same?

Then I remembered from some childhood game the principle of tracing pictures by placing a light underneath. I tore off a prescription blank, put the original beneath, and leaned it on a transparent lamp shade. The letters were more visible. My hands shook so violently that I botched the first attempt, but with the aid of a paper clip to hold the two together, I could hold the shade steady with my now-free hand. The second copy was more successful; the third even better. I used a pencil first, then went over it in ink, and finally, erased any leftover pencil marks.

I practiced tracing the mysterious words and symbols (beneath the three drugs was written something that looked like "Misu et jac caps. #50," and below it "Sig. cap t tid") over and over on ordinary paper. I didn't want to waste the hard-won sheets on the hospital pad. Then, taking an artist's pride in my work, I made an exact duplicate on a blank prescription.

But at the last minute, I had another idea, a way to avoid having to go through the whole process soon again. Where the word "Repetatur," followed by "1, 2, 3, 4," was printed at the bottom, I hastily circled the "4," then had second thoughts and panicked again. Would a doctor ordinarily permit four refills? Impulsively, I crushed the perfect copy and tried to do another, this time circling the three, not the four.

"Hey, what are you doing up so late?"

I leaped back guilty from the lamp, hiding the blank behind my back.

Dressed in a frumpy green chenille robe, her sallow face shining with cold cream, Enid had descended the steps as she did everything—noiselessly, stealthily—insinuating herself into a room rather than coming in directly. I had found her hangdog heroine worship more and more disturbing lately. It was not me she admired, I was

92

sure, it was the Other Me—the unreal one, the only one anyone at Wisconsin knew.

"God, you scared me," I said, quickly collecting all the telltale scraps of paper, the rejected prescription copies. I noticed that my hands were trembling again.

"Sorry," she said abjectly. "Got a test tomorrow?"

"Yeah, French," I said. Enid was a sociology major and was studying Spanish. I knew she wouldn't check.

"You'll be too tired to take it," she said, coming closer.

"That's *my* problem, isn't it?" I said, more acidly than I had intended. "Anyway, you're up pretty late yourself, aren't you?"

She was hurt. "I thought you might like some company. I saw you go down before, and I was waiting for you to come up." Or had she been watching me from the dark hallway, I wondered.

"Thanks, but I really need to study. I'll see you tomorrow. Okay?"

"Well, okay," she said mournfully. "I don't see why you take notes on such tiny pieces of paper, though."

I felt my heart begin to pound. Enid was no fool. Even if she hadn't been hovering in the hall before I had scooped up the crumpled sheets from the pad, her observant eyes might have taken in everything. Everything? No, she couldn't know. Impossible.

Smiling faintly—enigmatically? knowingly?—she slithered from the room.

It was 2:30 A.M. when I finally went upstairs, still filled with feverish nervous energy. The extra afternoon pill had guaranteed a restless night. I'd made three good copies, though I wasn't as satisfied with any of them as I'd been with the one I'd impulsively destroyed. But I realized I probably couldn't do much better that night. And the next morning I took a bus to the first on the long list of outlying drugstores that were to keep me supplied with Desoxyn for two and a half more chaotic years.

That summer—the summer of '51—my brother was married on the big lawn behind our house on Long Island. The reception was held under a huge turquoise-and-white striped tent. My mother had chosen the color scheme, just as she had chosen to have the wedding at our house. "We have so much more room," she had said decisively, and Beth's family had acquiesced.

As maid of honor, I was wearing a festive, frilly, and quietly suggestive pale turquoise dress that was cut perfectly for me. Alan, the bride's brother—dark, brooding, and very good-looking—was interested in me, and I knew it. I had met him before—before losing weight, before Dr. Weinstock, before Desoxyn. He had hardly glanced at me in those days. Safely enveloped by my layers of fat, though, I had contemplated him often and long. Now he was doing the looking. I was, as always, painfully conscious of the falsity of both my appearance and personality, and of the hopeless game Alan and I would begin to play, but—made reckless by the combination of Desoxyn and champagne—I couldn't resist playing it.

We began to dance cheek to cheek as the five-piece band played a medley of Rodgers and Hammerstein show tunes. Suddenly, Alan drew back and looked at me. His eyes were beautiful—a deep, mahogany brown with long, straight, black lashes, not unlike Mike's.

"You've changed a lot, haven't you?" he said. His voice

94

was soft, with a humorous edge. He was intelligent, rumored to be brilliant ("His hobby is astronomy. He builds his own telescopes, you know," I remember my mother saying to my aunt a few days before).

"Yes, I guess I have." I was aware of a heady, compelling, masculine odor as he drew me close again, and I was powerfully drawn to him, as I knew he was to me. But as the hours passed and the effects of the pill I'd taken just before the wedding faded, I became increasingly anxious in his arms. I was already afraid of displeasing him, yet aware that in the long run I would have to do just that. I would have to let him down; worse yet, let myself down. A normal sexual relationship between us was impossible. Even in this initial encounter, I knew the relationship was doomed, as were all my relationships now. Still, I managed to keep my anxieties to myself, and we spent the entire evening dancing. When he finally left, at 2 A.M., we made a date to meet in the city, where I was starting a job the next day.

My father had persuaded a friend of his to hire me as a proofreader for the summer. His firm published *True Confessions, True Romances, Secret Stories,* and the job was perfect. I was determined to control my drug-induced tendency to be unnaturally garrulous and gregarious. I didn't move from my desk all day; there was no need to mingle with the editors and the rest of the staff nearby. One false relationship at a time was all I wanted to take on.

The material I was proofreading fascinated me. Women were involved in lurid affairs, had children out of wedlock, abandoned those children, abandoned their husbands, were themselves abandoned; were raped, seduced, molested. But there were no tales of nice Jewish girls from middle-class homes on Long Island becoming drug addicts; no "How I lost weight and traded in my old personality for a new one" or "How I sold my soul to the devil for a Dexedrine capsule" titles. My story, in 1951, was clearly not a usual one.

After our first date, Alan called me at the office and we went out almost every evening. If he called, I took an extra pill to buoy me up. I felt that I had to maintain the same level of seeming confidence and vivacity I had set at the wedding, and that I felt he expected. If he didn't call, I took a capsule to cope with the disappointment. Within days, I had become completely dependent on him, just as I had been with Mike and Larry. And as before, after a few brief skirmishes over my bra, we, too, worked out a sexual routine.

After dinner in the city—usually at the cozy, inexpensive Café Brittany on 9th Avenue—as he drove me back to Cedarhurst, he slowly worked his hand beneath the skirt of my dress and began to stroke the insides of my thighs. "So smooth. Your thighs are so smooth," he said softly. Weren't everybody's thighs smooth? I wondered. How many other thighs had he stroked in order to be able to make such a statement? But I was flattered. Even if my breasts were awful, at least I had smooth thighs.

After about ten minutes, he worked his fingers beneath my underpants. Still driving with one hand, he began to stroke my genitals with the other. The sensations were exquisite, and I could quickly feel a moistness. Was this supposed to happen? I wondered if perhaps there was something wrong with me. But I didn't want him to stop.

As I became more and more aroused, I wanted to tell

96

him to pull over, to join me in this strange wonderland. What was there in it for him? Surely caressing me must bore him. My fears were based entirely on the ultimate prospect of losing him. If he was bored, he might drop me. But I didn't dare suggest that he become more involved. Suppose he agreed and, with both hands free, again grasped for my breasts? As with Mike, I couldn't risk it. So I could only wait till he thrust his fingers inside me—a strange, pleased expression on his face as I gasped at the thrilling, unfamiliar sensation, a mixture of pleasure and embarrassment.

Our frequent dates were beginning to attract the attention of both our families, who saw the relationship as a charming follow-up to that of Frank and Beth. "Maybe we should have waited and had a double wedding," hinted Alan's mother, and I could only smile faintly. Couldn't she see that marriage—any of the things normal girls my age might undertake—was impossible for me? The whole relationship is a phony, a fake, I wanted to scream. But I remained silent, and the summer rushed to an end.

On Saturdays, I often drove to Alan's home on Shore Road in Brooklyn, where he lived with his parents and was indeed building his own telescope in the basement. I knew that after a few capsules, I shouldn't be driving, but one day in mid-August, I took my parents' car anyway.

Agitated and overwrought from the medication, I headed for his house. My mind wandered restlessly, anxiously, to the afternoon ahead, and to what wise and witty things I could say when I got to Alan's. Just thinking about that made me nervous, and I put my right hand in my pocketbook and felt around to be sure the enchanted vial was still there. My other hand lay loosely on the steering wheel. I was oblivious to the traffic light ahead, or to the fact that I was much too close to the car in front of me. When it stopped for the light, I plowed into its rear.

Paralyzed, my hand still in my pocketbook, I sat there and watched the driver emerge from his car. Looking dazed but furious, he walked unsteadily toward me.

"What the hell's the matter with you?" the man asked, his teeth clenched with anger as I tried to apologize. "Goddamn dizzy dames."

He was right. I *was* dizzy.

The police came and we exchanged license numbers and gave reports. I carried the scene off with surprising aplomb, once I realized the man wasn't seriously injured. Unlike liquor, the Desoxyn was undetectable.

Considerably shaken despite my outer poise, I continued to Alan's, taking another half-filled capsule for comfort on the way.

After the accident, the danger I was in seemed more vivid to me. And I had concrete evidence that the damage being done could affect other people, too. I knew now I needed help, but I didn't know what to do, whom to see. Going back to Wisconsin could only mean the continuation of the pill habit. But even at home now, people had begun to accept the Other Me as the real one. Telling my parents seemed out of the question. I couldn't bear to think of their horrified faces. How disappointed they would be to find that my new slimness, my vivacity, the eloquent letters from Wisconsin, and my "courage" in sticking it out there had all come out of a plastic container. And of course there would be no question of their continuing to underwrite my expensive habit. They'd want to put an immediate stop to it, and that was unthinkable.

I had stopped seeing Dr. Weinstock now that I was my own source of supply. And I dared not return to Dr. Schmidt. She, I knew, would also insist that I give up the pills. "You see, Cho-Cho, it is chust as I said it would be," I could hear her crowing. "You were not ready to be thin. You are still a fat girl in a thin body." No, Schmidt was out and there was nowhere to run.

All summer, Ross had been traveling in Europe. He had written regularly, but I had answered only briefly, if at all. I had been completely engrossed with Alan. Now, as the summer was coming to an end, the relationship was clearly waning. Alan, like Mike, was cautious; he sensed that something was terribly wrong, though he didn't know what it was.

"Is there something you want to tell me?" he'd asked suddenly one night after he'd driven me home.

"No. Why? Why do you ask?" My God, was he on to something?

"I don't know. There's something about you—something I can't figure out."

"You know us exotic Wisconsin types," I said. "Inscrutable, enigmatic; all the mysteries of the Midwest locked in our seductive glances."

He didn't question me further.

In late August, at the height of my indecision about what to do next, and filled with anguish at the slow and what I felt to be inevitable deterioration of my relationship with Alan, I got a strangely persuasive letter from Ross:

*Dear Thérèse [we called each other by the romantic
names in the novels we'd read in French class, and
this one was particularly apt: Thérèse Desqueyroux
was a woman who had temporarily gone mad],*

*Where will you be living this term? Jer [Ross's
roommate] and I will come to see you* aussitôt que
vous revenez. Courage pour l'avenir. *We await
your return.*

It was signed *"Votre ami de Paris."* Well, God knows, *"un
ami"* was what I needed. I returned to Wisconsin.

I had waited so long before making up my mind to
return that there were no more rooms left at Walden. In
any case, I felt that my increasingly frenetic behavior
would be noticed by my friends—Enid, especially. Better
to keep some distance, as I had been doing at home, from
those who might observe me too closely.

Again, a room was found for me by the housing office—this time in Norris Hall, another Langdon Street
dorm. My room was on the first floor, at the end of a
long, damp corridor. The room had latticed windows on
the street and on the sides.

My roommate, Natalie Elfenbein, a placid, studious
redhead from Chicago, had a fat face, a surprisingly
beautiful figure, and what I contemptuously felt to be an
inordinate attachment to her mother. She telephoned
"Mummy" almost every night, and returned to the room
with tears in her eyes. I was not sympathetic. I feared and
envied her ability to concentrate, her beautiful breasts,
her loving family life. She was horrified when, my first
night at Norris, after Ross and Jerry knocked on our win-

dow to say hello, I climbed out—recklessly breaking the dorm rules—to wander the now-deserted streets of Madison with them till midnight. That became a nightly pattern.

"*C'est* Alyssa," cried Jerry, as I emerged through the casement window. "Alyssa, beware! Beware *la fenêtre étroite!*" We were all three now enrolled in Samuel Rogers' advanced course in the twentieth-century French novel and loved to playact the characters in Gide's *La Porte Étroite*.

Though I could barely concentrate on any of my other courses, in Professor Rogers' novel class I was inspired. Instead of confusing me, the capsules seemed to lend quicksilver to my mind and hand, and Professor Rogers almost invariably selected the essays I wrote in class, as though in a feverish dream, to read aloud.

My other subjects were a disaster. In a fit of drug-inspired overconfidence and momentary enthusiasm, I had signed up for a course in Greek. The daily memorization and translation were impossible for me. It required exactly the kind of concentration I now totally lacked. But I hesitated to drop it, since my decision to learn such a scholarly language had inspired a kind of awe in my family. With a sickening sense of oncoming disaster, I let the day for dropping courses pass.

Meanwhile, my success with men continued—exhilarating, but painfully confusing, because I believed it was based entirely on my drug-induced vivacity. But there was an underlying sadness to this vivacity, a mellow edge, a subtle shadow. I suspected, ironically, that it was this fine shade of difference from others, the mysterious

shadow cast by my secret awareness of my drug dependence, that was making me more popular than ever.

On the train between Chicago and Madison, I met
Lloyd, an artist and part-time instructor at the university,
who did a large watercolor portrait of me that I couldn't
connect with myself—a high-cheekboned beauty with lus-
trous eyes staring sadly at the viewer. And in the
Rathskeller, where I was spending more and more time,
Drew, a slim, wiry, graduate student with penetrating
green eyes and a passion for classical music, introduced
himself. He sent me flowers and records and wrote frantic, pleading letters to go with them. I continued to pose
for Lloyd, but I refused to go out with him, or Drew, or
anyone else.

Always, in the background, there was Ross. Sometimes
we would meet by chance in the music listening room of
the Student Union; or, if I missed him there, I'd meet
him and Jerry in the Rathskeller for a chocolate Coke
before returning to the dorm. In any case, they were back
a few hours later to knock on my window for our nightly
walks.

Sometimes, Ross or Jerry or both would stop dead in
the middle of the street, shut their eyes, and cry out,
"Alyssa, *je suis aveugle! Aidez-moi! Je suis aveugle!*" Then, as
they stumbled and groped wildly in the air, and we all
became convulsed with laughter, I'd lead them to the
Toddle House, where they consumed piles of pancakes
while I looked on.

During the hours between, they had been studying at
the apartment they shared off campus. My time wasn't
spent so profitably. More and more unable to concentrate, I'd spend the time till they came taking long,

soothing showers and washing my hair. Isolated in the shower with nothing to distract me, I would often feel my pulse racing, my heart pounding. Sometimes, I thought I was having a heart attack. Nervously, I started to pick at imaginary sores on my skin. Gradually, my chest and stomach were covered with small, red, rash-like spots. But nobody knew. I kept myself covered.

Soon, as the water streamed down on me, I began to hear mysterious voices. When the volume was low, they were incomprehensible whispers, but when I raised the volume, they ominously chanted "Inga-bugga, inga-bugga" over and over again—sounds I dimly recalled having first heard when as a child I had laughing gas for a tooth extraction. If I raised the volume even more, they took on the driving rhythms of a railroad train.

Terrified yet fascinated, I'd remain in the shower trying to identify the source of the voices—half-knowing I was imagining them; half convinced they were real. Words came to my mind from past sessions with Schmidt: delusional, schizophrenic, obsessive—words she had used to diagnose my condition. Now, they came back to haunt me.

I would leave the shower, trembling, get dressed, and join Jerry and Ross.

I spent Christmas in New York City, where my parents had taken an apartment in the Hotel Dorset for a few months as a break from the suburbs. My mother was still thrilled with my new figure and attributed my newfound energy to what she imagined was my own pleasure in being thin at last.

I realized that my parents, like everyone else, had

grown somewhat accustomed to me in my lively and out-going incarnation, though I had noticed my father's eyes on me a number of times when I tried to sneak a capsule out of my bag. Once, in a restaurant, I had been too care-less. "What is that you just took, Jo?" he asked sharply.

I was scared. My father had always been keenly obser-vant of me and what I ate in restaurants in a way that my mother, absorbed in studying the other people in the room, or her own reflection in a nearby mirror, wasn't. When I'd been gaining weight, it was he who'd say quietly, "Jo, that's the most fattening part." Now he'd seen me swallow a capsule. Had I made a disastrous blunder?

As casually as I could, I said, "Oh, it was nothing. Just an aspirin."

"Since when do you have headaches?"

Though he'd never done anything like it before, for a terrible minute, I thought he was going to ask to go through my pocketbook. But, either satisfied with my an-swer or fearful of going too far, he dropped the subject.

I continued to avoid my cousin Toni, who had recently married and had invited me to visit her in Philadelphia. I was too ashamed to see her; I knew that she of all people would penetrate the sham. And I felt, completely unrea-sonably, that, like Frank, she had deserted me by marry-ing.

Vacation was over, and I didn't go back to school on time. I knew I was failing most of my courses. What dif-ference did it make? My parents, still thinking I was the responsible student I'd always been, simply assumed I had an unusually long time off. They didn't ask ques-tions.

104

As the days slipped by, I got a letter from Lloyd, the artist. "Where are you? People are noticing you're not here. I miss you. Please come back." Just as the letter from Ross the summer before had seemed to will me to return, so now did the arrival of Lloyd's note come as a kind of sign. His seductive words seemed to draw me back irresistibly into what I began to see as the eye of the storm. I feared returning, knew I shouldn't, but could think of no other alternative. Besides, I realized that the Other Me was inescapable wherever I was. The voices in the shower had followed me to New York as well, and my nervous picking still kept the pitted sores on my chest from healing. I was certainly no better off here than at Wisconsin.

So once again I was deflected from seeking help at home. But I made a decision. I would return to school, but when I got there I would put an end to my addiction once and for all. I would speak to my advisor, speak to the dean—to someone, anyone, who could help. I took off for Madison once again.

I didn't have to worry about who to see when I got there. There was a letter waiting for me at Norris Hall. "Please see Dean Smith at your earliest convenience. You are currently failing four out of five courses and are on academic probation." This was the chance I needed, I thought.

Dean Smith was an efficient-looking woman in a black suit, with businesslike horn-rimmed glasses and brown hair cut in a trim feather cut. "Well, Johanna, what's behind all this?" she said, looking at some papers. "I see from your records that you've been an excellent student up to this term. Any special reason you're doing so badly now?"

It was now or never. How to present it?

"Well, you see," I began, "I was taking these pills to lose weight, and . . . uh . . ." My voice trailed off.

"Yes?" she said sympathetically.

"Well, I guess they don't really agree with me. I mean, they make me very nervous and jumpy. And I never sleep." To my embarrassment, my eyes were filling with tears.

"Well, why don't you just stop taking them? You don't look overweight to me."

Why indeed? I thought to myself. How simple it sounded: Just stop taking them.

"Well," I hesitated. How much would it be safe to say? "I guess I'm afraid to. I mean, I'm afraid my body's gotten kind of used to them. I mean—I don't know what would happen if I did stop." And that at least was true.

"Sounds to me as if you need a complete rest. I think a few days in the hospital would be a good idea. In fact, I'm going to insist that you go there. And I guess, in view of this . . . this *problem,* and of your previous good grades, we'll just give you Incompletes instead of F's on these courses you're failing. Fair enough?" She smiled brightly.

Yes, it was more than fair. The hospital would be worth a try. Maybe there I could be helped, would be able to pull myself together and stop taking the pills.

And that afternoon, I checked into the clinic—the same one from which I had emerged so triumphantly with the stolen prescription pad just about a year before.

CHAPTER 7

I spent almost all of that first drug-free day and a half dozing, the logical result of months of artificial wakefulness. I did manage to call my parents, and told them the same story I'd told the dean. And I called Toni, to whom, for the first time in years, I felt I could talk honestly. To her, I came as close as I'd ever done to confessing the full extent of my addiction and my desire to get over it.

But the minute the phone rang and I heard Jerry's voice, the afternoon of my second day at the hospital, my determination to remain completely drug-free evaporated.

"Alyssa, *où es tu? Et pourquoi, ma chérie?*"

My God, how could I hold my own with him and Ross in our continuous repartee without the pills?

To my temporary relief, Ross took over before I had time to answer Jerry. He was clearly worried, but for some reason convinced I was being kept in the hospital against my will. "Jesus, Jo, what's going on? I ran into Natalie about an hour ago and she told me you'd taken off like a shot for the hospital after you saw the dean yesterday, and wouldn't even tell her why. And why'd you tell her not to tell anyone else where you were going? What's all the secrecy about, anyway?" Without waiting for an answer, he went on. "Listen, Jer and I'll be over in an hour to spring you."

I froze. I couldn't think of a reason to tell them not to come. What to do now? My relationship with Ross was of growing importance to me. He had always been completely reliable, always there with a sympathetic word when I cried in the music listening room—though like everyone else who tried to get to know me, he was baffled about the cause of my unhappiness.

I also knew he was physically attracted to me. Often he tried to kiss me, and while I felt none of the magnetism toward him I'd felt toward Mike or Alan, there was a certain appeal in his straightforward desire. Over the Christmas vacation, he had visited me a few times, and without Jerry around as a buffer, a new tension had arisen between us.

"I think I'm in love with you," he shocked me by saying one night when, completely dressed as always, I had reluctantly submitted to his kisses and caresses.

"Oh my God, don't be," I said.

"Why not?"

"Because I'm not what you think I am. You wouldn't like me if you really knew me."

"Of course I would. I'll always love you—always. Anyway, how can you be something you're not? What do you mean?"

Was it the chemical me that he loved, not the real me? Could a chemical change you completely? Could it give you ideas for essays you wouldn't have otherwise? Could it make you witty, warm, self-assured? As I lay in the hospital, I wondered—could it be that the Other Me was in fact actually a real part of me, a part that I simply hadn't known existed before I took the pills?

I had skirted Ross's question that night. I kept my secret. Yet his declaration of love had reached me. Ross was nothing if not sincere, and mixed-up though I was, I knew he meant what he said. Would he feel that way, I wondered, would he be the rock I could cling to, if he knew me as I really was, whatever that might be? I couldn't take the chance.

My pocketbook still held a half-full bottle of pills. I hadn't worked up the courage to throw them away. And the hospital staff, with little or no experience with drug addiction, hadn't even bothered to ask for them when I checked in. Nor had the resident discovered the sores on my chest in his routine examination. When I clutched the robe to my breasts, he had discreetly inserted the stethoscope beneath it, meanwhile focusing his eyes on the wall behind me.

After Ross and Jerry's phone call, I scrambled to reach my purse. An hour would be just enough time for a pill to take effect. Keeping a wary eye out for the nurses, I extracted one under the covers and swallowed it dry. By the time Ross and Jerry came, I was almost my old self— or rather, what I'd come to think of as my "new" old self. But I convinced them I should stay in the hospital for a few days. After all, I had taken only one pill. There was still a chance for me.

"I have a low-grade fever," I said when they asked what was wrong, drumming up a professional-sounding phrase, "and some *mal de tête* thrown in. They think it might be mono."

Ross and Jerry seemed unimpressed, so I put a dramatic hand to my forehead, rolled my eyes upward in a pantomime of suffering, and added, "Or maybe smallpox, at the very least. Now let's see, what did that doctor say were the first signs? Low-grade fever? *Mal de tête?*"

We began to laugh. "No kidding, though, you'd better not come again," I said. "Whatever I have really might be catching, and you *do* want to be all pink and healthy for your classes, *n'est-ce pas?*"

As they reluctantly left the room, I called after them, "*Faites attention à votre santé!*" Then I lay back, relieved. The reliable chemical had done its work.

The next day I received two letters. The first was from my father:

> *Dear Jo,*
>
> *Enclosed is the check which you need.*
>
> *As we told you on the phone, we feel that you are handling yourself extremely well. We have every confidence, as you should have, that this interruption in your steady progress [from fat to thin, and in what he mistakenly took to have been the benefits of my sessions with Schmidt] will indicate to you as time goes on that you can handle yourself as well if not better than most.*
>
> *Of course you can do as you think best, but I would like to suggest that it would be a reasonable thing for you to suggest in a diplomatic way to the doctor in charge there that perhaps he or she would care to speak to Dr. Schmidt or communicate with her by mail. You can say that your dad suggested it but that you are passing it along without any opinion about it*

one way or the other. We are looking forward to
hearing from you, Sweetheart, and presume we will
do so in the next few days.

All our love,
Dad

How typical—and tactful—was that suggestion. My father was used to being in charge—and to my willingly following his advice. But there was no way that I would resume contact with Dr. Schmidt. And now that I had taken a capsule again, the letter's trusting tone was unbearable. I put it at the bottom of the drawer next to my bed.

The second letter was from Toni and was even more upsetting.

Dear Jo-Jo:
  No pleasantries at all—and you shall see why soon.
This is all too important for that. Jo-Jo—you have
reassured me, in your call, that your love for me is as
strong as it ever was, by laying down, along with the
pills, that very pose of mockery and sardonic humor
that was our stock in trade. Do you think I miss it? Do
you think I can do anything but thank God that we
have finally ousted that block to a deep, candid
relationship with each other? It's the greatest relief of
my life. In fact, in some ways, we've been pretending
with each other for years—even before the pills. Why,
times beyond number, as we were growing up, I've
bitten my tongue on a statement or observation I was
afraid might seem sentimental or cloying, because
humor was the keynote of our relationship; feeling
stifled and sad because of it, and yet knowing full well

111

that had you uttered a sentimentalism I would have given you the same comic treatment that you would have given me.

So we can let down with each other now, can't we? We can be our real selves and not go through the ridiculous motions of apologizing when we fail to be amusing—because we have owed each other an apology for years for being nothing but amusing.

In the whole world, I know there is nothing worse than, as you put it on the phone, to "live a lie." And oh, Jo-Jo, it takes such a terrible lot of courage to un-live it. But you have the guts—and Jo-Jo, that shows a kind of gallantry that, even if you're not finally successful in straightening yourself out, simply cannot be overlooked.

So you see, at this time in your life, you are being coerced, by forces outside yourself, for the purpose of self-preservation, to make this fight. You have no alternative. You must attempt it now, in order to go on living . . . and if you can accomplish this thing now, the way should be pretty clear afterwards.

I think of you very often. Nothing that has even happened to us or that will ever happen can change my concept of you as the bright, shining person that you are.

I carefully placed her letter underneath my father's at the bottom of the drawer next to my bed, knowing I wouldn't reply. It was too late. My panic at the prospect of Ross and Jerry's visit, followed by my almost immediate capitulation to the alchemy in the plastic container, made me see that right now I could only cut down on the pills; I couldn't give them up.

I managed to get through the term, but that summer, without the framework of my school routine, I again began to lose my hold on the tenuous reality I had created for myself.

Afraid of spending too much time at home, where, since the winter hospitalization, my father was watching me with increasing suspicion, I impulsively signed up for three courses at Columbia summer school. "They'll make up for some of those Incompletes I got when I went into the hospital," I said, and he agreed.

Relieved to see that my time would be used "constructively"—one of my father's favorite terms for activities deemed useful or educational—he and my mother left for a month in Los Angeles, where my Aunt Lil and Uncle Perk had moved.

The decision to go to summer school seemed like a sensible one, but it wasn't. I knew nobody there, and the academic pressure was intense. Even with the three daily pills, I couldn't seem to study or connect with people. The magic wasn't working anymore, except that my rigidly disciplined eating habits were unchanged. I felt strange—eerie and isolated—almost as I had during that unhappy summer when I was sixteen at the tutoring school.

Frightened, I thought of writing or calling Ross, who had written from Camp Onota in the Berkshires, where he had taken a job as a counselor. But what good would it do? And was it fair to keep involving him in my life when I gave so little in return?

I tried to lessen the sense of isolation, the fear of going

under, to at least rev myself up to the point where I could handle my classes, by increasing the pills again. Within a week, the dose was up to five; by the week after, to six or seven. And again, I couldn't concentrate, spent sleepless nights, began to pick at my chest with obsessional attention until the sores bled, and heard the voices in the shower chanting "Inga-bugga, inga-bugga" louder and louder in a crescendo of water. Though I couldn't focus on the lectures, slavishly I continued to go to classes just to be near people. While in class, in a grotesque and unconscious parody of my once well-organized notes, I would write the alphabet or my name over and over and over in alternating lines of meticulous script or print— first in small letters, then in capitals. By the time a class was over, I had filled four or five sheets.

One day the phone rang. It was Enid. She had left Waterford, Illinois, her hometown, to get a summer job in New York and had taken a small apartment near the Columbia campus.

"Jo, I hope you don't mind my calling," she said, pleading, as ever, for my favor.

I was so desperate for company that I was actually glad to hear from her.

"No, I don't mind."

"Have you got time to talk?"

"Lots."

"Oh, good." She was delighted. "Listen, I met some guys at this brokerage firm I'm working at downtown, and I've decided to have a party tonight." Typical of Enid, I thought sadly. They didn't invite her out, so she asked them. "I thought you might come. I mean, if you don't have too much studying."

Had there really been a time when I had studied, read, put work ahead of pleasure? "Okay, I'll come."

Three or four men in business suits were at the apartment when I got there, already somewhat dizzy from the extra, eighth pill I'd taken just a half hour before. Still, I felt ill at ease. My Wisconsin poise had vanished.

"How about a drink?" said one of them—Enid had just introduced him as Jim.

I knew from long experience that mixing liquor with pills made me reckless and out of control, just as I'd been the night I first danced with Alan and began our dead-end relationship. But now I needed to be exactly that.

"Fine." My hands were shaking. Maybe the alcohol would help me relax. "Is there any bourbon?"

"Sure. Want something with it?"

"Ginger ale." It was the one mixed drink I liked the taste of.

Jim was not especially attractive to me. Nor was he really any more importunate than others before him whom I had consistently repulsed, afraid that they would see my imperfect body. But that night, made even wilder than usual by the combination of Desoxyn and bourbon—and above all by my desperate loneliness—I succumbed.

Enid left for another party with the other men, and I stayed with Jim, sipping my fourth bourbon. I was feeling less tense, more confident, as I'd often felt when I took just the right amount of medication in the past. And I wanted to hold on to the once familiar feeling.

Marveling at my cool daring, I let Jim run his hands over my body, over my breasts, still safely harnessed by the special bra. I tried to forget what he might think of

115

the extra-wide panels on the back of the bra that he could probably feel through the lightweight dress fabric.

As Jim became more and more excited, he began to raise the skirt of my dress and grope for my underpants. I didn't interfere. I knew where his groping would lead, and yet I felt no impulse to stop him. What difference would it make? What difference did anything make? The very impersonality of the situation had a perverse appeal: an almost anonymous partner in an almost anonymous setting. Whatever Jim thought of my body, chances were I'd never see him again. And above all, I didn't want to be left alone again—not that night. If I gave in, he would stay longer.

As it turned out, I needn't have worried about my breasts. Aside from some perfunctory passes at the top of my dress, the action was all below the waist. Amazed at my quick compliance, and no doubt afraid I'd change my mind, Jim moved fast.

I can remember only the intense heat, my own sweaty body with my dress, still zipped up in back, pushed up above my hips; his pants pulled down to his knees, and the indelible image of the dirty Indian bedspread on which we scrambled. I recall no special pain or pleasure, just a sense of complete amazement at myself—that after my passion for Mike, after Drew's cajoling notes, Lloyd's pleas, Ross's unspoken appeals, I had ended up in this ugly, airless room on the Upper West Side doing it—the act I had feared as a child—with a stranger, a man I can only vaguely remember.

Alone in my room, I finally reached out to Ross. He seemed the only anchor left in my world gone awry.

Though I hadn't answered his first letter from camp, there in my box, just a few days after the episode with Jim, was a second.

Dear Jo,

It seems as though several weeks have passed since my first letter to you, and still no reply. Please don't think this is simply a summer correspondence or that I just adore to receive lots of mail. I'd like to know why I haven't heard from you. Are you all right? I heard in a roundabout fashion that you decided to go to summer school at Columbia, but certainly that sheds little light about your state of mind. If all is well, I think it's a good idea for you to go.

Camp life is pretty awful and the kids are likewise. My new epithet is "Uncle Ross," and it's really disconcerting. Seriously, I don't think of myself as the likeable type. I got my kids (6) to bed tonight by telling two stories. One eight-year-old kept screaming for The Iliad. *Precocious brat! And just before that, a mob of them came in to celebrate a birthday party. Oh God . . .*

Whenever I have the chance to, I try to get someone to go into town for booze, some of which I'm drinking right now. Not hearing from you is helping drive me to the bottle! I've heard from Jer and he, too, has become "bourbonized."

Please write to me AT ONCE and LET ME KNOW WHAT YOU ARE DOING! What courses are you taking?

Write and tell all. I want to know all about you.

I had come a long way from those early summer days when I hadn't replied to his letter, not wanting to involve him in my life again and frightened of the strong emotions I aroused in him. Now, I was far too needy myself to worry about what bad effects I might be having on anyone else.

So at last I wrote, in a shaky, spidery script quite unlike my usual writing. Both the handwriting and the content, discursive and rambling, reflected a day's consumption of seven to eight pills and possibly some drinks as well.

> *Blue Monday*
> *July 21, 1952*
> *1:00 A.M.*

Dear Ross,

It's one o'clock A.M. and I can't sleep for fear that I won't write in the morning—which really isn't so startling for me, except for my latest extreme (as in "going to ———'s," in case your little brats have made you dull-witted and slow), which (the extreme, that is) is a substitution for almost no sleep of a constant ability (and willingness) to sleep as long as possible.

One bargain I would like to make before starting: that you don't suddenly, mysteriously stop corresponding with me. I really have a lot of nerve demanding bargains when it was I ("me" sounds better, doesn't it?) who delayed so in writing back— but unless you have any strong objections—do you mind? I don't mean that we have to write immediately upon reading each other's letters and/or postcards (I'll

118

even agree to that, if you think I'll ever delay this long again), but I'll agree not to stop writing entirely (and you know what a lousy correspondent I am)—if you don't mind—if you will.

Life may be "awful" at camp (I'm quoting your letter) but "nightmarish" is the only word to describe how things have been going with me. In fact, that's the chief cause of my not writing up to now . . . I think I can honestly say that I've never been so unhappy in my life. (And just as you in particular would be familiar with my twilight melancholia in the listening room, you above all know that I've gone through some really miserable times.) I won't inflict the details on you, Ross, and either depress—or even worse—bore you with them. (I apologize for that— you were always sympathetic; and if you were secretly bored, you didn't show it at all.)

Yes, I'm going to Columbia—but I've figured out that even at best I won't graduate next June—and frankly, since total withdrawal (with refund of tuition) is allowed, I'm considering just quitting and getting a job. I feel like a parasite as it is. But that's not the real trouble—I'm not sure what is, so . . .

Well, I could go on indefinitely, but since I suspect that the quality of this letter is in reverse proportion to its quantity, and since the "little darlings" must be screaming by now for their "Uncle Ross," I won't keep you any longer. I never intended anything on this scale and hope (again) it didn't bore you.

Jo-Jo

P.S. What's all this about being "unlikeable" (sp.?) to

kids? Again—no details—but I'm quite sure you're
wrong.
P.S.2 Anything more re Jerry? I think of him often.

Finally, at the bottom of the page, in a wild, large hand
was scrawled:

Je suis pleine de remords! Pardonne-moi, je t'en prie,
de n'avoir pas écrit.

He answered:

Dear Jo,
You can't imagine how glad I was to receive your
letter today. Fate seemingly had crossed our letters and
there is therefore no need to discuss "receive and stop"
correspondence.
It would be wonderful if I could get to see you
sometime during a weekend. I would try to arrange to
have the day off. Coomprenezzvoo? Fortunate indeed
that I have regained my eyesight. In fact, it's
miraculous. No longer can I shout "Je suis
aveugle!" . . . I worry about your moods. What is
this melancholia? Have no fear that I shall stop
writing, but please don't feel obligated to write to me
immediately or at all if you don't want to. If, on the
other hand, you feel that writing to me would help you
out of the state, please do. And get me straight from
the beginning—NOTHING that you say bores me.
How many credits will you be short? You know that
you can take courses through correspondence? When

you say "quit," you do mean Columbia, don't you?
The alternative (U of W) would be terrible.
   I think that you definitely ought to utilize your spare
time. Why don't you try to find a room with a piano
where you could do some practicing?
   Please let me hear from you soon. I think of you.
                                                    Just Plain Ross

Finally, despite Ross's written support and my feeble
attempts to pull myself together, I realized I couldn't go
on as I was. I was up to eight or nine pills a day and could
no longer keep track of when I'd last taken one. I had
stopped going to classes and stayed holed up in my room,
concentrating all my frenetic energy on keeping my hand
steady as I meticulously copied out pages of the poems in
my Romantic poetry course, none of which I remembered once they were copied. If a letter or word didn't
look neat enough, I threw out the page and started the
meaningless process over again—as attached to my me-
chanical task as Dr. Manet was to his mindless shoemak-
ing in *A Tale of Two Cities.*

At last, I turned to my father, who had returned from
California a few days earlier. I knew there would be no
more "Jo can do anything"s now, no more of the long
wished-for praise I'd wanted for so long, and received in
recent years under such false colors. But I also knew that
in spite of his shock and disappointment, he'd take some
kind of action. He wouldn't let the situation continue.

I called him at his office. "Dad, I can't finish these
courses," I said.

"What are you talking about? Why not? Now you listen to
me, Jo, all you have to do is make up your mind and you'll

do just fine." For the first time, I noticed a tone of weariness in his voice. How many calls like this had I inflicted on him and my mother. But I had no time for guilt now.

"Dad, I can't," I said. "It's that medicine I was taking. I can't work when I take it."

There was a long pause. "I thought you had stopped taking it entirely in the hospital at Wisconsin," he said. The weariness had been replaced, as I'd dreaded, by a new note of suspicion and anger.

"Well, I did," I lied. "But then, when I got back to school, I thought it would help me keep my weight down, and . . ." I didn't want to tell him that I needed it now to sustain the Other Me.

"Well, I don't understand it. After you went to all that trouble to stop. But you'd better go up right this minute and see Sy Kolker."

Yes, Sy would help. Even though he'd originally been the one to recommend Dr. Schmidt, at least I knew him.

And again Sy put me into New York Hospital. I was forced to be fairly honest with him about the extent of my drug use, but I didn't mention the voices, the sores, or the Other Me, and he seemed unconcerned—or unaware—of the psychological ramifications. "Well, of course you can't sleep or study. Those appetite suppressants'll really get you going," he said jovially, after glancing at the label on the plastic container. "But it's not addictive," he added reassuringly. I looked down silently. "All you need is some rest at the hospital and you'll be fine."

My parents were relieved. An Authority had spoken. An Authority had taken charge. If it was as simple as all that, there was no need to be too upset. A few days—a week—in the hospital would take care of everything.

CHAPTER 8

As in the hospital at Wisconsin, I slept and dozed for the first two days. This time, I had left my pills at home, hidden in a paper bag behind some sweaters in my bureau. And as the third pill-free day passed, and then a fourth, and then a fifth, sixth, and seventh, I discovered that what Sy had said was at least partly true: The Dexedrine was not physically addicting. There were no painful withdrawal symptoms—no physical reactions, besides the initial uncontrollable desire to sleep.

Toni, whom I called after testing myself during that first week, came to visit.

"You've got to stick with it this time, Jo. I know you can do it."

Aside from her and my parents, I saw no one but Sy and the nurses. My parents, still kidding themselves that I was being "cured" of what they regarded as a strictly medical problem, agreed to tell anyone who called that I was away on a trip. Frank and Beth were in Italy, where Frank had begun work on a Ph.D. in Italian. I felt safe in the hospital, cocooned by my anonymity and relieved, for the time being, from the need to live up to my image of the Other Me.

I allayed my terrors about putting on weight by following a more rigid diet than ever, convinced that the slightest deviation would send my weight soaring again. Sy had ordered some menus totaling 1500 calories a day, but I ate only a scrupulous third of the lowest calorie foods.

Afraid that even my letters would reveal the old, imperfect, pre-Dexedrine me, I cut off my correspondence with Ross. I wrote him only briefly that I was going into the hospital for the same problem I'd had when I was hospitalized while in Wisconsin, and told him not to try to reach me for a while—that I'd be in touch when I came out.

He agreed, sending back only a short note of encouragement.

I left the hospital after two weeks. Only a few days remained till the fall term was to begin at Wisconsin. I had to decide what to do. How could I go back? Perhaps, if I could avoid all my former friends, I could make it there again as a new person. No, it would be impossible. Once more I thought about dropping out.

On the other hand, how could I stay in New York?

So, for the last time, I decided I would return to Wisconsin. The university was, after all, enormous. I would find a different niche for the new me—whoever that was. And this time I was determined to stay off the pills.

I arrived in Madison and called no one. As for courses, I carefully avoided signing up for any Ross or Jerry might be taking. I moved once again—into another school-run dorm, as far from Norris Hall as I could find, and was assigned a roommate again, a foolish girl with an appalling New York accent.

"Moi name's Mickey Dick," she said when we met, giving me an appraising once-over. "What's yaws?" Mickey (short for "Marcella") had an obviously fixed nose with unnaturally sculptured and constantly dripping nostrils. I had noticed that, despite their waxen perfection, such noses often dripped as though distressed at their new and unfamiliar shapes. She was heavily—and carefully—made up, but pretty in a vulgar kind of way.

She would be my first test case, I decided. I must impress her as I had impressed others in my former incarnation. As her eyes flicked over me expectantly, I wondered how I looked. Probably just as I had in those Walden days; maybe even thinner and more attractive. But how different I felt. After telling her my name, I could think of nothing to say.

"Do you know Ashley Goldstein?" she said when I began to unpack, embarrassed at my own silence.

I suppressed a desire to laugh at the unlikely juxtaposition of names and stammered, "Uh, no, I don't think so."

"He's an A E Poi," she said, dabbing at the inhumanly perfect nostrils with a Kleenex, and looking to see if I had gotten the full impact of the remark. "I think he's gonna take me out tonight."

For a moment, I was baffled. Then I realized she meant the fraternity. "Oh, you mean 'A E Pi,'" I said, emphasizing the long "i," and aware, even as I said the words, that they sounded as if I were correcting her pronunciation.

Apparently, Mickey hadn't taken offense. "I won't go out with anyone who isn't an A E Poi," she said. "My sister told me that's the best Jewish fraternity. I mean, they're all Jewish boys, y'know?" Suddenly, Mickey looked anxious. "Yaw Jewish, aren't cha?"

"Yes."

Mickey looked relieved. We had clearly exhausted our small supply of conversation, and she ran off to find a more responsive audience.

I had failed. Would I have made an impression with the pills? Would I have even wanted to?

Two weeks went by before what I most feared occurred. I ran into Ross and Jerry on the street.

"My God, where've you been?" said Ross, relief and joy spreading over his face. "I went over to Norris Hall, but Natalie said you'd come for your things and might have gone home. How come you didn't let us know you were here?" I could see he was hurt.

"Alyssa, *c'est toi enfin!*" said Jerry, almost simultaneously. "*Chère* Alyssa, where have you been? We've missed you. We need you. We need you to guide us. *Je suis aveugle! Je suis aveugle!*" he cried, and he closed his eyes and held out his hand for me to lead him, as I'd done so often in the past. I didn't take it, and surprised, he let it drop to his side.

"Well, I guess I just felt like making some changes this year," I said lamely. How would I have answered if I were taking Desoxyn? I wondered if I would have had a better reply—something funny, or interesting, at least. Now I stared miserably at the pavement. I tried to avoid Ross's curious glance. He must have noticed something wrong with me already.

126

"Listen, I'm late to class," I said. "I've got to go, okay?" And without looking back to see the expressions on their faces, I rushed through the brilliant autumn leaves and headed for Bascom Hill.

When I felt it was safe, I backtracked to my room, where I sat, paralyzed by the unexpected confrontation. Well, maybe the worst was over. They had seen me, no doubt realized I wasn't the same person anymore, and would drop me. I felt a sense both of relief and of terrible sadness at the thought. How much I was giving up. Until I'd run into them, I had been able to shut out such thoughts.

I was wrong. That afternoon there was an envelope in my box, addressed to "Mlle. Johanna Rosengarten, a/k/a Alyssa." I recognized Ross's square, assertive handwriting at once. He had somehow discovered my whereabouts. On a stiff piece of white paper cut to look like an official invitation was written:

Messieurs Ross et Jerome
(Les Aveugles)
request the pleasure of
Mlle. Alyssa at an
intime dinner party on
le vingt-neuf septembre
à sept heures et demi.

No refusals are permitted.
This by order of *les rois soleils*.

Jerry had scribbled a note on the bottom. "You've got to see our new *appartement*. It's *très* chic. We'll be by to pick you up at 7:15 tomorrow. Otherwise, you'll never find it. We're so exclusive we don't even have a house number."

I spent that night and the next day in a panic unlike any I'd experienced while on Desoxyn. I felt myself to be in a tight, compressed, self-contained box—a box without a key. It was stifling.

The thought of taking a pill crossed my mind for a terrible moment, but I immediately ruled it out. I remembered how quickly I had given up in the Madison hospital the year before, the minute I'd heard Jerry's voice on the phone, and I was determined not to give up again. I tried to think of other solutions—of calling to beg off somehow, anyhow. But even for that I lacked the courage. Finally, with the feeling of a prisoner awaiting the jury's verdict in a murder trial, I realized I would have to go to Ross and Jerry's.

At 7:15 sharp the next night, Mickey called to me from downstairs. "Jo-Jo, some guys are here for you." I glanced in the mirror. My face looked the same. If only the inside of my head could match up. I grabbed the bottle of wine I'd bought to give them and went down.

On the way to their apartment—which was entered through the rear door of a house that backed up on a junk-strewn lot near State Street—there was no need for me to talk. Jerry was busy telling me about his courses, how they'd found the apartment, how he'd seen Enid the day before and crowed to her about finding me. My heart sank at the news. More people to cope with, I thought.

"You should've seen the look on her face when I told her. Positively *affreuse!*" he said, doing a perfect imitation of Enid's gawky stance and abject expression.

Ross was quiet, observing me. I tried to think of how I

would have responded to Jerry in the past, but again could think of nothing to say. Trusting myself to be myself did not feel like an alternative.

We got to the apartment. "Isn't it marvelous?" said Jerry, waving an arm to indicate the two tiny rooms. "The 'Villa on the Lot,' we call it." He pointed out the dusty, iron, wood-burning stove, its door on broken hinges, which was the only source of heat besides the gas oven. He showed me the cot in the living room–kitchen that doubled as a "chaise longue" by day, a bed by night; the tiny "second bedroom"—what must have been the pantry of the original house—with barely enough room for a bed.

I saw the comic aspects of the place and tried to summon up the phrases I used to quote from Peter—phrases Ross and Jerry and I had laughed about and made part of our special jargon. But somehow the phrases "the living end" or "all tarted up" or "not to be believed" wouldn't come out, and I could say nothing.

By the time dessert came, an impenetrable pall had fallen on all of us. Even the three bourbons I'd had before dinner, and the wine I'd brought, hadn't helped. I was immobilized by what I saw as Ross and Jerry's expectations of me—a standard I couldn't possibly live up to. What must they be thinking? I remained frozen, totally lacking in spontaneity. And grief-stricken, too. In one evening I had lost two friendships it had taken me years to build; had lost the love and loyalty of two people I had really cared about and who cared about me. But of course, I realized with a jolt, it wasn't really me they had cared about anyway; it was someone else.

"Thanks for dinner, but I've got to go," I said, as they

began to clear the bridge table that doubled as a desk and dining table.

They didn't try to stop me. Jerry only cocked his beautifully shaped head to the side, a sad, bewildered expression in his eyes, and said, "Good-bye, then, Alyssa. Come again." I doubted that he meant it. Ross said nothing at first, then suddenly whirled around.

"I'm going to walk you home," he said firmly.

"No, don't. Please. I'd really rather walk home alone." Without waiting for a reply, I ran out the door, and, stumbling over the rocks, broken springs, and old tires in the lot, I made my way back to the street and then to my room.

That night, for the first time since quitting the Desoxyn five weeks before, I couldn't sleep. The evening had been a disaster; the real me—whoever that was—a flop. My fears had been confirmed. I had been mute, completely ill at ease, cloddish, dull.

As I sat motionless on the edge of the bed, Mickey came in. "How ya doin'?" she said. "Didja have a good time?" My having been called for by two boys seemed to have raised me several notches in her estimation. Well, *that* wouldn't happen again in a hurry, I thought grimly.

Before I had a chance to answer, I heard the phone ring down the hall, and Mickey ran to get it. She came back slowly. "It's for you."

I picked up the phone. It was Ross. "Look, I don't know what was wrong this evening, but if it's anything I did, I'm sorry."

Oh my God, no! He was blaming himself. Couldn't he see that what was wrong was me? When I didn't answer, he rushed on. "Anyway, I want to talk to you alone. I'll meet you in the music listening room tomorrow evening. About seven. All right?" We had made such arrangements a hundred times in the past.

"All right," I said, and hung up.

Suddenly I knew what I had to do. I had my insurance. Though I had no more pills, some inner doubt had led me to pack one last prescription pad and one model prescription in the flap of a suitcase when I left New York. Within minutes, as Mickey watched in astonishment, I had pulled the suitcase down from the high closet shelf where it was stored, knocking clothes off their hangers in my haste.

And that night, my hands trembling almost as much as they had on the night of my first forgery, I traced the prescription that was to start me on my final binge.

CHAPTER 9

I didn't wait to meet Ross in the listening room the next evening. Eager, now that I'd taken such a drastic step, to re-establish my identity as the Other Me, I knocked on his apartment door at around five o'clock the next day. Jerry opened the door. When he saw who it was, he looked pleased but wary. How quickly I had put him off with my sober—and somber—silences, I thought. I would have to do something about that at once.

"Well, I mean, doesn't a representative from the French Seeing Eye kennels even get asked in?" I said. "I hear there are two sightless *parisiens* here who need help. Their former guide tells me she's *très fatiguée* with the job and that she'd prefer that they switch to one of our *chiens extraordinaires*." I handed him a stuffed dog I'd bought on the way over.

Jerry grinned and put the dog on the cot. "Come in. *Entre dans le palais.* Ross isn't home yet, but he'll be here soon. God, it's good to see you. I thought you were mad at me or something. You were acting so strangely—and eating so strangely, too, now that I come to think of it. Ross thought so, too."

"Just one of my little aberrations," I said gaily, dismissing one of the worst evenings of my life with an airy wave.

"Well, I'm really glad you're over it. *En vérité*, you had us worried."

The old magic resumed. When Ross came in, he too was won over, the previous evening dismissed as a "bad mood." I was off and running again.

The four drug-free weeks had reduced my tolerance for the large doses of Desoxyn I'd taken before, and I started trying to hold back on the amounts I used. But with a fanatic and foolish consistency I was soon back to three capsules a day, then four, then five.

Now everything began to happen faster, as though versions of all the disastrous results of my previous drug dependence were being repeated, but at 78 rpm instead of 33.

My ability to concentrate went first, and with it my grades. The voices came back, louder and louder, and within a few months, the sores that had almost healed on my chest were picked raw again. I rarely slept, and often I didn't return to the dorm till late at night. Mickey, startled at the change in me but intrigued, covered for me or managed to leave the door unlocked after the last check.

Usually I ended my solitary wanderings at Ross and Jerry's door. They were no longer as delighted to see me as they had been at first. They were trying to work, and my unpredictable arrivals and just as unpredictable departures were becoming a problem.

One bitter cold night in February, when I left them and went back to my dorm, I found the door locked. Either Mickey had forgotten to unlock the door for me or someone had come by and relocked it. It was 12:30, and I had no money with me. I couldn't even go to the Park Hotel, where I'd spent my first few miserable nights in Madison. I'd have to go back to Ross and Jerry's.

Their windows were dark, and I stumbled as I walked up the broken wooden steps that led to their door. I knocked, and after a minute Ross came to the door in the dark. I realized that since it was Jerry's week on the cot in the kitchen, Ross hadn't wanted to wake him by turning on the light.

"Jesus, Jo, is that you again?" The annoyance in his tone was painfully clear.

"The door was locked. I couldn't get in," I said, my voice trembling. "I'm really sorry to bother you. I know I woke you up, but couldn't I sleep here? I mean, you could just give me a blanket on the floor." As my eyes grew accustomed to the dark, I tried to read the expression on Ross's face—a combination of anger, pity, and hurt pride. I had rejected his professions of love—refused to believe them—months before, and yet I couldn't seem to let him be.

An icy wind was blowing. Though my indifference to the freezing weather had returned when I resumed taking the capsules, Ross was not similarly immunized. He had only a towel wrapped around him. "Come in, it's freezing," he said, pulling me in and shutting the door behind me.

For a moment he was silent. Then he said, "It's too cold for you to sleep on the floor. You'll have to sleep in my bed."

"What about you, though?" I said stupidly.

"It's big. We can both sleep there."

"Okay. Thanks." I knew I wouldn't really sleep. The

Desoxyn and the awkwardness of this new situation would take care of that. But at least I'd be able to lie down, and being near Ross would be reassuring.

In the dark, he led me to the small bedroom. I put my coat on one chair, took off my shoes and skirt, and lay down under the covers, moving as close to the wall as possible. Ross got in beside me.

The mattress was soft and lumpy and gently rolled the two of us toward the middle. After a few attempts to stay on the edge, I remained there. I had on tights, under-wear, a sweater, and a bra. Ross had dropped his towel on the floor and was naked. I knew he was wide awake, though he was silent. I wasn't surprised when he shifted to his side and put his arm around me, pulling me closer.

"Jo, you know I love you," he said roughly, kissing me on the mouth with sudden passion. How different his kisses were from Mike's. Ross had wide lips and I could feel—almost painfully—his strong teeth against my mouth. Almost within seconds, he seemed wildly excited, and for a moment I was frightened by his intensity.

"Are you a virgin?" he asked.

What should I answer? The memory of Enid's apart-ment—the heat, the dirty Indian bedspread—flashed through my mind. I was suddenly ashamed again—not so much at the act itself, but, as I had been at the time, at its meaninglessness.

"No."

Ross reached behind me and shut the door to the other room. "Take off your clothes," he said. Mutely, I obeyed. How could I not, I thought. I had come here of my own free will, uninvited; had disrupted his life, his night; had tormented him in the past with my refusals either to have him or to let him go. I would take off everything, be truly naked before him, let him see, at last, how wrong he had been to desire me.

He was breathing rapidly as, with nervous fingers, I finally undid the three hooks of my wide-strapped bra. I could feel my soft breasts, released from their harness, droop. Well, he had asked for this. Now let him realize what a sham I was.

But Ross didn't seem to notice. As soon as I was undressed, he rolled onto me. Between my legs I could feel his penis, sheathed in what I realized must be a condom. Somehow, as we had lain in the dark, he had managed to slip it on, and I was surprised, briefly, to think that he had one so readily available. I didn't think of him as someone who slept with girls often enough to be prepared so quickly. Through the rubbery surface, his penis was large and very hard. And suddenly I, too, was excited. Though there had been virtually no foreplay, aside from his harsh kisses, the penis rubbing against my genitals and his long body above me set me aflame. Reaching down, I put his penis in me. The sensation was exquisite, and within seconds I felt an extraordinary moment of wild pleasure that left my vagina throbbing. At the same time, Ross groaned and I realized that he had experienced the same swift pleasure.

After a few minutes, he rolled to the side. "I'm sorry. Are you mad at me?" he asked quietly.

"Of course not." No, I wasn't mad. Yet, in spite of the intense enjoyment the experience had given me, I was disturbed. Somehow I felt that if Ross became my lover—my "boyfriend"—our relationship would be altered in such a way that he would no longer be my friend. And at the back of my mind lurked the fear that if he hadn't been so aroused, my breasts would have repelled him, that if I hadn't been so overstimulated by the pills, the whole thing wouldn't have happened. My frenetic, drug-induced abandon would not have existed. This pleasure, like all the others I had experienced while on the pills, soured on examination, too. No, I thought immediately, I wasn't angry, but I wouldn't repeat the experience.

"Darling, we didn't expect you for another week," said my mother after she got over the shock of seeing me walk into the breakfast room of our house in Cedarhurst one morning in late May. "Why didn't you call? I could have met you at the airport."

"Just got through with exams earlier than I expected, and figured there was no point in hanging around," I said. I didn't tell her I'd lost still another term to Dexedrine and despair; that in my last-ditch attempt to take finals I'd written what I thought was a brilliant essay on Chaucer all on one line of my blue book; or that after that I'd given up and left without saying good-bye to anyone—not to Ross, not to Jerry, not to Enid, all of them caught up in the giddy elation of graduating that made me feel even more like an outcast.

Distracted by the intricacies of planning the Memorial Day weekend at our country house in Massachusetts, my mother accepted my answer without further questions. The preparations for the weekend were all wonderfully, frighteningly familiar. We'd owned Silverbrook since I was eight and it was still referred to as "the farm," though my father had long since given up on raising chickens. How often I had been torn between wanting to go up with my parents and my fear that once there I'd do nothing but eat. The isolation of the country house, on a dirt road a mile from the nearest neighbor; my awareness of my own loneliness—that my only friends were my parents' friends—would make me feel restless, unhappy, trapped.

Almost as though reading my mind, my mother said, "Why don't you come with us? Peter is coming. And Ron Street." Ron was Peter's latest "friend." I remembered uneasily that the capsules were running low. I had meant to get a prescription filled before I left Madison, but in the haste of my departure, hadn't had time. Quickly I went to my bedroom and checked the container in my purse. If I kept my intake to five capsules a day, there were enough for today and the three-day weekend. I'd have to get a refill Tuesday morning, but I said I'd go.

The weekend went smoothly. It was a relief to be away from school, to feel taken care of again. Ron—tall, blond, attentuated, a painter of huge floral watercolors—turned out to be fun. With Peter and him, I drove to Tanglewood and to Jacob's Pillow. The time went quickly and relatively painlessly.

The first hint of trouble came Monday morning at breakfast.

"Clae," said Peter, "why don't we stay another day? Herb has people working for him who could carry on, hasn't he? Anyway, you know what I always say: You can't take it with you."

"Not with you around to help spend it," I said, confident that his suggestion was out of the question.

"Outrageous brat," Peter said, laughing.

But to my amazement, when my father came in, he

didn't react as I'd expected. "Maybe I *could* stay," he said. "Any special reason you have to go back today, Jo?"

I tried to repress my feeling that the question was more meaningful than it sounded and, caught unprepared, said, "Well, I guess I'd rather go back today, but if everyone else can stay . . ."

Stupid, I thought to myself. Idiotic. Why hadn't I made up some excuse? I would have just enough pills left for today, none at all for tomorrow. I felt my heart begin to pound. I couldn't do without the pills. My world would collapse; I would become the cipher I had been for those five weeks last summer and fall.

I cursed my casual pill consumption of the weekend. Why hadn't I at least thought to keep one in reserve? Now there was nothing I could do. I didn't even have an empty capsule in which to siphon off a third or a half of each full capsule—the stopgap I had used so often in the past.

By Tuesday morning, I was desperate. My mother had slept late, and the packing took till noon. I realized we wouldn't get home till four or five. My mother had planned a picnic lunch for the trip home. "We'll find some picturesque little spot," she said with enthusiasm. I knew, too, that she, Peter, and Ron were sure to want to stop at three or four antique stores on the way. No, I'd have to be bold.

As we approached Winsted, the nearest town with more than a general store, I said, as casually as I could manage, "Mom, could we stop at the drugstore? There's something I really need."

"Of course, dear. While you're there, I'll run into the

grocery store and pick up some cucumbers for the picnic."

I saw my father eyeing me keenly. "What is it you need, Jo? Can't it wait till we get home?"

"Well, I . . ." Why hadn't I had an answer ready?

To my relief, my mother—assuming it was "that time of the month"—interrupted. "What difference does it make what she wants? You heard me say I could use some cucumbers anyway."

My father was silenced.

When we got to town, my mother pulled into a spot right in front of the drugstore. Glancing back to be sure my mother was heading for the grocery store and my father was still in the car, I walked into the dim interior of Ivery and Whitmore.

Trying not to avert my eyes, I took the carefully folded prescription I had forged in Madison but not had time to fill there or at home from my wallet, and handed it to the druggist. The pin on his gray pharmacist's jacket identified him as Mr. Whitmore, a mild-looking, gray-haired man with half-moon glasses over which he peered benignly. He looked at the slip quickly, then up at me, and I froze. "Been taking this long?" he asked.

"Oh, no, not very," I said. "Just a month or so. For my weight."

"Uh-huh," he said, looking up again. "Been hearing some talk that they may cut out refills on this stuff."

So that was it. Why had I circled the "2" after "Repetatur" on the prescription? I had, of course, originally expected to fill it—and refill it—near Madison, where, despite my original fears, no one had ever questioned the refills. My greed would be my downfall, I thought grimly.

"I probably won't be needing the refills," I said, as calmly as I could. "Can you do it right away, though? Some people are waiting for me outside."

"Sure, sure. No problem. No trouble at all." And he turned and moved behind the shelves of medicine that separated the prescription section from the rest of the store.

"Could I see that prescription, please?"

My heart stopped. It was my father's voice. I had been oblivious to his entrance.

The druggist, startled, re-emerged, the paper still in his hand. He looked from my father to me uneasily.

"I have a feeling my daughter shouldn't be getting that prescription filled. It's for some kind of diet pills, isn't it?" he said sharply.

"Why yes, it is," said Mr. Whitmore.

My father's voice was shaking. He was no more used to such scenes than I was, but I could see he was determined. I was frozen, unable to speak.

"We live in New York, and I'd like to bring it back with us to our family doctor," he said more calmly. "So if you don't mind, I think I'd better take it with me."

"Doesn't matter to me," said Mr. Whitmore. "I've just been telling your daughter here they may be putting out some new regulations on this medicine soon, anyway." And he handed the slip to my father.

Terror made me brave. "Dad, I've got to have those pills. You've got to let me have them."

"Not this time, young lady," he said. When I was a child, I had always been able to tell when he was really angry at me by his suddenly calling me "young lady." "We'll have to see about this when we get home." I knew his voice when he had made up his mind. I would have to give in for now.

Together we left the store. My face was flaming with rage and embarrassment, but there was nothing I could say. How could I explain my desperation, my need? For the rest of the trip I was silent, my father and I avoiding each other's eyes. And I could see from the moment we got home that there would be no sneaking out, no furtive visits to the nearby drugstore. My father was keeping track of every move.

Refusing dinner, I lay on the bed of my beautiful turquoise-and-yellow room in torment. So it had come to this: I was an addict, terrified of what would happen to me without my supply of magic. Desperate, I tried to conceive of a plan. For once, I could see no way.

There was a knock on the door. It was my mother. I didn't know if Dad had told her yet of what had happened. "Darling, what's the matter? Why are you lying there like that?"

Mom sat down on the edge of the bed. Her dark eyes were sympathetic. "What's all this Dad's been telling me about the pills? I thought you had stopped taking them last year."

So she knew. Anger, accusations, reproaches—any of these would probably have kept me silent. But her sympathy was more than I could bear. I began to weep.

"Mom, I've got to have those pills. I can't explain it all now. I've just got to have them. You've got to tell Dad to let me have them."

My mother was frightened. "Well, my God, Jo, if they're that important . . ." For the first time, I could see the beginnings of serious doubts about me in her eyes. "Maybe we should get Dad up here."

142

"No, no," I said, then thought better of it. "All right. Yes. But you've got to help me."

"I don't understand why you can't wait."

"Just get Dad, okay?"

When my father entered the room, I turned away from him. "Well, what seems to be the trouble?" He was, as ever, calm, seemingly unruffled.

In all the years of our life together, I had never openly challenged my father. Whether out of fear or respect, I had never dared. Tonight was different. "The trouble is that I want that prescription. I've got to have it, and I've got to have it filled."

"Not until I've had it checked out," he said, startled, I could tell, by my assertiveness.

Suddenly, I began to scream. "I've got to have it, don't you see? I'll fall apart without it; I'll be nothing. I'll get fat. You've got to do something. Now, now, now!"

Panic-stricken, my mother headed for the phone. "I'm calling Fred Simon right now," she said. Fred was our family doctor on Long Island.

"Yes, yes. Call him. He can call the drugstore for me. He can do something tonight," I said, frantic. I couldn't believe that I was behaving this way, saying these things to my parents.

"Thank God you're in, Fred," I heard my mother say. "It's Jo-Jo. No, she's not sick. At least, I don't think so. But . . . could you see us tonight? No—I don't think it can wait until tomorrow."

I blessed my mother. Dr. Simon would see my desperation, would convince my father. I remembered his gentle manner when he came to make a house call. Well, he was in for a shock. This was a far cry from swollen glands. "All right," she concluded, "we'll be right there."

As it turned out, Dr. Simon didn't have to do any convincing. In the car, on the way to his house, I blurted out the whole story, starting with the first prescription from Dr. Weinstock and on through Radcliffe, Barnard, Wisconsin, Columbia; the stolen pads, the forgeries, the lies about my hospitalizations. After all, they knew the worst already. And I knew I was finally cornered. I tried to describe my despair, my terrible fear of what would happen to me without the pills—to my body, to my whole being, to the Other Me. But most of all, I told them of my desire to be free from the tyranny of the drug. Even as I spoke, I realized how desperately I wanted that freedom now, how sick I was of the forgeries, the lies, and most of all, of the terrible dependence, the fear that I couldn't exist without it.

They listened in silence. "I see," said my father, more sympathetically than I would have thought possible. "Now I understand a lot of things. I'm going to speak to Dr. Schmidt tomorrow. We've got to get you some help."

"But why didn't you tell us sooner?" said my mother.

"I didn't tell anyone. Don't you see? The whole illusion would have been destroyed if someone knew."

But at the same time I was asking *myself* why. Why *had* it taken so long to reach this point with them? Maybe because, during the past four years, some of the same magic had seemed to operate at home as had operated at school. With the help of the medication to free me, I had been able to communicate more with, and feel closer to, both my mother and father than I had in the entire eighteen years that had gone before. If I gave up the pills, I would have to risk losing the closeness, would no longer be the mercurial, charming, frenetic child that had so en-

144

tranced them and the rest of my small world for four years. And I was ready.

But not that night. Not so abruptly.

By the time we got to Fred Simon's, they had agreed that I needed the pills for the time being. With Fred's cooperation, I could have the medicine. But it would be the last I could have. The next morning my father would start to look for a hospital or sanitarium.

Dr. Simon wrote out a new prescription. "Don't want you arrested at this stage of the game," he said, with an attempt at lightness. And I realized that, in a final ironic twist, this last prescription would be the first legal one I'd had in years.

My father called Dr. Schmidt the next day, and after filling her in on what had happened, asked for her help. We had come a full circle, for now, four years later, she again suggested Great Oaks.

PART TWO

PART TWO

CHAPTER 10

"Me and my mother in Westchester County." Pause. "My mother and me in Westchester County." Another pause. "Me and my mother in Westchester County."

Ignoring the incantation behind me, I remained riveted to the wire fence, watching my usually erect and buoyant parents, looking stricken and suddenly old, walk heavily to the parking lot across the road. They didn't look back as they got into their car and drove slowly beneath me and then out of sight around the corner of the main building, where I was now an official resident of the second, "less seriously disturbed," women's floor.

I felt a fleeting desire to shout "Wait for me, wait for me!"—as I had so often in childhood. But that desire was unexpectedly replaced by an exuberant rush of relief. I was at last cut off, set free, though the sight of the crossed-wire fences that lined the square cement porch from ceiling to floor, reminded me paradoxically that I was being imprisoned—even wanted to be imprisoned— in order to win that freedom.

"Me and my mother in Westchester County. My mother and me in Westchester County."

I turned around. The dark-haired girl I came to know as Nina was pacing back and forth, her arms, then as always, crossed tightly against her chest. And in the fading light, as my eyes darted from Nina to my other companions on the porch, my relief gave way to a terrible fear.

Standing not five feet from me was a girl of about twenty with horribly acned skin, huge, dark, long-lashed eyes that were terribly crossed, and dandruffy hair twisted into greasy sausage curls. Behind a food-stained, off-the-shoulder peasant blouse, she had enormous, pendulous breasts unrestrained by a bra, and wore a dirty wrap-around skirt that suited her needs well, since she kept her hands inside it constantly, masturbating freely. She mouthed soundless sentences and giggled senselessly as she inched toward me. Why was she coming closer?

Frozen, as I had been in remembered nightmares, I prayed for the return of the nurse who had brought me up in the elevator and then promptly left to retrieve my papers, which she had left downstairs.

I forced myself to turn away, and saw a trim woman of about forty dressed in what looked like a smart tennis outfit eyeing me malevolently from the far corner of the porch, an irritated smile playing over her attractive, pixieish, somewhat simian features. "Babe" Hawkins (I was told her name later) spoke in the amused, country-club tones that I learned to dread and fear in the months to come. "Of course, it's the goddamn Jews who rule the world and spoil everything," she said, looking directly at me, but then quickly at Nina and the other girl, too, making the target of her attack ambiguous. "They start all the wars, and now they're running all the businesses."

150

My God, I thought, the porch, the second floor, the whole hospital, was filled with these loonies—insane racists, sex maniacs, homicidal maniacs, for all I knew. What the hell was I doing here? Surely I wasn't as crazy as they were. But if I stayed around them, maybe I soon would be. And what had happened to the nurse—Miss Addison, I remembered now ("Call me 'Addie,' hon")— who had brought me from the admissions interview with Dr. Cunningham?

The interview had been brief. Dr. Cunningham, the administrator in charge that day, was a courtly Southerner, the type one saw in ads for mint juleps—white beard, rotund little belly, cavalier good manners, even a narrowly striped black-and-white vest covering his gentlemanly pot.

His questions were strictly factual.

"And how long has this charmin' young lady been takin' this, unh, Dexedrine?" he said, pencil raised, looking from me to my parents for all the world as though we had been co-conspirators in my eight-year descent. My mother's eyes filled with tears, and I felt I could read her mind. The one thing about psychiatry that was universally believed in that era was that parents were to blame for their children's problems. Heredity, physiological unbalances, brain malfunctions, a child's distorted perception of reality—these were considered extremist theories.

I was, as ever, troubled by this simplistic view, and felt, not for the first time, a moment of anguish at seeing my proud mother's humbled form. But why in God's name was he questioning them, not me, anyway?

I was still somewhat high on the pill I'd taken that morning at the hotel in Washington before driving to the Oaks. Was that why I felt such confidence? Or was it the

151

realization that the lies could really be over now, could be over for good? It was time to tell everything—even to this seeming jackass.

"Four years," I said evenly. "And I suppose you know all about what came before that? The overweight, the underweight? The—"

"All raht heah," he said, tapping the file in front of him with his pencil and beaming a benevolent smile. He paused for a moment, then went on. "Well, well, fo' years," he repeated, as though impressed that I'd set some kind of record. "That is suhtainly a long time. And can y'all remember just how much . . . how many of these, unh . . . you were consumin'?"

"Anywhere from five to fifteen capsules a day," I said.

"My, my." He seemed genuinely shocked. "Well now, missy, you're not gonna do that any more down heah, ah hope." And he waggled a finger at me as though reprimanding a small child.

I looked at him, startled. Was he serious? Could he be as simple as he appeared? Was I really supposed to pledge perpetual abstinence, to reply, in the same arch tones, "Well, ah hope not, Dr. Cunningham. Ah'm not heah fo' a vacation."

Dr. Cunningham went on. "Now if y'all will just give me any of those little devils you might have left in yaw bag, we'll try to make it a little easier for you heah." He stood up, came around the desk, and extended his hand, as if asking a naughty child to hand over a stolen cookie.

I reached in my pocketbook and gave him the plastic container I'd won in my last desperate confrontation with Dr. Simon. Good, I thought. At least they knew where to begin.

"Well, ah do thank you," said Dr. Cunningham, with a courtly bow. He sat down again and tilted back in his chair. "Now, ah hope y'all won't mind if we search through yaw belongin's. It's a part of owah routine heah."

"Not a bit," I said.

My parents watched, horrified, as I was led across the hall by Addie, the nurse, who had soft brown eyes and drooping jowls.

"Now honey, you just take off all those pretty clothes and put 'em on that chair over there," she said.

To my relief, I was given a sheet to cover me as she checked the hem of my skirt, my pockets, the lining of my pocketbook.

"You don't mind if we keep this, do you, hon?" said Addie, as she put my nail file into a small box marked "Rosengarten." I wondered briefly how long it would be till I saw it again. "It's just that some of the patients get a little upset sometimes, and then . . ." Her voice trailed off. "Not you, of course, honey. I can see that right off." I wondered what she could see "right off." That I wasn't psychotic? That I wasn't likely to slit someone's throat? To slit my own? Still, I felt strangely flattered and let it pass.

When we returned to Dr. Cunningham's office, he seemed to have wound things up with my parents, and sat back again pleasantly in his large chair.

"So, missy, that wasn't so bad, was it?" he asked.

I didn't answer, wondering why he never called me by my name. Was it an attempt to objectify the new patients, some psychiatric way of keeping a distance, or just a form of gentlemanly behavior with which I was unaccustomed? The possibility that he might keep forgetting my name, or perhaps didn't care enough to remember it, also crossed my mind.

"Now what ah think," he said, leaning forward now with what I took as an attempt at shrewd incisiveness, "is that for the first few weeks at least, this heah young lady will be betta off on owah second floor, raht heah in owah main building, than in Small Oaks. Small Oaks is that pretty l'il house y'all probably passed by out thay-uh in the middle of the grounds," he explained, looking at my parents. "Yaw dawtuh will go theah when she, unh, shall we say, 'graduates' from Two."

Then he looked down, apparently embarrassed at what was coming next. "Now theah are some patients up on Two who are 'actin' out' quite a bit moah than yaw dawtuh is—unh—raht now." I was struck by his use of the term "actin' out"—his first use of professional terminology, and even more so by the fact that the confidence Addie felt in me was clearly not shared by Cunningham. "But they're not dangerous," he added reassuringly. "No suh. We wouldn't have 'em on Two if they were dangerous. Soon as they start any funny business, back up to Four they go—far, far away from the likes of you all."

But how much "funny business" were they allowed to start, I wondered, before they went "back up"?

"The point is," he wound up, looking past me to my parents, "we want to keep a real close eye on this young lady at fust." So, I was to be kept under lock and key for an indefinite period. But I didn't mind. The important thing was that, as I'd expected, during the search of my possessions, Addie had failed to note the slit in the inside arch of my left sneaker, where I'd hollowed out a small hole and stashed a desperation cache of five capsules. I had come to Great Oaks hoping for the best; but then, I'd hoped for the best before.

Addie reappeared with a folder, just as the girl with her hand rotating gently under her skirt had reduced the distance between us to about arm's length.

"Now, Dorothy, you leave Jo-Jo alone, hear? She's gonna be livin' with us for a while, and I want you to be real nice to her." Dorothy flashed a surprisingly sweet smile and shuffled back a step or two.

"Sorry I got held up, hon," Addie explained. "Dr. Cunningham was in there goin' at it hammer and tongs with Lee. That Lee Rodman"—she said the name fondly, as though discussing a mischievous child—"I swear, if that boy ain't careful, he's gonna end up right back in the Cottage as an inpatient again."

She didn't explain who Lee was, or what the Cottage was, either, and I didn't ask, happy only that she was again safely at my side.

"Well," she said, "guess I'll show you around a little bit on the way to your room. You're lucky. You won't have a roommate. Tonight, anyway. We just moved Ellen over to Small Oaks this mornin'. But we'll see how long *that* lasts."

Lee. Ellen. The cast of characters was growing. But I was in no mood to ask who they were—why Lee was arguing with Cunningham, why Ellen was a risk for Small Oaks, or even, most important of all, why they were fellow mental patients of mine.

Addie led me from the porch and into a long, dim, empty but clean hallway. I was expecting the worst, having read *The Snake Pit* a few years before. But in contrast to the neat hall, there was, everywhere, the pungent odor of urine washed over with antiseptic—an odor I recognized from ladies' rooms in gas stations.

There were no doors on any of the rooms. Clearly the patients were not to be trusted behind closed doors. As we passed the rooms, I tried to glance into each quickly. In one, a young nurse was talking softly with an enormously fat girl who looked up dreamily and emitted two loud belches as I passed by.

"That's Harriet Mandelbaum," said Addie, with no further explanation.

Many of the other rooms were empty. Where did their residents go during the day? I wondered.

Halfway down the hall on the left, Addie stopped and unlocked a door. "This is the nurses' office, where we keep all the medications and give our reports when we change shifts. You'll have to wait outside. No patients are ever allowed in here." She went in and, to my great relief, opened the top half of what I now realized was a two-part Dutch door, so that I could see her as she glanced over my papers. Looking nervously over my shoulder to be sure Babe and Dorothy were still on the porch, I stayed as close to the half-door as possible.

"No medications for you tonight, I see," Addie said. No, and none ever again, I thought to myself, not if I could hold myself together here.

Addie emerged, re-locked the door, and led me across the hall. "And here is what we call our 'day room.' This is where you can watch TV, or relax, or just be with the other patients, if you like." I glanced at the sagging couches with their ripped, imitation leather upholstery, at the barred windows, and at the out-of-focus TV. From the patients I'd met and what I'd seen so far, I was sure I wouldn't "like."

In the middle of the floor, a woman who had pulled out all her dirty-blond hair except for an Indian-style strip down the middle, stood flailing her arms about to the voice of Perry Como singing "Don't Let the Stars Get in Your Eyes." Her feet remained stationary. She had the vacant stare of a mongoloid, though Addie whispered to me, "Don't let her looks fool you. Rosemary's smart enough when she wants somethin'."

I noticed an old upright piano with no ivory on the keys standing against one wall. I felt a surge of pleasure at the sight of the familiar object. Lightly, I ran a finger down the keys. Only three or four of them played.

"'Fraid some of the patients got to that one a long time ago."

"Is there another around that works?" I felt a strange urgency to know that a functioning piano was on the grounds somewhere.

"There is one up on Four," said Addie. "If you listen real hard, you can hear Tria playin' on it right now."

In the background, over the voice of Como, I heard the faraway strains of a Chopin nocturne. More mysteries. First Lee. Then Ellen. Now Tria, who must be considered "seriously disturbed" if she was on Four.

"Come to think of it, though," Addie said, after a minute or two, "I don't really think there is another piano around. And I expect you wouldn't want to venture up to Four to use that one." She laughed grimly. "No sirree, you wouldn't want to go up there."

We left Rosemary, now seated dully in front of the snowy TV screen, and re-entered the hall.

"Addie, I want a cigarette right this minute! Now! Do you hear me?" Babe Hawkins came striding down the hall. I noticed that she had a graceful, elegant carriage even when she was in a hurry. "What the hell is the nurses' office doing empty? Where are all those dim-witted student nurses? What the hell kind of yid place is this anyway?" she asked sneeringly, looking at me. "Just because there's a new patient, do I get completely ignored?" She was shouting louder and louder. I saw Nina, who had paused briefly in her pacing, standing in the doorway of the porch to watch the fireworks. Behind her stood Dorothy, giggling and holding her skirt up.

"Now, now, Babe, just hold on a minute," Addie said soothingly. Her failure to be terrified by Babe impressed me enormously. "We've just been so darn busy today, movin' Ellen out, movin' Jo-Jo here in."

"'Jo-Jo'?" Babe said with a snort. "You call that a name?" I could hear Miss Clark my first day in the second grade telling me, "That's no name for a nice little girl."

But mercifully, Babe soon turned her fury back to Addie. I was suddenly touched at the picture of this commanding woman, who, I suddenly noticed, shared some of my mother's authoritative charm, having to beg for a cigarette. It was evident they were meted out one at a time. Of course, I thought. The matches. The possible burning. My God, we could all be set on fire by this rabid anti-Semite. And my fleeting moment of compassion passed.

An out-of-breath student nurse came running down the hall, looking at me uneasily as she approached. I realized with a start that she was scared of me. Don't be afraid, I felt like saying, I won't hurt you—and then thought, but I am here on Two, like the others. And with good reason, like the others. And I do have to be watched—just like the others.

158

"Sorry I'm late, Addie," said the nurse. "Ellen just wouldn't stop talking. Then she wanted to go over to the A to talk to Lee, and I had to be sure she had grounds privileges. I'm afraid she's getting high again." High? On what? I wondered. The "A." What was that? Grounds privileges, I figured, must be the right to walk around the grounds. Alone? Accompanied?

I was suddenly conscious of an overwhelming fatigue. I hadn't had a capsule since before breakfast, and its energizing effects had worn off. But I didn't care. I could go with the fatigue now. I could sleep, if necessary, for a week. And when I woke up I could be as lethargic and uninteresting as I wanted.

I thought briefly of Ross, or Jerry, of Toni, of Frank and my parents, and realized that if any one of them had come to remove me from this madhouse at that moment, I would have actually fought them off. Though I was probably in more physical danger than I'd ever been in my life, and though some of the patients frightened me, I had an enormous sense of homecoming. In this house of horrors, I felt safe at last.

Addie took me to my room—a small square with barred windows almost too high to see out of, and two metal cots that were just like the ones I remembered from camp. "The bathroom's across the hall," Addie said, but I was too tired to check it out. "Now you take a little rest and dinner'll be up in just a few minutes."

That was Tuesday evening. When I awoke, it was ten o'clock Thursday morning.

159

CHAPTER 11

Dorothy's hand was gently stroking my shoulder. I restrained an impulse to scream, pulled away, and made a dash for the nurses' office.

Inside, Addie was pouring a colorless liquid into tiny glass containers.

"Addie, help me. Dorothy's in my room and I don't know how to get her out."

"Well, good morning," said Addie cheerfully. "Do you know how long you've been asleep, young lady?" She looked at her watch. "About a day and a half! Fact is, if you hadn't woke by yourself, I was gonna go in there and get you up myself in a few minutes, 'cause Dr. Block—he's in charge of all the new patients—he's coming up to see you at twelve."

"Addie, I didn't wake up by myself. Dorothy's in my room, and I don't know how to get her out."

"Now honey, listen to me," Addie said firmly. "Dorothy is harmless. All of 'em here on Two are. Dr. Cunningham told you that, didn't he? She just likes you, that's all. She's been walkin' in and out of your room to check on you ever since you fell asleep."

160

Terrific. I'd made a hit on the second floor already.

"I don't *want* her to like me."

"Let's see about a breakfast tray for you. Then I'll show you how to get rid of Dorothy, if she bothers you that much," said Addie, a note of reproach in her voice. She picked up the phone and dialed, covering the mouthpiece while she waited for an answer. "We don't usually serve trays between meals, but we had special orders from Dr. Block on you." Then she turned back to the phone and ordered the tray. "Now," she said, when she'd hung up, "let me show you how to deal with Dorothy."

I followed her meekly down the hall till we got to my room, where Dorothy was sitting on the bed. "Dorothy, I told you to leave Jo-Jo alone the day she got here, and I meant it. Now scat, out, vamoose." Looking stricken, Dorothy shuffled out of the room. "See," said Addie, "that's all there is to it."

I felt, again, a rush of admiration for Addie's calm control. Would I ever feel unafraid of Dorothy, or Nina, or Babe?

"Where'd you say the bathroom was?" I asked, though I remembered perfectly well. I wanted her to go with me in case anyone was in there.

"Right across the hall," Addie said, pointing at still another doorless room and looking at me shrewdly. "Don't worry, no one's in there now. Most of 'em are at the A, or on the grounds, or at O.T.—Occupational Therapy," she explained when I looked puzzled. "You'll be perfectly safe. Oh, we unpacked for you while you were asleep." I noticed for the first time that my clothes were hung in the small closet, and was sure the staff had gone through all of them. Had they found the capsules?

Apparently not, to judge by Addie's face.

The minute she left, I leaped to the closet and picked up my sneakers. Prying the thick rubber in the arch apart, I saw my secret hoard, safe and sound. But why, I wondered, was my relief tinged with disappointment?

The bathroom was empty, as promised. Aside from the omnipresent odor and the three doorless booths, it looked like a public bathroom anywhere. Trying to breathe through my mouth as I entered, I used the toilet, then rose and glanced in the mirror—a flat, metal sheet that distorted my image. Of course, I thought; no glass.

My hair, uncombed for a day and a half, had come almost completely loose from its ponytail and hung about my face in Medusa-like strands. The clothes I'd slept in were wrinkled and dirty. I really looked as though I belonged on Two now.

There was, I noted gratefully, a curtain on the shower stall. Keeping the two flimsy towels Addie had given me with my toilet articles on the sink near me, ready to grab in case anyone came in, I took a hasty shower and washed my hair, looking with loathing at my breasts. The towel barely covered me, but I made it back to my room and into clean clothes unobserved. Thank God I didn't have a roommate. I thought of all the times I'd had to wait till Natalie or Mickey left the rooms we'd shared at Wisconsin before I could slip into or out of my bra. Often I got into bed with it on under my nightgown, and put it on again under the sheets before I got up.

I finished dressing, put my wet hair back in a ponytail, and combed down my bangs without a mirror. There was none in the room, and Addie had taken the one from my purse the day I entered, to put in my box with the nail file.

Addie reappeared. "Well, you look a lot neater. I had 'em put your breakfast out on the porch. Hope you like pancakes, 'cause that's what they brought."

Pancakes. My God, I couldn't eat pancakes. In an instinctive gesture, I reached for my bag, thinking in a panic, "But the Dexedrine won't have time to work. I can't eat without a pill." Even if I'd wanted to pry open the sneaker, I couldn't. Addie was watching me closely. Resigned, I followed her past Rosemary, who hadn't budged, and Nina, who was pacing the day room today, to the porch—empty of patients for the moment, and almost pleasant in the pre-noon sun.

On the tray were a glass of milk, two thick pancakes, some melting butter on a dish, and a small jar of syrup. There was a fork and spoon, but no knife. Five hundred calories at least, I computed quickly, maybe more. But I couldn't request special low-calorie meals here, I knew that. And I also knew that I couldn't go on living with a half grapefruit for breakfast and hard-boiled eggs for lunch.

Deliberately, I picked up the syrup and started to pour it over the pancakes. To my amazement, I poured only half, then stopped, just as I would have if I had been taking the Dexedrine. I used some butter, but not all that was on the plate. Then I picked up my fork and took a bite.

Suddenly I remembered the evening eight years before when I'd finally broken my anorectic fast and responded to my father's anguished, "Jo, you have to eat. You're ruining your health."

Then, I'd known almost immediately that something cataclysmic had taken place. Now I wondered: Without

163

the Dexedrine as an ally, would the helpless submission to some unfillable need start again?

But this time no one was watching me at all. Addie had gone back down the hall to tend to Rosemary, and I realized I could run back to the room and extract a capsule from my sneaker if I wanted to. But I didn't. I slowly ate half the pancakes and drank half of the milk.

Giddy with my newfound power to stop eating, I stood up and walked to the edge of the porch, then back to the tray. Perhaps, even after two days, there was still some of the drug in my system. No. I remembered Dr. Weinstock telling me how quickly it passed out of the body.

As I stared at the food, another, older recollection came to my mind. I could almost hear my mother's voice saying angrily, "Nancy, these pancakes aren't done enough. Take them back." I was eleven or twelve, and my mother had come down to the breakfast table in one of her inexplicable bad moods.

My mother had risen late. She had removed the evil-smelling triangular patches she pasted on her face at night to prevent wrinkles, but their faint outlines were still etched on her skin. Her dark eyes, unglorified by the mascara that would transform them later, looked like angry black buttons, and she had carelessly tied one of her innumerable kerchiefs into a jaunty turban on her head. Her robe was silk and exquisite—more suitable for a party, I thought, than a breakfast. She had applied lipstick unevenly, and I averted my eyes from the dry, ragged edges of her mouth, over which she nervously ran her tongue.

We had all been exceptionally on edge that morning, I remembered, but why? I couldn't recall, though I could hear in my mind the little bell on the table that my mother rang furiously to summon the cook. "Nancy, don't you hear me? These pancakes aren't done enough. Take them back."

I could have wept. It was ten o'clock and I had been up since seven, first reading in bed, then taking my bike out for a ride. I was starving, but knew that weekend breakfasts together were part of my mother's concept of happy family life that I didn't dare challenge.

"They're okay, Mom. They're done enough for me," I protested weakly.

"They're raw inside." She looked at me with disgust. "My God, can't you wait a few minutes?"

Conscious of my gluttony, I gave up. I was often hungry long before meals were served, even when I hadn't been up for hours, and was already slightly overweight for my age and height. But that day I was particularly sorry I'd said anything, since by doing so I'd drawn my mother's fierce gaze.

And, again, I remembered that there was a special reason I had felt it so important to keep the peace that day. What was it? I tried again to recall what had happened later, but I couldn't.

Slowly I refocused on the unfinished portion of slightly underdone pancakes in front of me, waiting for the impulse that would drive me, powerless to resist, to eat the rest. But again, I looked at the food, felt no urge to eat more, and walked to the other side of the porch.

Outside, I could see student nurses and aides trailing the patients around the grounds. Directly beneath me, a blond, bony woman was croaking over and over, "That other brown one, that other brown one." I saw what must be Small Oaks about fifty feet up the drive that seemed to go from one end of the Oaks to the other, and another barnlike structure across the road from it. To the left of Small Oaks, almost hidden behind some trees, was the pointed tip of another building. An A-frame. The A? I wondered briefly. But I took it all in only dimly. Somehow, by some miracle, I had eaten a normal meal. But why? How? What new magic was taking place?

Addie suddenly reappeared in the doorway. "Enjoy your breakfast?" she said cheerfully.

What should I say? That it had been a kind of revelation? A breakthrough meal? The possible evidence of some unknown sorcery? "Enjoy" wasn't exactly the word to describe what I'd felt, so I simply said, "Oh, sure, it was fine. I like pancakes."

Dr. Block was medium height and somehow square-looking, though not fat. He was square in a robotlike way, with movements that seemed almost jointed. Even his face, in the dim light of my room, had a square, masklike opacity.

"Well, Jo-Jo, how are you getting along here on Two?" This was progress. Someone in authority was actually using my name. "Must be a little scary, I imagine."

I noticed now that the reason his expression was so stiff and his face so opaque was that he must have once been terribly burned or wounded (during a battle in World War II, I later learned) and had needed extensive plastic surgery. This had reduced the range of his facial expressions and his ability to move easily. But his voice was deep, warm, and vibrant, and I liked him right away.

"Yes, I guess it is," I acknowledged.

166

"Well, you probably won't be here very long. We have our fair share of alcoholics, but we don't get many cases of amphetamine addiction, so we want to be sure not to rush things. In fact, you may be the first," he said candidly, "unless they had some before I got here two years ago. Anyway, we almost always start new patients who don't show dangerous or psychotic tendencies on Two till we can watch them for a while, and get a more complete history than in admissions. Often, when in-contact patients like you come in, they're too upset to talk much."

If I'd been upset in admissions, it was more because of Dr. Cunningham's inanities than anything else, I thought, but didn't say so. I had never heard the phrase "in contact" before, but it was clear from the context that he meant "in contact with reality."

"Of course, you turned over all the capsules to Dr. Cunningham, right?" he said, looking at me with intent, expressive brown eyes that did a lot to compensate for the impassivity of his other features.

"Oh sure," I said, ashamed once again, as I'd been with Addie, of my secret supply.

"Because it would certainly be a waste of our time and your father's money if you hadn't."

"Right," I agreed, looking down guiltily.

"Even though you're kind of a test case here at Great Oaks, I did a lot of work out at the VA Hospital in California with guys who got addicted to drugs during the war, and I know how devious addicts can be." Inwardly, I squirmed. "Fact of the matter is, I got pretty attached to morphine myself while I was going through all this"—he pointed casually to his face—"so I know how hard it can be to break a drug habit. They gave it to me as a pain-

167

killer first, then I couldn't stop taking it. That's one reason addiction interests me."

I was amazed at his openness. Dr. Schmidt had never admitted to any faults, or said anything about her own background. And it was thrilling to be talking to someone who understood, from firsthand experience, at least part of what I'd been going through.

"I hope you'll be my doctor—my psychiatrist, I mean," I blurted out suddenly.

"Well, maybe," he said, with a suggestion of a stiff smile. "Those decisions are generally made by a group of us. There are a lot of factors to be considered. Meanwhile, let's get a few more details about what brought you to Great Oaks."

For the next hour he went over some of the same material as Cunningham. But whereas Cunningham's style had put me off, I was inspired by Block's warmth to talk freely about the weight gain, the pills, the Other Me.

Finally, he glanced at his watch. "I've got to be going. Just try to relax and don't let the other patients get to you—especially Babe," he said with a wink. "I'll be up to see you tomorrow, but about an hour earlier. This is lunch time for most of the patients. Okay?"

"Okay." I realized I'd really look forward to it.

A lunch tray was waiting for me—again on the porch. "You're gonna get spoiled at this rate," said Addie, "but Dr. Block said he didn't want any interruptions. Otherwise, you'd have got your tray in your room like the others." I wondered about the other, more "in contact" patients. Did they all eat on trays in their rooms?

"I'm not really hungry," I said. It was as simple as that. I had eaten breakfast very late; I wasn't hungry.

168

"Be a long time till dinner, hon. We eat at six," said Addie, "though of course you could stop off at the A this afternoon for a snack." So you could buy food at the A. It must be a store of some kind. "We're sendin' you for a look-see of the grounds with Miss Cavalino this afternoon." I remembered her as the student nurse from my first day. "Sure you don't want to take a look at the lunch? You might change your mind."

"No, I don't want anything," I said.

Miss Cavalino must have been reassured by Addie that I wasn't likely to give her much trouble, because she began chatting as soon as she'd unlocked the clanking metal doors that barred the entrance to the elevator. She was quite ugly, with sallow skin, small, close-set, muddy brown eyes, and a dumpy body. I marveled at the ability of this girl—like others I'd known in the past, any one of whose physical defects would have caused me enormous mental anguish—to sail through life happy and confident, planning a nursing career, planning marriage (she was engaged, she told me even before we had emerged from the building, whipping out a picture of her boyfriend), and apparently not at all aware that imperfect humans such as she had no right to feel this way.

It was a beautiful day. The heat that had seemed so oppressive inside was cooled by a steady breeze. And it was a relief to be able to take a breath without inhaling the noxious fumes on the second floor.

"Where would you like to start?" she asked.

I had a fair notion of the buildings in the immediate area, but which was which? And where was the Cottage— the one Addie'd said the patient Lee might be returned to? I envisioned something out of Hansel and Gretel. I decided on the nearest safe-looking haven. "Let's start at Small Oaks," I said. We headed toward the house, which looked just like a thirties, suburban, Tudor-style residence anywhere, except that it had bars on the windows.

"I hear this was once Dr. Cunningham's private house," said Miss Cavalino. "He and some other doctors bought up the land around it when they decided to start the hospital. Anyway, after a few years Cunningham moved into town. Guess he got tired of hearing 'em screaming up on Three and Four all night."

I had been so soundly asleep that I hadn't been aware of the night noises at the Oaks.

"What's on Three?" I asked.

"That's the most seriously disturbed men's ward. I'm going to have to go up there next week, and boy, I'm scared to death."

I wasn't sure I appreciated her frankness, nor the realization that though Cunningham had said dangerous female patients were put "far, far away on the fourth floor," he had failed to mention that dangerous male patients were just a floor above me.

We circled the house and entered a good-sized kitchen where a plump nurse, who wore her thick gray hair in a high, neat bun, was writing something on a big clipboard. Why were they always writing? I wondered. Addie was always writing, too.

"Mrs. Johnson, this is Jo-Jo Rosengarten," said Miss Cavalino. "She's a new patient on Two."

"Hi, Jo-Jo Rosengarten," said Mrs. Johnson. She looked cheerful and happy, like Addie. Perhaps, I speculated, you needed an even more cheerful disposition than most to cope with the patient population of a mental hospital.

"Go right on through," said Mrs. Johnson. "I think the side porch is open anyway, 'cause Lee and Ellen just asked me to leave it unlocked for 'em. I figured since Lee's an outpatient now, it was okay."

Lee—the one who had quarreled with Cunningham, I recalled—and Ellen, my almost roommate. I was to meet them at last.

We passed through a central hall, a living room furnished in much the same way as the day room on Two—except that the furniture was in slightly better condition—and onto a small screened porch.

Facing me from the far side of a creaky couch was a young man in his mid-twenties with the kind of good looks that brought to mind such movie-magazine adjectives as "dashing," "sophisticated," and above all "devastatingly attractive." He had long, slightly uptilted hazel eyes, topped by satanically arched brows, one of which he raised frequently to emphasize a point as he spoke, black wavy hair swept back without a part, and pale cheeks with a slight suggestion of puffiness that kept him from being conventionally handsome. His nose was slim and fine, and he had a small but sensual mouth, from which the lower lip came out ever so slightly, like that of a rebellious child.

As we entered, he glanced up at me but didn't interrupt his conversation with the girl—Ellen, I assumed—whose heavy back, in a sweater that revealed several rolls of fat, was turned to me.

"Would you mind sitting here for a few minutes?" said Miss Cavalino. "I've been walking patients around the grounds all morning and I'm knocked out."

"Not a bit," I said. We sat on some rickety lawn chairs

171

opposite Lee and Ellen, who went on with their conversation as though we weren't even there.

"Now, Ellen," Lee said in a teasing tone, "you're becoming far too indolent. You know what they say, 'Idle hands are the devil's workshop.' And God knows yours are idle. 'You toil not, neither do you spin.' Consequently, I have reached the inescapable conclusion that you are either a creature of the devil or a lily of the field. Recommended treatment: something for you to do besides wear out the cushions and that pretty, if somewhat overweight, *derrière* sitting on the Small Oaks veranda."

Awed, I wondered if Lee always talked that way. Other than on a stage, I had never heard anyone toss off such extravagant verbal pyrotechnics with such casual ease—a speech with literary allusions, quotations from the Bible, foreign words. The sardonic dryness of his delivery saved it from sounding pompous.

For the second time since my arrival, I felt a sudden desperate craving for a Dexedrine. That would be what I needed if I were ever to talk to Lee as an equal. I wanted to leave, yet felt magnetized to the seat.

Ellen laughed delightedly. "Why, Lee Jessie Rodman, you are terrible!" What was their relationship, I wondered. Romantic? Platonic?

Now that I was sitting across from both of them, I could see Ellen's face, too. In spite of the fact that she was plump in a way that seemed bloated and unnatural to me, she was extremely pretty, and reminded me of my memories of Snow White in the Walt Disney movie—a pageboy of smooth, shoulder-length black hair parted in the middle framed a calm, serene brow, round dark eyes, and a short, slightly upturned nose.

Her mood darkened suddenly. "Fat chance of my being able to do anything *here*. Oh God," she said, "why won't they let me go to England and be analyzed by Ernest Jones? That's my only hope."

I was startled at her abrupt mood swing, though she was still charged with all the energy of what I came to recognize as one of her "up" stages. Ellen was charming, sweet, and, I later learned, hopelessly stuck in a manic-depressive cycle.

But I knew nothing about her then—about the shock treatments that hadn't worked before she came to the Oaks, or the other hospitals where she hadn't been cured. And that day—the sun shining, Ellen laughing, and Lee gently teasing her—the two of them looked like characters you might have glimpsed at a country club.

But this was no country club. What on earth were Lee and Ellen doing here?

"Ernest Jones could cure me, I know it," Ellen went on. "But these stupid doctors"—she drew out the word "stupid" contemptuously—"just won't let me go."

Was it true? Was Ellen being kept prisoner even though she wanted to leave, Snow White trapped in the dark forests of Great Oaks?

"Of course," she continued, "Dr. Block tells me I'm just dramatizing things." Dr. Block was probably her therapist. Soon he'd be mine, too, I hoped. But Ellen was clearly not satisfied with him, not satisfied with anything about Great Oaks.

"We've been through this before," said Lee patiently. "You know there are shifts open at the A. And the good Lord and Dr. Cunningham willing, I will soon be in a position personally to offer you gainful employment."

"You hope," said Ellen. Now she was doing the teasing. What did Lee hope? "I wouldn't work in that excuse for a store anyway. Me serving ice cream cones to Harriet Mandelbaum and Rosemary Kelly. Noooo thanks. I didn't go to Radcliffe for that. And come to think of it, I don't think that's what you went to medical school for either, *Doctor* Rodman."

Lee was a doctor? I was completely confused.

He looked as though he'd been slapped. "That's hitting below the belt."

"God, Lee, I'm sorry," said Ellen, her tone suddenly sympathetic. "It's just that this place . . ." Her voice faded off.

"I know. It's all right." He seemed serious now, almost paternal. "I didn't say you should make the A your life's work, any more than I want it to be mine. But at least it would be a plan. And you know what I always say: A bad plan well-executed is better than no plan at all."

I thought the epigram wonderfully original, but Ellen ignored it. Her attention had suddenly focused on me. "Well, and what have we here? A new victim, it seems." Her smile took the edge off the bitterness of her comment.

"Yes, this is Jo-Jo," said Miss Cavalino. "She's a new patient on Two. Jo-Jo, this is Lee Rodman and Ellen Edwards."

I was in a panic, terrified that I'd have to say something and be discovered for . . . for what? After all, Lee and Ellen didn't really expect anything of me. Nobody did. I had to keep reminding myself of that.

So, much as I might have liked to be eloquent and witty like Lee, or despairing and dramatic like Ellen, I knew that here I didn't really have to be either. I had no expectations to live up to, no Ross and Jerry to please. At the thought of Ross and Jerry, I felt a stab of guilt at having left without letting either of them know where I was going or why.

For an awkward moment, as Lee and Ellen looked at me curiously, I thought of staying. I'd have to start talking with the "in-contact" patients sometime. But not yet. Not today.

As Ellen's soft "See you," trailed after me, I rushed out the side door of Small Oaks, the surprised Miss Cavalino hurrying behind, and headed toward the safety of Two.

"Back so soon?" asked Addie.

"I want to write a letter," I explained. "Do you have any paper?"

"I don't have any stationery," she said, pausing to think for a moment, "but you can use the backs of some of these report forms, if you like."

Before I went to my room, I paused. "I saw Lee and Ellen on the porch of Small Oaks, and Ellen said something about Lee's being a doctor. Is that true? I thought he was a patient here."

"Oh, it's true, all right," said Addie. "I mean, both are true. He's a doctor—a psychiatrist, in fact—and he's a patient here."

A mentally sick psychiatrist. The idea was shocking.

"And he isn't the only one either," said Addie. "Oh my, not by a long shot. We've got another, and a whole pack of psychiatrists' children."

Speechless, I started down the hall.

Dear Ross,

 *I'm writing to you from Great Oaks, a mental
hospital in Somerset, Virginia. The sheets of paper
I'm writing on are the backs of the nurses' report
sheets.*

 *For all the years I've known you—and more—I've
been living a lie. Sounds corny, I know, but it's true.
Somehow I couldn't help myself. I felt I had to be
somebody else for people to like me, and unfortunately
you fell in love with that Other Me—or thought you
were, anyway.*

 *I became that other person by taking a drug called
Dexedrine—Desoxyn, really, which is another form of
the same. The medicine changed me completely, but
I'm not exactly sure how. That's what I hope to find
out here—who I am without the pills.*

 *I guess I'll have to start relearning how to live
almost from scratch—anyway, from the time I was
about fourteen, when I started destroying my life in
various ways. I'm going to try anyway. I don't know if
I'll ever have the courage to meet you again, or
knowing what you do know, if you'd ever want to.*

 *I think this is the most difficult letter I've ever had
to write in my life, but I felt I had to let you know
what was going on. That much at least I can do.
Please let Jer know, too. I'm truly sorry for any pain
I've caused you. You deserved (deserve) better.*

I recopied the letter, sealed it, and started for the door,
my eyes falling on the sneakers in my closet as I passed
by. I thought again of Ross and Jerry, and then of Addie,

176

Dr. Block, Dorothy, Nina, and the others—the first to be present at my rebirth.

Putting down the letter, I picked up the left sneaker and pried out the capsules, still neatly wrapped in a piece of Kleenex. I walked across the hall, dropped them in the toilet, and watched as they swirled around and then, quickly, disappeared.

CHAPTER 12

"Can I be of service, Jo?" Lee raised an eyebrow and leaned toward me across the counter of the A, where he seemed to be in charge—at least for the afternoon. Miss Cavalino and I were continuing the tour I'd so abruptly cut short the day before.

The counter was just big enough to fit three tall stools in front of it. Ellen was sitting on one of them, her head down. She looked settled in, with two empty Coke bottles, her purse, and an open pack of Viceroys spread out on the counter in front of her. Apparently, though she didn't want to work at the A, she didn't mind being a patron. Or perhaps, I thought, intrigued again, she just wanted to be with Lee.

"Can we interest you in some candy, some cigarettes, some champagne or *paté de foie gras?*" Lee continued.

"Unh, no. Not really. I—I don't smoke, I mean, I'm just looking around," I stuttered awkwardly. As if to prove it, I turned away and surveyed the A.

"Look away," said Lee with a smile. "There's absolutely no charge for looking." Seeing Lee's eyes on me, I made an elaborate pretense of studying the back wall with its high, rectangular, sliding windows, and the jukebox underneath them.

"Well, now that you've had a good, long look, what do you think of our humble establishment?"

I wished I could have said, What's this sporty ski house doing on the grounds of a mental hospital, especially one without a hill in sight? Or mentioned that the sliding glass doors across the front—wide open now for the summer— and the few small round tables scattered inside and out, gave it the equally unlikely aspect of a European street cafe.

Instead, I said nothing, relieved that Lee was temporarily distracted, for Rosemary Kelly, dragging her feet, came in with another student nurse. She stopped halfway to the counter and pointed wordlessly at the jukebox.

"Could Rosemary get a dime, please? I think she wants to play the jukebox," said the nurse.

Since I hadn't wanted to buy anything myself, I'd temporarily forgotten that all my money had been taken away the day I arrived. A charge account of some kind, I realized, would be the only way to buy anything at the A.

I saw Lee write something on what looked like a stenographic pad, heard the ring of a cash register—apparently out of sight beneath the counter—and watched as he lifted the hinged piece of wood that closed the counter off to come out. Presenting the dime to Rosemary with a courtly flourish, he said, "Madam."

Ignoring him, Rosemary shuffled to the jukebox, put in the money, and pushed a button. The box began to blare "It Takes Two to Tango," and in a moment she began her strange arm movements, jerking her head spasmodically at the syncopation.

Lee returned to his post behind the counter, and I took the opportunity to look more closely at the area around him to see what the A had to offer. Besides the cigarettes, in a metal dispenser to his right, boxes of candy bars, soap, toothpaste, shampoo, and a few other simple drugstore items were neatly displayed. No aspirin, razors—or shaving lotion. I was learning fast. Miss Cavalino had told me some of the alcoholics had ordered the shaving lotion by the case. A tower of hot drink cups rose from beneath the counter, so I assumed coffee was available, too.

It was all pleasant enough, but I couldn't figure out why a person with Lee's obvious intelligence would want to run this tiny store. And he did want to run it. I'd found that out from Addie the night before, along with the information that the store had been a completely patient-built and patient-run experiment until recently. "But Cunningham doesn't think the patients should be in charge anymore," she said. "They took forever to finish it, and the last manager got depressed and let everything fall apart." That explained Lee's conflict with Cunningham. But why was it so important to him?

The fat girl from Two, Harriet Mandelbaum, waddled in and heaved herself onto the stool next to Ellen, who pulled back in revulsion. Harriet was a basically attractive but grossly overweight girl of about eighteen, with white, delicately freckled skin, large, melancholy eyes, and thick, raven-black hair.

She ordered a double Coke, and began to drink greedily from a large paper cup, making loud sucking noises as she drew on the straw. After every two or three sucks, she would swivel her enormous bulk around to stare knowingly at me. Though she was smiling, I sensed something

180

unfriendly in her eyes, and she seemed to time her hostile burps to coincide with her glances.

Just as Dorothy's pendulous breasts had seemed a terrible extension of myself, so now did Harriet's obesity reflect my own worst fears, both past and present. Seeing her was like looking back in time. That might have been me at eighteen, I thought with a shudder.

But gratefully, I reminded myself that my response to last night's dinner had been much like the one I'd had at breakfast. There'd been fried chicken, mashed potatoes in gravy, and canned string beans. Almost automatically, I'd removed the skin with its crusty coating and had eaten the stripped chicken and the beans, which I carefully pushed to the edge of the plate, far from the threatened encroachment of the gravy. But no potatoes and no dessert—a pool of melting vanilla ice cream with strawberry sauce.

I'd gone to bed early, grateful that the TV in the day room had been adjusted. Babe, Dorothy, and most of the other patients were watching it, and left me alone.

I woke up in a panic the next morning—my heart pounding, my body wet with sweat. I'd had a dream in which, as Dr. Schmidt—now in Cunningham's chair at the Oaks—shook her head silently and pessimistically from side to side, my body began to inflate painfully, starting with my feet. I grabbed for my pocketbook to take out a capsule, then remembered with horror that it was empty. Unable even to scream, I looked down helplessly and saw my legs balloon out, then my stomach and my breasts, till I had reached nearly 225 again. Finally able to force out a strangled "No, no!" I awoke in a tangle of sheets.

Not even bothering to put on my bra—usually the first thing I did in the morning—I rushed to the nurses' office in the baggy hospital nightgown I'd decided to wear in case anyone came to check on me at night.

There was Addie, back for the day shift. "Don't tell me Dorothy's givin' you trouble again," she said good-naturedly.

"No. It's not that. Addie, I've got to get to a scale; I've got to weigh myself."

"Nothin' to worry about. We've got one right here in the closet." Now at least she'd have something to write about in her notes. "Miss Rosengarten in a panic. Demanded scale. Looked wild and disoriented."

I stood on the scale and moved the bottom weight to 100. Fingers shaking, I slowly inched up the top weight . . . 31 . . . 32.

The last time I'd been on a scale was the morning I left Cedarhurst for the Oaks. I'd weighed 138 then, safely below 140. What would the pancakes and the chicken have done to me? I continued to move the bottom weight up: 34, then 35, then 36. At 37 the arrow began to shift downwards, and at 37½ it was suspended in midair. My heart beating wildly, I stepped off and then on again, waiting to see if perhaps the scale had erred. But no, miraculously, the arrow moved quickly upwards, briefly touched the top, and then went halfway down again.

It was all right then. Not only hadn't I gained without the pills, I had actually lost half a pound. I would tell Dr. Block about that, too.

Ellen distracted me from the train of whirling thoughts Harriet had inspired. "May I have a light please, Lee?" she said, taking a cigarette from the pack on the counter.

"Certainly, m'dear. Always at your service." Lee picked up some matches from under the counter. He gave Ellen a light, and then, still holding the burning match, took a cigarette from his shirt pocket with his other hand and swiftly lit it, with a graceful turn of his wrist. I thought it a very intimate gesture—lighting both cigarettes with one match—and felt strangely jealous.

Ellen looked more glum than she had the day before. Suddenly, even before she'd begun to smoke the cigarette, she stubbed it out. "Oh my God, I can't breathe. What have those doctors done to me?" she said, gasping for breath. "I can't breathe, I tell you. I'm dying! The stupid doctors here are trying to keep me from breathing! Oh God, why won't they let me go to England? Ernest Jones could help me."

Calmly, Lee continued to fill the cigarette rack. I was amazed that neither Miss Cavalino nor the nurse with Rosemary were doing anything to help. Then, as Ellen didn't turn blue or collapse, it occurred to me that probably this wasn't the first time she had claimed she couldn't breathe, though in fact she could.

"Oh my God, my chest! I feel this terrible pressure on my chest!" she cried out again. There was still no response. "If Kip was here, he'd help me," she said accusingly, looking at Lee. Kip—another patient? an aide? a doctor? "But *you* do nothing, *Dr.* Rodman. The great Dr. Rodman does nothing," she said, her chest heaving. I thought it mean of her to keep calling him "doctor," knowing how he felt about it, but if Lee minded, he didn't show it.

"Have you tried loosening your bra?" he said drily, and I burst out laughing. Lee winked at me conspiratorially as Ellen, still gasping for air, gave him an angry look. I was enormously flattered, but felt my face flushing.

Embarrassed by my inability to say anything to him, I

183

turned nervously to Miss Cavalino. "Okay, let's go now. You said you'd show me the Cottage and the O.T. shop." Surprised, she got up from her seat.

"Leaving so soon?" Lee asked, emerging from behind the counter. Was I imagining it, or did he sound disappointed? "You haven't even sampled one of our incomparable A-frame Cokes. And let me assure you that you won't find a cheaper or a better one anywhere else on the grounds." I was so flustered that it took me a minute to realize he was kidding. The A, of course, had no competition.

This time I had to answer. He was too close for me to hope for deliverance from Rosemary or someone else.

I paused for a moment. "Unh, I—I've got to get back to the store—I mean, the floor—soon," I lied.

"You do?" said Miss Cavalino loudly. "Addie didn't tell me. Why do you have to get back?"

My face flaming now, I took off toward the road, Miss Cavalino trotting beside me.

"Why didn't anyone tell me you have to get back?" she persisted.

"I don't," I said. If I hadn't been so upset, the look of astonishment on her face would have been funny. Well, let her think I was a little nuts after all. One advantage of my situation, I thought grimly, was that I could get away with crazy behavior like this.

As we followed the road through the grounds, I noticed a large, modern, one-story building under construction. I tried to regain my equilibrium with a joke. "Are the patients building that one, too?"

Miss Cavalino didn't get it. "Oh no. They took too long on the A, I guess. It's gonna be a center for psycho-drama, and dance therapy—things like that."

I wanted to ask what psychodrama and dance therapy were, but didn't have a chance because she was pointing ahead. "Up there's the Cottage." I was curious to see the place where Lee had lived until recently. "It's for the men what Small Oaks is for the women. They keep about eight patients there—same as Small Oaks."

No gingerbread house, the Cottage was another relic of suburbia cum iron bars, but this one in red brick, like the main building. Disappointed at its ordinariness, I turned back.

"The O.T. shop's in that white barn across the road from the A," said Miss Cavalino. "Want to go up?"

"Sure."

We walked back and ascended a creaky wooden outside staircase that I thought had great romantic appeal. It led to the reconstructed hayloft of the old white barn I'd seen from the porch on Two.

While Miss Cavalino went to look for Evvie Gordon, who was "a wonderful sculptor" and in charge of O.T., I looked around. The gabled and eaved second-floor interior was cozy, though spacious. With patients kneading clay, knitting, making lanyards, and playing chess, it could have been one of the arts-and-crafts bunks of my camping days. But what a motley crew of campers! Among them, Babe Hawkins—a safe distance away—was cursing under her breath and stabbing a shuttle between the threads of a loom. Rosemary, who'd come over from the A, was twisting and turning in the middle of the floor, and a giant man, who looked and sounded like the village idiot, was playing chess with a male attendant.

In a few minutes Miss Cavalino brought over a slim,

cheerful, but harried-looking woman with dark auburn hair and greenish eyes.

"This is Evvie," she said.

Evvie gave me an appraising glance. "Would you like to start something, some kind of project? A lanyard, maybe?"

Why not? Making a lanyard would be a way to "keep busy," my father's panacea for all psychic ills. And since I was starting my life again at about age fourteen anyway, why not pick up where I'd left off? I had a sudden grotesque picture of presenting Dad with the lanyard, or a bookmark, or a belt, as I'd always done after my summers at camp. What would I say? "Look what I made for you at the crazy house"?

But Evvie was waiting for an answer.

"Okay," I said.

As Evvie left to find me the lanyard materials, a small, squat woman of about forty with unusually heavy arms and legs but a startlingly beautiful face—high cheekbones, deep-set violet eyes, a slash of scarlet mouth—rushed up to me. From her disheveled hair and sloppy dress I guessed she was a patient, and I drew back, afraid she might attack me. Instead, she stopped in front of me, looked at me searchingly, and said in a throaty, Tallulah Bankhead voice, "You look familiar. Where do I know you from? Haven't we met?"

I froze. She did look familiar. Oh my God, no. What would happen to my newfound anonymity, my chance to start life over, if some relic of my past was around to haunt me?

"I—I don't know. I don't think so," I said weakly.

"Cedarhurst. My God, Cedarhurst," she said. "You're

Clae and Herb's daughter." And as the dawning recognition of Fay Hess, who, with her husband, Howard, had belonged to the same golf club as my parents years before, struck me, I felt the first moment of real despair I'd experienced since I arrived. The one thing I knew I couldn't confront was the old me or the Other Me. If Fay knew or remembered me as either, and tried to pull me back into that milieu—even into her memories of it, or of me—I'd be finished.

But a closer look at Fay's equally terror-stricken face revealed that she was as frightened at the prospect of losing her anonymity as I was. A recollection of my Aunt Lenore talking to a friend about Fay on the telephone came back to me. "Yes, it's a shame—especially with three kids involved. I don't care how upset you are"—the word "sick" was rarely used for mental illness then—"it seems to me you have an obligation to stick with your children."

We stared at each other, seeming to read each other's minds. "I won't tell anyone at home if you won't," Fay said finally. "And I won't bring it up here either."

"It's a promise," I said.

"I'd like to forget the Five Towns and all that garbage anyway," she said bitterly. "Those silly bitches, with their weekly visits to the beauty parlor and their goddamn fund-raising luncheons. To give your mother credit, she really wasn't like a lot of them, but all most of those bastards ever think about is money, and who's got the biggest house and the most expensive mink coat. Christ, they make me puke."

Though Fay had not included her, I knew all too well that my mother, too, had succumbed to the pervasive preoccupation with appearances. Because of it, I remembered bitterly, she had gone off one day when I was about thirteen and disappeared. Suddenly, inexplicably, just dropped off the face of the earth.

Frank was away at school by then, my father was unreachable—out of town on a business trip—and nobody else seemed to know where she was.

Four days later, she'd finally called from Peter's *atelier* in the city.

"My God, Mom. Where have you been? I've been so worried."

My mother's voice sounded far off and vaguely irritated. "I don't know why you were so upset, darling. After all, you should've known I was all right. If anything was wrong I'd have let you know." I sensed a lapse in logic, but didn't interrupt. "Now look, I'm not going to be home for another few days, but if you like, you can come and meet me for lunch at Monte's tomorrow."

Monte's, a restaurant on Central Park South where I often met my mother and Peter, was cool, green, and soothingly familiar. Large semicircular booths lined the walls, and I spotted the back of my mother's wide-brimmed hat across the room. Peter was facing her and waved. I started toward them.

My mother turned around. "Darling, I hope you won't be angry."

I was paralyzed. A bandaged, distorted face, swollen and black and blue, faced me. The eyes were slits, and beneath the bandaged nose with its flat, distended nostrils, the beautiful even teeth, surrounded by skin still yellow with iodine above the lipstick, shone in a smile—a smile both heroic and grotesque.

"But why didn't you tell me, Mom?" I said, filled with a sense of helplessness and betrayal. I forced the words out slowly, trying not to look at my mother's face. "How could you just disappear like that and not even let me know where you were?"

"I knew if I told you, you'd want to stop me."

This was true. She had asked my opinion several times.

"You know everybody says you'd lose all the character in your face if you had it fixed. Don't, please, don't," I'd replied. To me the idea was somehow grotesque, unnatural, and most of all, frighteningly irrevocable—a change that couldn't be undone, that would alter my mother beyond any hope of going back again. In some mystical way, I felt it would alter her intrinsic being as well, and somehow confirm the overweening preoccupation with herself, her singing, and her appearance that had obsessed her for the past few years.

Startled at the shock still on my face, she hurried on, eager to change the direction of the conversation. "But darling, this isn't the way it will look later. All this swelling will go down in a few weeks. You're going to be proud of your crazy mother, you'll see."

"I *was* proud of you, Mom."

"Well, now you'll be even prouder," she said gaily. She had donned sunglasses now, and the macabre smile flashed beneath them.

I remained standing, unable to bring myself either to sit down or to leave. Her frightening disappearance and the change in her face had done more than confirm my mother's self-absorption and suspected indifference to my feelings. It had also doomed once and for all my attempts to link the face of the smart woman in furs sweeping out the driveway in the Packard with that of the heavy, lonely, and unattractive child my mother, in a few moments of intimacy, had described herself as having been. ("Darling, stop worrying. You'll grow out of it, you'll see. I was just like you at your age, believe it or not—well, maybe not quite your size.")

"Really, Jo, you're taking this much too seriously," she went on. There was a note of genuine surprise in her voice. Clearly, she was hurt and irritated by the strength of my reaction. "I thought you'd be happy for me. You know how much I hated that bump in my nose. Now stop acting silly and sit down. You'll see, I'll be home in a few days and you'll forget all about it."

I sat down, but somehow, I knew that no matter how she looked in a few weeks, I wouldn't forget all about it— then or ever.

Fay was looking at me closely. "Well, and what brought you here? You look all right to me," she said accusingly. "Got any symptoms?"

"What do you mean, 'symptoms'?" I asked. I'd heard the word only in the context of physical illness.

She looked surprised at my ignorance. "You know— sweating palms, headaches, trembling, that kind of thing. Lots of people here have some."

"No. No symptoms. Not yet, anyway." After all, I'd only been off the Dexedrine for three days. Anything could happen. "But take my word for it, I belong here."

Fay didn't ask me why. "Met any of the others?" she asked. "Any of the A crowd?"

I mentioned Lee and Ellen.

"Lee Rodman," Fay said throatily, "is a charming bastard. Smart as a whip and witty as hell, but cold as ice." She drew me aside, and then added, *sotto voce*, "You know, Jo-Jo, the

190

first month he was here he got one of the student nurses pregnant and she had to leave, practically under cover of darkness. They almost threw him out of the Oaks, but his doctor, Kerner, pleaded his case, so they kept him on. *I'd steer clear,*" she advised. "He's a heart-breaker."

I was shocked. Something about the Lee I'd observed didn't match Fay's description, nor did it square with Addie's affectionate tone when she'd mentioned him. I wanted to ask more about him—about his relationship with Ellen, and why he was at the hospital—but was afraid it would show too much interest.

"Ellen's a mess," she went on. "We both had shock treatments at other hospitals." Shock treatments, which I knew from Schmidt weren't used at the Oaks. "As you can plainly see, they didn't work on either of us. I guess she got here about three years ago—two years after me."

Then Fay had been a patient at the Oaks for five years, Ellen for three. I was appalled, though if I'd investigated the subject, I wouldn't have been. Without the wonder drugs that were soon to come, short-term hospitalization for serious mental illness was unheard of.

Fay switched the subject. "Who's your doctor going to be?"

"Dr. Block. At least, I hope so."

"A capable guy," Fay said. "But much good *that* does. Christ, I've got Pickens—supposedly one of the best—and I still can't get out of this place." She said this almost in a moan, and I supposed she was thinking of her children back home. "I've tried it as an outpatient and I always end up coming back in to Small Oaks or Two. Once I even had to go back to Four, where I started."

I tried to think of what terrible things could have happened to her as an outpatient that would have forced her to constantly return—especially in such bad shape that she'd once had to go back to Four. I realized that for the first time in three years, I was feeling lucky—lucky that I wasn't as badly off as Fay; that I was still young, and hadn't had to abandon my children and home for shock treatments. I also realized that without planning or worrying about it in advance, I'd had my first conversation with one of the "in-contact" patients.

CHAPTER 13

"You're going to see Dr. Poole at three this afternoon in the annex to the main building. Room 46," said Evvie, two weeks later. She was reading from a scrap of paper on which she'd taken down some notes when the phone rang in the O.T. shop a few minutes before.

I let the tiny colored beads I'd been picking up with a hair's-width needle drop off the end. "Are you sure? I just saw Dr. Block this morning and he didn't say anything about it. Why would I be seeing someone else the same day?"

"Oh, I'm sure, all right. They just called from the main building when they couldn't find you on Two. As for why, I haven't the foggiest."

I was uneasy. Things had fallen into a kind of routine—a routine, I had to admit to myself, that was not altogether unpleasant.

The focus of my days had become my talks with Dr. Block. At eleven o'clock, on four days a week—the usual number of therapy sessions for patients at the Oaks—I returned to the floor to see him in my room. ("My office

193

floats. I'm a man without a country," he said.) I confessed my terror of going on another monstrous binge, of feeling the need for Dexedrine again to transform me.

He was casual and reassuring. "Well, I guess that could happen. But I have a feeling it's not going to—especially if we can find out something about what got you started on all this."

I recognized the analyst's ploy—the same, actually, as Schmidt's had been: If you can find out the cause, you'll have the cure. How contemptuous of her and her probing I'd been. But Dr. Block was different, different from Schmidt, different from Cunningham. His calm, uncritical manner continued to disarm me. And I noted with pleasure that he didn't take notes.

"They won't make me leave because I seem too normal—I mean, you know, not acting crazy or having symptoms—will they?" I asked at the conclusion of our session this morning. To Ellen or Fay, who were constantly complaining about wanting to leave, I wouldn't have dared to say such a thing.

"No worry about that, Jo-Jo. Don't forget, you've been a pretty mixed-up girl. That may not be obvious to a lot of people around here right now, but believe me, we've got your history straight. You need to go way back and find out who you are. Not only who you are, but where you're going to go from here. Finding that out'll take time. It isn't going to happen overnight."

With Dr. Block, I had decided, the time would be well spent.

But now I was to see someone new. Why?

It seemed I had no choice but to wait and see.

Ten to three. There were no chairs, and I stood uneasily in the long corridor of the new wing—fluorescent lights, clean new black-and-white linoleum tile, a doctor's name on every door. Only twenty vertical and thirty horizontal feet from Two, I estimated, remembering how the annex abutted the main building. Yet in the shiny new hallway there was no sign that this was part of the same mental hospital.

I was, as usual, early for the appointment. My mother's lateness had bred in me a punctuality on which I prided myself, and one of the things I'd liked about Dr. Block was his scrupulous promptness. At eleven sharp of every morning we were scheduled to meet, he had materialized at my door, the stiff smile I'd come to welcome on his lips.

Don't brood about Dr. Block, I told myself sharply. He probably doesn't even know about this meeting. If he had, he'd undoubtedly have mentioned it. I'd have to ask him in the morning.

Three P.M. Nurses and aides arrived, leading patients from all the floors. Doors opened—every door except Dr. Poole's—and during the next ten minutes there was a steady movement in the hall, as patients emerged from the offices, many looking dazed and disoriented, to be taken in hand by the waiting attendants as their replacements went in.

Three-ten and the hall was entirely empty again, except for me. I put my ear up against Dr. Poole's door but heard nothing. I tried to fight the resentment that being kept waiting always aroused in me. How often I had been made to wait—first as a child sitting on the Spruce Street curb straining to see the long overdue Packard; then as a teenager on cold street corners after some of my appointments with Schmidt. "Be on the corner at five-ten sharp," my mother would say, and I always was, hoping against hope as I shivered in the icy wind that this time she'd be on time. But she was invariably at least fifteen minutes late—more often a half hour or more.

As I stood there, my anger mounting, I recalled, too, a November morning years before, just after I'd transferred to the Woodmere Academy. A short Thanksgiving Day play was planned, and as the best reader in the class, I'd won the largest part—that of Prudence Alcock, a Pilgrim housewife in the first colony. The role hardly made up for having to stay in the second grade, yet it was some comfort, and I took it seriously, seeing it as another way to show that I had been wrongly held back.

"Mom, come to the play, you've got to come," I'd begged when she got home at night. I didn't consider asking my father. To ask a commuting father to take time off for such a daytime event in that era was unthinkable.

"Well, of course, dear. What time does it start?"

"Nine. That's when we have assembly."

"Ungodly hour," she'd murmured, but added, "Don't worry, darling, I'll be there."

Before the play started, I scanned the audience from behind the curtain, my neck rubbing against the white cardboard of the pilgrim's collar I'd made for my costume. The lower school was small, and guests were always seated on tiny children's chairs at the back of the hall. There were, indeed, some guests, but not my mother.

"Time to begin, Johanna. Now take your place on stage," my teacher said.

196

"Couldn't we start a little later?" I pleaded. "My mother isn't here yet."

"Don't be foolish. You know assembly is from nine to nine-thirty. We can't run the school just to suit you."

By 9:20 the play was over, and as we took our bows, I noticed the door to the auditorium open on the left. Elegantly dressed—with gloves, a hat, her sable neckpiece draped artistically around her shoulders—my mother swept into the auditorium.

Seeing me onstage, she smiled and waved gaily, at first unaware that the play was over. I looked down, my eyes filled with tears, and waited for the curtain to close.

My mother appeared backstage. "I'm sorry, darling, but I never thought they'd start right on the dot of nine." She said this in an aggrieved tone, as though the school were somehow to blame for being so slavish about time. "I don't know how they can put on a play at that hour and expect anyone to come anyway. I mean, it's almost impossible to get here so early. And then, Al took the longest time getting the car, and . . ." There were, as always, other reasons: Nancy had awakened her late; she couldn't find her hat.

"Never mind, dear, I'll be at the next one," she'd said.

Wordless, I'd turned away. There was nothing to say. But I knew, in my heart of hearts, that she could have been there if she'd really wanted to—could have gotten up with my father, could have come without a hat, could have told Al to get the car earlier. If she'd really cared about my feelings, she'd have been there.

I'd never told Schmidt about my mother's lateness; not how I felt about it, anyway. It occurred to me, as I stood there, getting madder and madder, that it might be a good thing to discuss with Dr. Block.

Three-fifteen. I knew I didn't have to wait now. Poole could come looking for me. God knows, I'd be easy enough to find. Yet I was curious—not so much about Poole himself, as about the purpose of the meeting.

At 3:25 the door at the end of the corridor opened and I saw a tall, broad-shouldered, and good-looking man of about thirty-eight coming toward me with a tentative smile on his face. He had an odd walk—with one shoulder raised slightly higher than the other—and he was carefully carrying a cup full of steaming coffee.

I recognized the cup as one from the A. So if this was in fact Poole, he'd kept me lingering in the hall while he stopped for coffee. I felt, again, a rush of the anger that had begun to dissipate when I saw him, at last, coming down the hall.

"Miss Rosengarten?" he said. I nodded, surprised at his formality. Dr. Block had called me Jo-Jo from the start. "Sorry ah'm late, but we had a staff meetin', and it ran overtime." He took out a key and unlocked the door to his office.

How come the other doctors were already in their offices if there'd been a meeting, I thought, but I was so disconcerted by the combination of his extreme, if fading, good looks and the unexpected Southern accent—less pronounced than Cunningham's but unmistakable nonetheless—that I decided not to say anything about his lateness or the damning cup of coffee.

His office was tastefully but unremarkably furnished in Danish modern—with a desk against the right-hand wall in the corner near the window, a couch on the wall op-

198

posite, and a comfortable upholstered chair facing the window at a right angle to the couch.

He didn't say anything about where I should sit, so I quickly took the chair. He didn't seem to notice, and in fact had a remote, preoccupied expression on his face as he spent the next few minutes getting organized—clearing his throat, loosening his tie, putting his coffee and what looked like an inhaler from the pocket of his tweed jacket on the desk. Then he removed his jacket to hang it on the back of the straight desk chair.

I noticed that he moved slowly and cautiously, and seemed to wince with pain, especially as he took off his jacket. Almost involuntarily, I said, "Is something wrong?" then was annoyed with myself for sounding solicitous when in fact I was still angry.

"It's mah back. Mah back goes out every now and then and it's damned painful."

I was, again, conscious of his accent. Keep an open mind, I told myself. Just because Cunningham is a Southerner and a jackass doesn't mean that all his colleagues are jackasses, too.

"Mind if I smoke?" he said, taking a pipe from a pipe rack on his desk. Three or four minutes had passed.

"No."

He picked up the pipe, tapped it on the ashtray to empty it, and took a sip of the coffee. The way his chair was positioned, facing the wall behind the desk, kept him from looking at me directly. I wondered if this was by design—in order to put his patients at ease—by accident, or if he just didn't like looking people in the eye. What a contrast to Dr. Block's intense gaze. I would tell him about it tomorrow.

Poole's position made it easier to study him, however, and as he fiddled with the pipe, I took a closer look at his profile. Ten years ago, I surmised, he must have been unusually handsome, and he was still so attractive that I knew I'd find it uncomfortable to talk to him, even if I could get past the Southern accent. Handsome men had always seemed to me creatures from another planet, not real people with whom one could hold real conversations.

"Well, ah guess we ought to get started," said Dr. Poole, glancing at his watch and then, briefly, at me. His peculiar furniture arrangement meant that he had to look over his shoulder to see me at all. I was neither facing him nor not facing him.

I sat and waited for him to go on, but he took another sip of coffee, and gazed dreamily at the blank wall in front of him.

What was supposed to happen next? With Block, there had been no awkward pauses, no pauses at all, in fact. Unable to take the silence any longer, I finally said, "Would you mind telling me why I'm here? I mean, I just saw Dr. Block this morning, and he didn't say anything about my seeing you."

"Yeah, ah know. Well, we hadn't had our meetin' yet this mornin'. But since then, ah've had a long talk with John, and he's been tellin' me all about you.

John. So they were friends. And Block knew. Any hope that this appointment might have been unknown to him—the mistake of a bungler at a higher level—died.

"Oh really?" I said, waiting for him to continue. But again he said nothing. He just shifted in his chair, lined the inhaler on the desk up with some pencils, took another sip of coffee, and ran his other hand over his hair.

The silence lengthened embarrassingly, and I gazed at the diplomas on the wall over the couch. They undoubtedly offered proof of Poole's credentials, but I was beginning to wonder.

Well, no use leaving the matter in any more doubt, I decided. If I was supposed to say something first, I would start by suggesting the very worst reason I could think of for this meeting, and at least put my mind to rest on that score. Then we could go on from there—that is, if we could ever get a conversation going.

"My being here doesn't mean you're going to be replacing Dr. Block as my therapist, does it?"

"That seems to be the general ah-dea," he said, now getting up with a grimace and fiddling with the cords to the blinds.

I felt as though I'd been struck.

"John's—Dr. Block's—schedule was just too full to fit you in. Ah have the time and ah thought you'd be a raht interestin' case." He granted me a fleeting smile.

"Should ah open the window, do you think?" he inquired irrelevantly. "Are you feelin' too warm, too cold?"

"No," I said, still trying to grasp what Poole had just told me. What *was* I feeling? Hurt, maybe—rejected, shocked, perhaps—but certainly not too warm or too cold.

Dr. Poole was carefully lowering himself into the chair again. "But why?" I asked, when at last he seemed comfortable. "Dr. Block and I had so much in common. I mean, he had experience with addiction, and—"

"Well, ah cain't claim to have been an addict," Poole interrupted, "but ah sure can drink anyone under the table. Fact is, in medical school, we used to go out and get

201

plastered every night. Ah swear, ah don't know how ah ever graduated." He chuckled reminiscently.

I couldn't believe my ears. Was I supposed to admire him for his drinking prowess? To consider it somehow analogous to Block's addiction or my own? "Anyway, ah've never had a female patient from New York City. Ah think it would be good for my development."

Good for *his* development. But what about mine? Surely his never having had a patient from New York City would in no way qualify him as the best person to handle such a case; possibly quite the opposite. In fact, I was having a hard time figuring out why he and I had been put together at all.

But perhaps, I thought, he'd only been teasing and I just wasn't attuned to his humor yet. After all, the hospital was known world-wide. Surely to be a doctor there you had to be well qualified. And Dr. Block had apparently endorsed the choice. Perhaps he knew something terrific about Poole that wasn't immediately apparent.

"I'm not really from New York City, by the way," I explained. "I grew up in Cedarhurst, Long Island."

"Well, what's the difference?" he said huffily, looking at me as though I were nit-picking. "I mean, it's all the same, ain't it?" I knew the "ain't" was an affectation, perhaps meant to foster a folksy simplicity, yet it irritated me.

"No, it really isn't," I said, emphasizing the "isn't." "One's a big city, the other's a suburb, and they're quite a distance apart." He was looking skeptical, so I added weakly, "I mean, it's an entirely different way of life."

There was another pause. Poole shifted again, cleared his throat, used the inhaler, and blew his nose. Suddenly, he turned again to face me.

"Ah s'pose your daddy's a Democrat?"

I nodded. *Now* what was going on?

"An FDR Democrat?"

"Yes, as a matter of fact, he was. Why?"

Ignoring my question, he said, "You know, Miss Rosen-garten—"

"Jo-Jo," I interrupted.

"Miss—unh—Jo-Jo. That man just about destroyed this country in the thirties. Did you know that?"

"No, I didn't know that. And I don't believe it either."

I was outraged. How dare he attack my father's politics—or by extension, my own.

"Well, it's true," he said. "The man was a damned Socialist. Anybody with any sense could see it."

I continued to fume, furious with myself that I couldn't think of a biting and knowledgeable retort. At the same time, I couldn't believe the direction the conversation had taken. Were his remarks perhaps intended as some sort of clever psychiatric provocation, one that would cause me to rise to my father's defense? To attack him? To talk about how it had been at home? If so, the tactic had failed.

"May I ask why on earth you brought up FDR?" I asked.

"Why do you think?" He looked at me slyly.

Uh-oh. Poole's approach might be unconventional, but he was not above turning questions around, in tried-and-true psychiatrist style.

"To annoy me, maybe?" I said.

He chuckled again. "Well, Miss—Jo-Jo—funny name, ain't it?—ah'm not goin' to tell ya. I'm goin' to let you figure it out for yourself. What do you think of that?"

I felt like slapping him. "I don't think anything of it."

But my real opinion was that it was stupid, annoying, and above all, pointless.

"Bet you think ah'm one of those prejudiced Southerners, don'tcha?"

"Actually, I hadn't thought about it at all," I said, though of course that's exactly what I'd already concluded. Was he going to surprise me and prove otherwise?

"Well, ah want you to know, some of the Negroes ah've met are the finest people ah've ever known. Why, we had a fella workin' on mah daddy's farm—Billy Williams was his name, ol' Billy Williams—who never went to school a day in his life. But ol' Billy was smarter than half the guys I met at the University of Virginia in medical school. And that's a fact."

"Are you trying to tell me some of your best friends are Negroes?"

"That's exactly right," he said sincerely, totally unaware of the irony. Before I could come up with a reply, he began the slow ascent from his chair. "Well, our time is almost up. Guess ah'll be seeing you tomorrow about the same time."

I glanced at my watch. It was five to four. Our fifty minutes had been reduced to thirty-five, all of them worthless. On top of his seeming incompetence, he was also cheating on the allotted time.

Not that I wanted to prolong the conversation. Quite the opposite. But I'd learned through Fay that the hospital was costing my father a lot of money—about a thousand dollars a month, she'd said, with a sizable chunk going for the analytic hours. The idea that Poole could blithely dispense with fifteen minutes worth of my father's hard-earned money was galling.

"Do you mean three tomorrow, which is when I was here, or three-twenty-five, when you arrived?" I asked. This was not at all how I'd intended to bring up the issue of his lateness, but I couldn't resist saying something, and I no longer cared how it came out.

"Technically speakin', we don't have to start till three-ten," he said. "That first ten minutes of the ow-ah are considered passin' time."

"That still makes you fifteen full minutes late," I said. "And you ended early, too."

"Ah said ah was sorry now, didn't I?" He headed out the door. I had no choice but to continue our conversation on the move. "Don't tell me you're one of those nervous nellies that's always watchin' the clock. Y'all should try to be a little more relaxed, like me. But ah guess you Northerners are always rush-rush-rushin'."

Speechless, I let him go on. "Anyway," he said, locking his door behind him (didn't he have any other patients?), "ah'll see you tomorrow. And ah'll try not to be late, even though ah think you're makin' too much of it."

You won't be late again if I can help it, I vowed to myself, because I won't be here to be kept waiting. I had already decided to see Cunningham or whoever was in charge of assigning therapists and demand a return to Block. And if I couldn't get Block back, then I'd take someone else. Anyone else. I might not be in great shape myself, but Poole, I had decided, was a nut. He was certainly in the right place, I thought grimly—just on the wrong side of the gates.

CHAPTER 14

"Where's Fay?" I asked Evvie breathlessly, panting from my dash to the barn and up the steps to the O.T. shop. Before taking action, I knew I had to tell someone sympathetic what had happened, sort out my thoughts, find out whether and how a change of therapists was made. "Where did she go? Is she coming back?"

"I think she said something about going into Washington tonight," said Evvie, as she put lids on the paint jars. "She probably went back to her room to change."

"Oh, no," I groaned. Fay was living at Mrs. Callahan's, a rooming house three blocks away from the hospital that was often a first outpatient residence. If she was going to Washington, she wouldn't be back at the Oaks till tomorrow.

Evvie was looking at me curiously. She wasn't used to seeing me in such an overwrought state. "What's wrong? Can I help?"

For a moment I was tempted to talk to her. She was down-to-earth and commonsensical. But she was also Administration, and as such likely to regard my behavior—

and possibly my opinions—as pathological. For the same reason, I hadn't rushed to see Addie.

"No, it's not really that important," I said.

My heart still pounding, I left the O.T. shop and stood at the top of the steps. Where to turn next? As though drawn by some involuntary force, I headed for the A, impelled by such a need to talk that I forgot my fears about being with Lee.

To my relief, he was on duty behind the counter. Aside from Ellen—perched as usual on her stool—there were no other customers. I remembered that a large group of patients had been taken for a drive that afternoon, which explained the relatively quiet O.T. shop and the empty A.

My disquiet must have been immediately apparent because the first thing Lee said was "'Rest, rest, perturb-ed spirit.'" I recognized the line from *Hamlet* and couldn't help but smile.

"'Perturb-ed' isn't the word for it. Listen, do either of you know anything about Dr. Poole?"

"Poole? I thought you were seeing John Block," said Lee, raising an eyebrow. I was surprised that he knew who had been my doctor so far. Could it be he had been asking about me just as I had been asking about him?

"'*Were* seeing' is right. Now they've changed me to Poole and . . ." I stopped myself before making any leading statements, not wanting to influence what they would say. "Anyway, do you know anything about him?"

"Good-looking. Southern. A great ladies' man and a favorite of Cunningham's, I've heard," began Lee cautiously.

To my surprise, Ellen interrupted him. She and I hadn't really spoken to each other since our first encounter on the Small Oaks porch. "Why don't you tell her the truth?" she said.

Lee shrugged as though to say, "Do as you wish, but it wouldn't be my way."

"Listen, Jo-Jo," she said—I liked the way she said my name, softening the "o" so that it had an almost foreign flavor—"I'm sorry if what I'm going to say will upset you even more than you already are, but I've heard it on pretty good authority that his private life is as messed up as some of the patients'. He drinks a lot, and last year he had a fight with a bartender and threw his glass through a mirror behind the bar."

"Oh my God," I groaned. An alcoholic with a streak of violence.

"Is that how he hurt his back?" I asked. "I thought maybe he'd been wounded in the war, like Dr. Block."

Lee guffawed. "Not exactly." Now that Ellen had said what she did, he seemed more willing to speak freely. "Dr. Calvin Poole was laid low on the playing fields of Long Ridge Country Club. He took too wide a swing one day and threw his back out."

Ordinarily I would have found my misconception funny, too, but not if Poole were to continue as my doctor. Still, I thought quickly, it was a truism that many psychiatrists had troubled private lives. That didn't necessarily interfere with their professional effectiveness. And looking on the bright side of Ellen's story, at least he'd attacked the bar and not the bartender.

"What about his reputation as a doctor?" I asked.

Lee paused, as though considering his answer carefully—a habit I'd noticed on the Small Oaks porch, too. "Unorthodox. I've certainly heard it noised about that his methods are unorthodox. But he's been on the staff for about five years, so I suppose he must be doing something right."

"Oh come on, Lee," said Ellen. "You know he has a reputation for unreliability. Just because you're a doctor doesn't mean you have to cover for him."

I thought I again saw a look of pain in Lee's eyes, but he turned away to wash out a coffee pot too quickly for me to be sure.

"Well, tell us about it—I mean, if you want to," Ellen said.

"Not only do I want to, I'll explode if I don't tell someone," I said. And I tried to describe the "psychiatric hour."

"Certainly does sound peculiar," said Lee when I had finished.

"What I really have to find out is how to do something about it. I've got to try to change back to Dr. Block."

"I don't know," said Lee. "They've usually got some arcane reasons for the choices they make, even though they may be completely baffling to ordinary mortals like us. Cunningham moves in mysterious ways, his wonders to perform."

"So it's Cunningham I have to see," I said. I'd had a slim hope that perhaps some other administrator was in charge of such decisions.

"You mean you have found the eminent Dr. Cunningham not to your liking?"

"I thought he was a real idiot," I said. I couldn't believe I was speaking so freely to Lee and Ellen.

Lee was beaming. "You're remarkably perceptive, Jo-Jo," he said, and I felt as though someone had presented me with a blue ribbon. Then I looked worriedly at Ellen. Would she be resentful? No. She was smiling, too, apparently in agreement. If I were Lee's girlfriend, I thought—or whatever the Oaks equivalent for a girlfriend was—I'd have been jealous, I was sure. Ellen must have a more generous spirit than mine.

"Listen," said Lee, "Why don't you use the phone here to try to set up an appointment with Cunningham? The phone is supposed to be for A business only, but we can overlook that little technicality."

He wiped his hands on a dish towel. I'd noticed he'd done that several times since he finished drying the coffee pot, and wondered about it briefly. Then he handed me the receiver across the top of the counter.

To my surprise, I was given an appointment for the next morning. "I gather you'll be undergoing your trial by fire tomorrow," Lee said when I hung up. "Permit me to offer you a Coke on the house, and we can all drink to your success. Wish I could put something more interesting in it but there *are*, regrettably, rules which of course one may not break. I tried it once, so believe me, I know."

Was he referring to the episode with the nurse? I didn't dare ask, and we touched our paper cups in an imaginary toast.

At 11:00 A.M. the next morning I was ushered into Dr. Cunningham's office.

He looked up from the inevitable file on his desk, and waved at the same chair I'd occupied the day I arrived. Then he tilted back in his own reclining chair and regarded me with a benign smile. "So, missy, to what do ah owe the pleasure of this visit? Ah've been lookin' through

210

your file heah and ah see nothin' to be concerned about. Nothin' at all. Fact is, ah hear through owah grapevine that you have been doin' very well. Very well, indeed."

I saw my opening. "Well, if that's true, Dr. Cunningham, I think it's mainly because of Dr. Block." He started to say something but I rushed on. "I mean, I really got along well with him, and now—yesterday—I found out about the change to Dr. Poole. I'm sure you know about it, and I really don't think I'll be able to get along nearly as well with him. Work with him, I mean. That's why I'm here. I want to go back to Dr. Block. I know he's very busy with new patients and everything, but I can't believe he couldn't fit me in somewhere. We wouldn't even have to meet at the same time every day or anything. I wouldn't care."

Dr. Cunningham was smiling broadly. "Well, well, that was quite a speech, missy. You suhtainly are a persuasive young woman."

Could I have won so quickly? Emboldened, I added quickly, "Besides, Dr. Block and I had so much in common."

"Mm-hmm," said Dr. Cunningham, still smiling. "Now let's hold onto owah horses heah for just a minute." My heart sank. The smile, I realized, meant nothing. "Don't you think you are jumpin' the gun just a little bit? Dr. Poole happens to be one of the pillars of owah staff heah at Great Oaks. And ah've known him puh-sonally for years. His daddy and I went to school together, and let me tell you he's from one of the finest families in Richmond. His background is absolutely impeccable."

I saw another opening. "But that's just it, Dr. Cunningham. His background. I mean, I'm sure it would be just fine if I were from the South too. But I'm not. I'm from a suburb of New York City in the North, and I have this feeling that he and I might as well be talking different languages."

"Now, Miss Rosengarten," said Dr. Cunningham, no longer smiling, but using my name at last, "ah think there is moah to this, unh—little problem—than meets the eye." I decided Cunningham must be a student of the cliché. "Do you want to know what ah really think?"

"Well, sure." What else could I say, I wondered.

"Now missy, ah'm assumin' you know what a transference is. Am I right?"

Of course, you dunderhead, I thought. I realized he was testing me and answered as calmly as I could. "It's a strong attachment to the therapist, sometimes positive, sometimes negative, and usually based on your relationship to your parents, that you have to work out before you're cured, isn't it?" What was he getting at?

"Good for you!" he cried. "Smart girl! Now what ah think is that you-all have already begun to make a transference to Calvin Poole and you are fightin' it tooth and nail. Ah always say it's when the patients begin theah negative transferences that they come in here protestin' that they want a change. Course, in yaw case, it's been very quick—very quick indeed—but it happens that way sometimes."

I began to feel like Alice in Wonderland. Or was it me that was out of perspective, seeing things upside down? I struggled to stay calm.

"Dr. Cunningham, if you want to talk about transferences, I agree that I had a quick one—but it wasn't to Dr. Poole. It was to Dr. Block. So why break that off and start me with someone new?"

Dr. Cunningham was looking at me sadly, clearly disappointed that he wasn't getting through to me.

"Mah deah young lady, ah'm sure Dr. Poole explained to you that Dr. Block's schedule would not permit him to keep you on. And as for yaw good feelin's toward him, that was no transference, ah'm sure. Why, you just liked him. And why not? He's a mahty fine fella. That's why we keep him in admissions. All the patients like him. But"—he looked at me reproachfully—"they don't all want to keep him on as theah doctor. Now ah think you will have to allow us, in owah infinite wisdom, to make the final decision in this matter. Ah assure you we have thought long and hard about it."

I knew that my time was running out. Dr. Cunningham had looked at his watch two or three times. I decided I had nothing to lose now by being completely direct. "I'll never get anywhere with Dr. Poole. I'm sure of it." Keep calm, I told myself. He's just looking for signs of mental-patient hysterics to prove he's right.

He leaned forward with what I had come to think of as his "I'm-doing-this-for-your-good-and-I-know-better-than-you" look. "One thing ah learned many yeahs ago was to nevah say nevah."

"Dr. Cunningham, I hate to have to tell you this, but did you know that Dr. Poole practically boasted to me that he drank his way through medical school?"

He put his head back and laughed delightedly. "That Cal. Well, we all have to sow owah wild oats at some time or other."

"And he started criticizing my father's politics," I went on desperately.

Dr. Cunningham looked at his watch. "Dr. Poole is known to be a little unconventional in his methods, theah

213

is no denyin' that. But that's part of his technique. He likes to shake his patients up some. Ah'll bet he was just teasin' you. And you fell for it." He wagged his finger and smiled at me roguishly.

"But why? Could you tell me why?"

"Now ah think that's his business, don't you?" He sat back and looked at me as though this time I'd gone too far. "But whatevah he did, ah'm sure he knows just exactly what he's doin'. Now, missy, ah'm a busy man, and ah've given you a good portion of mah precious time. Ah think you had better decide to be a little moah open-minded in yaw attitude."

The irony in his comment, I could see, was not intentional. As I rose and approached the door, I decided on impulse to make one last request. Perhaps, since he'd refused my main demand, I could make some progress on a small point.

"Could I ask you one last question, Dr. Cunningham?" I said, amazed at my own boldness. Where was the paralyzing sense of defeat I had expected to feel if I lost my case?

Surprised, he looked up from his desk, where he was already moving my file to the "finished" basket with one hand and picking up his phone with the other. "At yaw service."

"Would it be possible to get the piano on Two fixed, or to put one that works in one of the other buildings somewhere else on the grounds?"

"So you are a musician, are you?"

"I'm not that good. It's just that I like to play sometimes. It's—it could be therapeutic." If he was going to trade in clichés, why shouldn't I? "And there must be other patients who might like to use one, too." A selling point, I thought.

214

He looked at me shrewdly, sighed, and put the receiver back on its base, apparently resigned to wasting a few more moments of his precious time. "Now, missy, have you asked yourself why this heah piano is so important to you?"

I had thought nothing Cunningham could say would amaze me anymore, but I was wrong. "What do you mean? Is there something wrong with wanting to play the piano?" No one in my experience had ever questioned the value of playing an instrument, and again I felt like Alice.

"Well, ah just think that sometimes owah patients are regressin' when they hold on to theah old forms of escape."

So that was what he considered my wish to play—a regressive form of escape. I, on the other hand, was sure it was a sign of health—a desire to re-establish myself, to find again the person I'd been, or would have been, without Dexedrine.

But Cunningham was going on. "Now we have a patient up on Four"—I knew he was referring to Tria—"who's been playin' away fo' years. And it pains me to tell you that that girl is no better now than she was when she got here."

"But surely it's not because of playing the piano," I said incredulously. "Surely, playing the piano isn't bad for her. It must, at least, be one connection with reality."

Cunningham didn't respond. Instead, he paused for a moment, and smiled at me placatingly. "Well, ah'll give it some thought." His hand reached for the telephone receiver again and hovered for a moment before landing. "And ah have to say that ah'm sure you'll eventually see that ah was right about Dr. Poole. In fact, ah'm willin' to bet that one of these days you'll come in here and thank me fo' not givin' in to you."

I tried to picture the scene—me in crinoline, first knocking shyly on the door, then entering and offering him a bouquet along with thanks—but the vision faded fast.

As I opened the door to leave, my head spinning from our final, astonishing exchange over the piano, he called out, "Oh, Miss Rosengarten, one last thing. Ah almost forgot, but Miss Addison—Addie, I guess you call her—and Miss Evvie Gordon and Dr. Block have all agreed that in a few more weeks, when there's an openin', you'll be ready to move into Small Oaks. Now what do you think about that?"

I felt I was being thrown a bone. That will hardly make up for losing my doctor and being told that wanting to play the piano is a neurotic escape and a regression, I wanted to say. But of course I didn't. Furthermore, I was not at all sure that I wanted to leave the security of Two, with its safe, measured meals on trays, and Addie's comforting presence, for the freedom of Small Oaks.

But this was no time to voice any doubts—and certainly no person to whom to voice them.

"Fine," I said, and closed the door behind me.

I stood in the hall for a moment and realized that I was trembling. I'd lost on both the points I'd hoped to win. I was suddenly reminded of the day in Miss Clark's gloomy office when she had so finally, so devastatingly, removed my last hope of entering third grade. I had lost a battle then and never really recovered from it. Would this second defeat deal a mortal blow to the shaky equilibrium I had been establishing at Great Oaks?

As I stood outside the door, my trembling subsided. I waited for the old feeling of hopelessness and despair to take hold. But I felt strangely light-headed, even giddy.

216

Come to think of it, I had dealt with Cunningham rather well. I hadn't knuckled under immediately, had maintained my poise, had marshalled reasons and arguments. Even more importantly, I had done it all without the help of Dexedrine—without even wanting the help of Dexedrine. Nor had it occurred to me to somehow obtain food to make me feel better. It seemed I wasn't quite as helpless as I had always thought myself to be. But how had it happened? Where had my eloquence and poise—however ineffective with Cunningham—come from?

Baffled but elated, I headed for the A, hoping Ellen and Lee were still there and that Lee hadn't closed up yet for the twelve-to-two lunch break. When I got there, he was shoving the sliding glass doors across the front.

I looked around, but Ellen was nowhere in sight, and the rest of the patients had already returned to their floors. Lee and I were alone for the first time. Ordinarily, I knew I'd have been terrified of saying something stupid—or worse yet, saying nothing at all. But now I didn't have to look for a topic.

I helped Lee replace one of the doors on the track from which it had derailed, enjoying the sense of being useful. Then, increasingly impatient to tell him what had happened, I watched as he strung a heavy metal chain through metal loops on the door and the wall. Finally, in silence, he attached a padlock.

His movements were careful, deliberate, and—in this case, I felt—irritatingly slow. Didn't he want to know what had happened?

When he'd tested the padlock, he wiped his hands on his pants and turned to me. "Well now. What was the result of your interview with the Grand Inquisitor?"

"I didn't get anywhere," I said, "but the crazy thing is, I'm not as upset about it as I'd thought I'd be. I don't know why, but it doesn't seem as important to me as it did yesterday."

Lee paused before speaking. "Maybe the magic of Great Oaks is casting its spell on you. You do realize that at least half the cure here is supposed to come from the total environment and the so-called 'interpersonal relationships'—not just the therapy."

Was that it? His remark made sense. Certainly the progress I'd made—however minute—had been more the result of my learning to cope with the patients on Two, at the O.T. shop, even now, at the A—than with anything I'd learned with or from Block. And if that were so, then whether Block or Poole or even Cunningham was my doctor wasn't nearly as important as I'd thought only yesterday. Perhaps I had it in my power to get better almost in spite of what seemed to be the obstacles that had been put in my way.

"Maybe you're right," I said, "because I certainly haven't changed my mind about Poole. Oh, and I have to tell you something funny. Dr. Cunningham told me that my wanting them to put a piano that works somewhere on the grounds was a neurotic regression."

Lee smiled briefly, but didn't say anything, and I began to feel uncomfortable as a long pause ensued. "So you play, do you?" he said finally.

"Well, not really that well." I was flustered. "It's just that I feel—I guess the word is 'disoriented,' or uncomfortable, or something—without a piano around. If it was here, I don't even know if I'd use it that much."

There was another pause as Lee stared at the ground,

seemingly deep in thought. What had I said, I wondered, that had put him in such a contemplative mood?

Suddenly he looked up abruptly. "I think I can solve at least part of the piano problem for you."

"You can? But how? I thought you and Cunningham had had a quarrel, too."

"We've got a piano out at our place—Kip's and mine," he said. I remained silent, both dreading and hoping for what I knew was coming next. "It's not right on the grounds, of course, so it wouldn't fulfill your requirements for ready access at all hours of the day and night." I knew his teasing was well-meant, but I blushed anyway. "Still, once you get to Small Oaks, you could come out there to use it sometimes."

I realized the possible implications of the remark at once and felt a sudden resurgence of the self-consciousness I'd felt with him for so long. But Lee didn't seem to notice my silence.

"That's really nice of you," I said at last. I hadn't even obtained "town privileges" yet, much less permission to visit someone off the grounds—and a male patient at that. And what would happen if I did? The story about Lee and the nurse resurfaced once again, and along with it, rankling and unbidden, the awareness of my own body and its imperfections.

But I didn't want to show my hesitation. "Dr. Cunningham did say I could move to Small Oaks soon—I mean, when there's an opening. Probably in a few weeks." Then I couldn't help but add, "I mean, if I want to."

"Why in God's name wouldn't you want to?" Lee asked incredulously. "Is it such paradise up there with Babe and the others?"

Should I tell him about my fears—about the pills, the overeating, the terror of losing control? No, not yet. There was some reserve in Lee that brought out a measure of reserve in me as well.

"I don't know. I've gotten used to Two now."

"You'd get used to Small Oaks, too," he said, and my doubts faded. As I listened to his confident tone, I had a sudden, piercing, poignant vision of Lee as a competent professional, sure in his convictions of what was right and wrong for his patients. What had happened to his confidence about himself, his assurance about his own life?

"Tell you what, Jo-Jo," he said after another pause, "you move to Small Oaks and I'll have a dinner party to celebrate. I've been wanting to have some people out, but I couldn't seem to work up the energy. Besides, I couldn't think of a good rationale. There aren't many causes for celebration around here. I guess you've noticed that."

As we stood there, and I tried to digest what Lee was saying, I saw Miss Cavalino coming along the road with Dorothy in tow. Dorothy was giggling and stopping at every few steps to touch her genital area through her clothing—almost as though to reassure herself it was still there. "Addie said to remind you to be back up for lunch if I saw you," Miss Cavalino told me. "Oh, and also to tell you that you had some mail."

My heart began to pound. My parents had been advised not to write, as well as not to call, for the time being, and no one else knew where I was. No one but Ross.

"Thanks, I'll go right up."

I turned to Lee. "Listen, I'll think about what you said. But I've got to go."

"What's the rush?" he said, holding an unlit cigarette

220

gracefully between thumb and forefinger. "Surely it can't be the *haute cuisine* on Two that draws you with such urgency."

"I—I can't tell you. Not now, anyway." And I hurried from the A once again.

Back on Two, I took Ross's letter from Addie and rushed to my room.

> *Dear Jo,*
>
> *To say that your letter was both a revelation and a tremendous shock would be to state the case mildly. (And by the way, I'd have answered sooner but I was on a trip to Grand Manan Island in Canada—do you know it? It's wonderfully isolated—and just got back.)*
>
> *I feel terrible that you were going through such tortures all these years and didn't feel free to tell me. I say "tortures," even though you didn't use the word, because I think of you as such an honest person, and to have felt you were being dishonest all the time must have been a form of torture to you—almost like being stuck in one of Dante's Circles of Hell—the Circle of Falsity?*
>
> *As for me, I in turn now feel terrible because I realize that you didn't trust me as much as I'd hoped, and because, since I didn't understand the problem, I couldn't help you. But there's no use in recriminations. You did what I guess you felt you had to do at the time.*
>
> *I think it's wonderful that you've had the courage to walk away from everyone and everybody in your*

past—even me, much as it hurts—in order to, as you put it, "start relearning how to live." I trust that Great Oaks is a place that can help you do that. I think I've heard of it, by the way.

Still, I can't believe that you will be that different now. I've been thinking and thinking about it since I read your letter last night, and I can't seem to convince myself that any medicine can turn a person into something that wasn't there to start with. Unless it's some medicine compounded by Dr. Jekyll, that is! In fact, I think we talked about this once years ago, or maybe you wrote me something about it, but of course I didn't know what you were getting at then. How stupid and insensitive I was! Anyway, I am sure there is some essence in you that I will always care for, whatever the "packaging."

I will be leaving for Harvard in a few weeks. I read a book a few months back—Red Star Over China by Edgar Snow—that absolutely fascinated me, and I've decided that I want to get an M.A. in Chinese Studies. Harvard is the best place to do it, and I was very lucky to be accepted into their program. Perhaps I will teach? I, too, am confused about the direction of my life. Only in a less dramatic form than you. But maybe it is selfish of me to tell you about my anxieties, or to complain, when your own current problems are so overwhelming.

I called Jerry in Appleton and read him your letter, as you requested. Of course he, too, was shocked, though he said that in retrospect it explained a lot of things. I promised to keep him informed about you. To do that, of course, you'll have to do same for me. He's

thinking of coming to New York City to try to get a job
as a translator with the U.N. Wouldn't it be
wonderful if we could have a reunion? But of course,
not till you're feeling better.

I want to hear from you. Always. I won't let you
drop out of my life so easily.

Ross

Dans l'avenir, à: *27 Conant Hall*
Harvard University
Cambridge, Mass.

As I finished the letter, I felt again the magnetic pull of the past and all it stood for. I remembered how one of Ross's letters years before had been the force that drew me back to Wisconsin—just as, the year after, it was my meeting with him and Jerry that had started me on the Dexedrine once again.

His intentions had always been blameless: to try to set my driftless life back on course. Instead, I had been drawn deeper and deeper down.

Now I was glad that he had written, and that he and Jerry knew the truth. But I knew I wouldn't write back for a long, long, time—if ever. Rightly or wrongly, I felt that the complete exorcism of the Other Me demanded no less a sacrifice.

CHAPTER 15

Three days later, with Dotty, a student nurse, beside me, I took my first walk down the six long blocks from the hospital into the "business area" of town.

I was thrilled beyond anything I'd have anticipated only three weeks before to have earned "accompanied town privileges." The cracks in the old sidewalk, the hedges that bordered the Oaks grounds on Main Street, and the old Victorian houses that lined the streets, all had an exquisite clarity.

But my elation about the excursion died fast when I got back to Two. "You're going to be takin' your meals in the dinin' room from now on," Addie told me almost as soon as I got off the elevator. "It'll help you get used to the routine at Small Oaks."

No more measured portions, I thought; no more safe trays; no more privacy for my fanatical scrapings of gravy and careful divisions of permissible food.

"I don't mind eating up here," I protested.

Addie looked up, surprised.

"Now don't be silly, Jo-Jo. You can't eat on Two forever. At least you'll have someone to talk to down there."

Oh God, she was right. I'd have to make conversation too. I knew Ellen ate in the dining room—and Fay, when she'd been at the O.T. shop. And of course Lee, when he worked two shifts at the A.

I'd been bypassing the A again. The more I thought about it, the more I'd become convinced that Lee's mention of the possible dinner had been the kindly impulse of the moment. I'd decided to save him the embarrassment of having to live up to his hasty suggestion by keeping out of his path.

Now I'd probably be forced to confront Lee in the dining room. But I had no choice. Addie was right; I couldn't eat trays on Two forever.

The dining room was set up cafeteria-style in the basement of the main building. Fluorescent lights gave everything a cruel brightness, and the tables were Formica, the chairs plastic-covered and institutional. But aside from the preponderance of nurses' uniforms and the presence of a few disheveled-looking "patrons"—I'd heard that patients from Three or Four were sometimes brought down one at a time as a treat—it had the hum of ordinary life.

I immediately noticed Lee, Ellen, and Art Schwartz, a Cottage patient I'd heard Lee was training for some shifts in the A, sitting together. Art was a graduate student in physics at Cornell whose presence at the Oaks, like that of Lee, had me baffled. I knew him because he often came to the O.T. shop, where, as his strong fingers molded clay into amazingly lifelike dogs and horses, he liked to play a somewhat professorial role, cleverly drawing out the opinions of those around him.

I tried to look away, but Ellen had already spotted me. She waved languidly and pointed to the empty chair next to her. I'd have to sit there.

The lunch, to my dismay, was going to be difficult to deal with. Though the food was served cafeteria-style, there were actually no cafeteria-style choices. It was a set meal—roast beef in a floury gravy, creamed spinach, oven-browned potatoes. The dessert was a chocolate sundae. No plain vegetables; no fruit. I knew I could have said no to any or all of the parts, but I worried that Lee or Ellen—Art, too, perhaps—were watching me, listening as I moved my tray along the metal shelf. I accepted the plate, with a large helping of everything, from the hands of the kitchen worker, who was looking at me curiously. New patients in the dining room must be a novelty. Feeling trapped, I put my tray down near Ellen, who smiled wanly, clearly in one of her more apathetic phases.

"I'll explain the intricacies of concocting one of our famous A-frame ice cream sodas to you this afternoon," Lee was saying to Art. He hadn't looked up. Good, I thought. Let me eat unobserved. Cautiously, I began to scrape the gravy off the meat.

"Don't tell me you're on a diet," Lee said suddenly. He'd been watching me all along.

"Uh, not exactly. Just trying to be careful," I said stiffly. But, humiliated, I stopped scraping and started to eat the meat, with what remained of the gravy still on it. The worst thing was that I was hungry, too. Hungry, and nervous—a deadly combination for me, I knew. And as Lee and Art continued to talk, Lee occasionally glancing over at me, I helplessly finished the meat, then the potatoes and creamed spinach, then the sundae, almost choking on every bite. And once again, as I had in my first breakfast on Two, I recalled the disastrous lamb chops, the peas and chocolate cake that had launched my 120-

pound binge years before. But this time, instead of tri-umph, I felt the bitterness of a terrible memory relived.

When I'd finished, I rose mechanically and took my tray to the attendant who was collecting them at the counter. Without a backward glance, I left the dining room and took the elevator back to Two.

"What's the matter, hon?" said Addie when I found her with Rosemary in the day room. She was trying to get Rosemary to eat, but Rosemary was turning her head from side to side like a baby refusing its mother's spoon.

"I don't want to eat down there anymore," I said. "Please don't make me eat down there." For the first time since I'd come to the Oaks, I began to cry. Rosemary was so astonished that she stopped moving her head and swallowed a mouthful of spinach.

"Well, sure, honey, but why?" Addie put down the spoon. She knew all about me, of course—how fat I'd been, about the pills, everything. Still, she looked puzzled.

"It's too hard. I feel as if everybody's watching me. Expecting me to act normal. Eat normally. I can't yet. It's all too new. Please, I want to keep on eating here—even if they don't let me go to Small Oaks. I can't eat down there. I'll get fat again. I probably gained four pounds today already."

Now I was sobbing. The confidence I'd felt when I'd eaten half the pancakes, when I'd left Cunningham's office, and more recently, on my walk through Somerset, had totally disappeared.

My black mood and swollen eyes were obvious even to Poole when I appeared for our afternoon meeting. He

227

had been there at 3:10 sharp the first day, 3:15 the next. I had expected the gap to widen daily. But to my surprise he was on time once again.

"Somethin' wrong? You're lookin' a bit peaky."

Dubious though I was about his ability to help, I was too upset to keep my problem to myself. I told him my alarming reaction to what had happened in the dining room.

"Now let me follow this," he said, lighting his pipe. "Ah gather you don't want anyone to know about your obsession with food, is that it?"

"Well, it isn't really an obsession anymore, is it?"

"Sure it is. Whether you're stuffin' yourself or not, you're worryin' about it all the time, aren't cha?"

"Well, not all the time. But a lot of the time."

"That's what ah call an obsession," he said with satisfaction. "Now, Jo-Jo, most folks here have got a lot worse stuff than you to hide, but a lot of 'em will go around tellin' anyone who'll listen all about it. Personally, ah don't see why you have to say anythin' at all. But if you feel you have to, why, ah'd just tell 'em the truth. Ah'd just tell 'em you were fat, that you got hooked on Dexedrine to lose weight, and that you're tryin' to get on top of it. They aren't gonna think you're so crazy. You've got to remember, you've got a *lot* of competition in that department here."

I knew he was probably right, and that what he said made sense, but I continued to eat on Two.

Another week and a half passed, and, my confidence still shaken, I continued to stay away from the A and spend most of my time in the O.T. shop. Sometimes, as I hurried over, I'd glance furtively at the rear windows of the A, and twice Lee had seen me and waved. I'd waved back, but I didn't go in.

One day I asked Evvie if she'd show me how to use the sewing machine. In my teens, I'd envied Toni after she took a course at the Singer shop in Philadelphia and began to make her own clothes.

"Sure, I'll show you," said Evvie. "I've got an hour free before we open up for the afternoon. Why don't you see if you can get here early."

Back on Two, I asked Addie if I could go out right after lunch.

"You better call her back. You can't go then. We're moving you over to Small Oaks after lunch today. Orders just came up. Helen Dougherty moved out and you're moving in."

With the sense of foreboding that I'd felt when I returned to Madison and all the pitfalls it represented, I accepted the decision.

A sunny room with double exposure. Frilly curtains, rose-patterned wallpaper, and a four-poster bed with a quilt—another world from the dim starkness of Two. I could breathe here without having to get used, over and over, to the smell of urine washed down with antiseptic.

But then there was also the kitchen, its icebox plentifully stocked with loaves of white bread, peanut butter and jelly, sugary canned fruit juices. "You can come in anytime you want a snack," said Mrs. Johnson cheerfully. "Only time it's closed is for reports." I knew about reports from Two. The nursing supervisor came around twice a day and once at night to review the notes made by the floor nurses.

I left my unopened suitcase on the bed and descended the steps. Back steps, just like the back staircase at Spruce Street I'd descended so often in my gluttonous midnight raids.

Ellen was sitting on a chair in the kitchen, and as she raised her head and murmured a soft "Hi," I caught, on her breath, a sickly sweet whiff of Paraldehyde, the white fluid I'd seen Addie pour into tiny medication glasses on Two. Paraldehyde, I'd learned, was the only medication besides Phenobarbital used at the Oaks for calming agitated patients. Ellen must have been starting one of her manic rises, I assumed, and her doctor had prescribed the medication to calm her.

"I gather we're housemates now," she said.

"Yes, I just moved in."

"Don't kid yourself about Small Oaks. You may not be as locked in as you were on Two, but you're still a bird in a gilded cage."

I didn't reply because, horrified but fascinated, I was watching her actions. When I'd entered the kitchen, she already had a loaf of white bread, peanut butter, jelly, and a bottle of milk on the counter in front of her. Now she was methodically spreading the peanut butter thickly on the bread, pouring herself a glass of milk, slathering jelly over the peanut butter, then putting a top on the oozing sandwich.

"Did you miss lunch?" I asked stupidly. It was only 1:30 now. "No," she said, her pretty face suddenly mournful, "I had lunch. I'm just hungry again."

Don't. Don't eat that, I wanted to scream. Don't do this to yourself. But I knew I couldn't stop Ellen any more than my mother could have stopped me years ago. From

230

what I'd heard about Ellen, I gathered that she alternated her eating binges with equally severe bouts of starvation, so it was unlikely that she'd ever become grossly obese. Still, the sight of her consuming one sandwich and then another—mechanically and without any apparent pleasure—had worked on me like one of the Chagall pictures of the Seven Sins.

"Did you want a sandwich too?" asked Mrs. Johnson pleasantly. Unlike Addie with her wiry peppiness, Mrs. Johnson exuded grandmotherly warmth. I was sure I'd never be as fond of her as I was of Addie, but she seemed nice, and I knew her question was well meant. Like the rest of the staff, she'd probably been appraised of my problem with food, but advised to treat me no differently from any other patient.

"No. I thought I did, but I don't." Yet I felt dissatisfied. I liked peanut butter and jelly. Now that I was at Small Oaks, would I have to go back to a life of total austerity to survive? Or could I, just possibly, eat the equivalent of the half-pancake and syrup I'd eaten on Two?

"Do you have any crackers?" I asked determinedly.

"Sure." She took out a box of saltines and handed it to me. I took one, and as Ellen poured herself a second glass of milk, I spread the cracker thinly with peanut butter and jelly, then ate it slowly, savoring the unfamiliar sweetness.

"Want another one?" said Mrs. Johnson. "Why don't you have a sandwich with Ellen?"

"No," I said, "I've got to do some unpacking, but thanks. That was just what I wanted." Maybe I could cope with the dining room after all. If Mrs. Johnson, or Ellen—or eventually even Lee—thought I had strange

231

eating habits, let them. I would do what I had to do. I returned to my room.

"Somebody's here to see you," Mrs. Johnson called from the bottom of the stairs about a half hour later. I was puzzled. Ellen or Fay would have come right up.

As I came down the steps I heard Lee's deep laugh. I wanted to run back up to my room and shut the door. How could I face him after my evasive behavior, my failure even to thank him again for his advice and help? Still, my feet carried me into the kitchen once again.

Ellen was gone, so there'd be no help from that quarter. Lee was lighting a cigarette. Then, as I'd noticed in the A, he wiped his hands on a kitchen towel. It dawned on me that he hadn't been handling anything wet. And I suddenly realized that sweating palms must be one of Lee's symptoms. The realization made him somehow less frightening.

"So they finally sprung you, eh?"

I smiled, remembering how Ross had planned to "spring" me from the Madison hospital.

"How did you know?"

"I have my sources. Actually, Ellen told me you were moving over." To my relief, he didn't say anything about my not having been in the A for a week and a half. "Well, now that you're out, we'll have to go ahead with that little *soirée* I was planning at our country estate. How's Thursday night? Okay?"

"Sh-sure," I said, flustered. "If I can get permission. That's only three days away." I turned to Mrs. Johnson. "Do you think I could get permission to leave the grounds so soon?"

232

"We could try," she said. "All we can do is try. I suppose Ellen will be going out, too. That might make it easier."

"But of course," Lee said. "She'll be Kip's special guest—as ever." I remembered how Ellen had said that Kip, Lee's housemate, had helped her the day she couldn't breathe in the A.

As soon as Lee left, I blurted out the question that had been on my mind for weeks. "Isn't Ellen Lee's, well, sort of girlfriend, Mrs. Johnson?"

She laughed. "Lee's girlfriend? Lee is a loner—especially since . . ." Her voice trailed off and I assumed that she must be referring to the story about the nurse. "At least he's been one till now. But he's very nice—even though I can hardly understand what he's saying half the time. Those words he uses! But no, Ellen is certainly not his girlfriend. She's Kip's girlfriend, if she's anyone's. Lee just kind of keeps an eye on her for Kip now that Kip's gone back to college."

I felt a combination of relief and uneasiness. This information put Lee's friendliness to me in a very different light. Could it be that he was, after all, as interested in me as I was in him?

Lee picked up Ellen and me in his secondhand olive Chevrolet promptly at six—a phenomenon I only later realized was a rarity.

"Martin's meeting us there," he said. I assumed he meant Martin Taggart, an outpatient Fay had told me was a member of the A Committee.

There was a magnificent sunset that evening, and I felt happy in spite of my anxiety as we drove out the back gate and into the increasingly rural area where Lee and

Kip lived. On that early spring evening, it seemed to me the loveliest ride I'd ever taken.

The "estate" turned out to be a quite ordinary, but somewhat dilapidated, white shingled house on about three overgrown acres. An old barn was the only clue to the property's former use as a farm.

Martin was waiting on the porch, and Lee introduced us. He struck me as smooth and cool. I put him in my growing category of mystery patients at the Oaks, who could certainly pass for normal. But then, I realized with a start, so could I.

We went in. Lee, seeming to revel in his role as host, mixed us all drinks and took us on a tour of the house, which he told us had come furnished with "motel room modern."

The house had six rooms. On the first floor, behind the front porch, were the living room we'd entered and what had probably once been a parlor. I saw a darkly burnished Steinway upright against the parlor wall.

"You don't find pianos like that in most motels," Martin said, and winked at me.

Lee's reply was uncharacteristically terse. "No, it's mine."

I was surprised. I'd expected him to say something about the piano—the original inspiration for the whole evening—to me at least, but he didn't. And when Martin, not seeming to notice his reaction, asked whether he or Kip played, an expression of anguish crossed his face. "I used to, but not anymore." I spotted a dusty carton with music in it and there was a Bach toccata open on the music rack, so I gathered Lee's playing days were not at a complete halt. But he clearly didn't wish to talk about the matter any further and slammed the door when we left the room, almost as though to shut it away from the rest of the house.

A kitchen with a picture window ran the entire length of the back, and on the second floor were three very sparely furnished bedrooms. Ellen had clearly been there before. She seemed agitated as Lee showed us around, perhaps upset that Kip wasn't there yet or, I began to fear, perhaps that I was.

We returned to the living room to wait for Kip to return from his evening courses. Kip's enrolling in school had impressed me as a sure sign he was cured, and I was very curious to meet him.

While we waited, Ellen and I were silent, while Lee and Martin talked about the A. "It just might snap some of those malingerers out of their self-indulgent, parasitic existences and back into reality," Lee said—rather unfeelingly, I thought. The drift of his conversation seemed to indicate that he regarded all mental illness—including his own, and, I suspected, that of all of us present—as essentially hostile and aggressive, no matter how passive and helpless we might appear.

I had never thought about mental illness—my own or others'—that way, and found the concept exciting and disturbing. Was that why I'd gotten so fat? Taken all that Dexedrine? I'd have to consider the possibility. Meanwhile, I sensed that Lee himself was the primary target of his own indictment.

Lee fixed us all another drink—Ellen and I were drinking bourbon and ginger ale, Martin and Lee bourbon on the rocks—and I began to feel more relaxed. I noticed Lee's drinks were twice the size of Martin's.

Meanwhile, Ellen grew quieter and more morose by the minute. I wondered what was wrong, whether she was unhappy that Kip wasn't there or whether the Paraldehyde she'd been taking at Small Oaks might not be

235

mixing well with the alcohol in the drink. At any rate, just as Kip bounded into the room with a joyful, "Why, how are y'all?"—a huge Labrador right behind him—Ellen took one look at him and, with a convulsive heave, threw up all over the floor and the couch. There was a silence as she sat there, seemingly in shock.

"I, I . . ." she began, but then stopped and began to gasp for air. "Help me, Kip, help me."

"We better get you back to the Oaks," said Kip, but Ellen remained immobile where she was, gasping and wheezing.

Kip leaned over, grasped Ellen under the arms, and lifted her to her feet. "Now, come on," he said, and, still dazed, she followed him obediently out the door, the huge dog close behind.

Lee, seemingly in control but with the glazed look in his eyes that I soon learned to recognize as his "third or fourth drink look," was, to my surprise, not the least bit sympathetic. On the contrary, he was outraged that Ellen had spoiled his party.

"Why, that hostile bitch! How dare she have the effrontery to throw up on my couch!"

"Maybe she couldn't help herself," I said meekly. "Maybe the drink disagreed with her, or something was bothering her, or—"

"Jo-Jo, forget the excuses. That was a devious and hostile act, and it was directed against me."

Since no one else was doing anything about the increasingly pungent mess, I managed to find some rags and sponges and started to clean it up myself.

Just as irrationally as Ellen's throwing up had seemed to him a spiteful act, so did my taking on this unpleasant task strike Lee as a saintly one. "You'd do that for me!" he said several times. "How nice! Jo-Jo, that is really nice, really very nice."

Two hours had passed, and Lee finally roused himself and began to put the steak and baked potato dinner on the table. Kip returned, plunged into gloom. "Now what did you-all say to Ellen to upset her like that?" he asked Lee, who calmly reiterated his contention that she was a "hostile bitch," and for a few minutes I thought they'd have a fight. However, Kip calmed down and Lee returned to the kitchen. In a few minutes he re-appeared, a napkin over his arm. With a flourish, he lit the candles.

I was silent during dinner. Lee, Kip, and Martin talked about Kip's classes at the American University. Kip said that some of his professors were "mighty erudite" but that what he liked most about being back at school were "all those nubile maidens floatin' around the campus." I saw that he shared Lee's passion for exotic and esoteric words, and rarely used a simple one when a more complex one would do. Like Lee, Kip was also about twenty-eight, and unusually attractive, with bright blue eyes behind round, horn-rimmed glasses, and a ruddy complexion. He had a beatific smile, and brought a burning intensity and boyish enthusiasm to everything he said. To this ingenuousness was added a sensitivity that was involuntarily revealed by his blushing often and unexpectedly.

I was still so distracted by what had happened to Ellen, and by the conversation, that I ate the steak and half the potato without worrying about overeating or what Lee might think if I refused dessert.

It was 9:30 when we finished. Kip said he was going to bed and would help Lee clean up tomorrow. Martin took

237

off in his car for Carlisle, an apartment development halfway between Somerset and D.C., where he lived.

Lee and I got into his car for the drive back to the Oaks. At first we were silent, alone for the first time all evening. I was aware of the silence, and sure that Lee found me a terrible bore. I was, consequently, completely shocked when, just before I got out of the car, Lee said, hesitantly, "How would you like to come out tomorrow morning around eight to have breakfast with me?" His naming an exact hour seemed to reflect that he'd already given the matter a great deal of thought. And I saw that while the night had grown chilly, there were beads of sweat on his forehead, and he wiped his hands continuously on his pants.

I was both flustered and tremendously flattered. At the same time, I was conscious that it sounded like a compromising situation. Again, memories of Fay's warning, of Addie's implications and Mrs. Johnson's "ever since . . ." raced through my head. Would Kip be there? And didn't Lee have a shift to work at the A the next morning? I seemed to recall that he worked Fridays. It seemed safe enough to ask. "Yes. I do have to work tomorrow," Lee said. "That's one reason I'd like you to come out. I have a terrible time getting up, and if you come, I'll be sure to make it on time. You could take a taxi," he said, almost pleading. "It only costs a dollar."

I could now see the breakfast appointment in a different light—more as a mission of mercy than a tryst—and one that would indirectly benefit the whole hospital. Many of the patients who gathered near the entrance of the A before each shift became very anxious when the doors didn't open on time.

I made a snap decision. "All right," I said. "I mean, if I can get permission again, I'll come."

Thus began a strange and compelling association—envied by some, termed a "sick dependency" by others, and generally misunderstood—that affected the rest of my stay at Great Oaks, and to some extent, the rest of my life.

CHAPTER 16

The next morning I decided to take a positive approach rather than beg for permission to leave the grounds. Bracing myself, I walked into the Small Oaks kitchen and, as casually as I could, said to Mrs. Johnson, "I'm going to Lee's to help with planning for the A."

Mrs. Johnson was absorbed in reading the reports left by the night shift, and looked up distractedly. "Well, I don't know, honey. After all, you don't really have unaccompanied town privileges yet. I wonder if I shouldn't ask Dr. Cunningham about it."

But before she had a chance to ponder how far her authority permitted her to go, I slipped out and hopped into the cab I'd called on the pay phone in the main building earlier. And off I went, on the same bucolic route I'd followed the night before—for the second time in twenty-four hours.

I'd expected Lee to be up when I got there, but the house was silent. Kip's MG was gone. I was at a loss as to what to do. I looked in the windows and saw nothing but last night's smudged glasses and overflowing ashtrays. I knocked on the door, louder and louder, but there was no response. Perhaps, I thought, Lee had been more influenced by the four or five drinks he'd had than I realized, and had forgotten all about the invitation.

I waited outside for about ten minutes, hoping Lee would miraculously appear—dressed, shaven, and apologetic. But no new sounds broke the silence, and I grew more and more uneasy. It occurred to me that if the door was locked I couldn't even call a cab to return. But I wasn't yet bold enough to try to enter the quiet house alone.

Increasingly uncomfortable, and also aware that Lee's shift at the A was drawing closer, I tried throwing stones at all the second-floor windows. No response. There was nothing to do but try the door, which opened easily. The sweetish smell of bourbon hung in the air. Feeling I'd already crossed one dangerous frontier, I glanced at the phone and considered calling a cab for a safe and hasty retreat. But the thought of the patients who would soon be milling about the doors of the A spurred me on, and I cautiously mounted the stairs.

The bedroom door was ajar and I saw dirty clothes scattered all over the floor. Obviously sound asleep, Lee was sprawled on the bed, a sheet covering his lower body. As I considered how to wake him, I had a chance to study him in repose—the chiseled features, the thin, slightly upturned nose with fine nostrils, the quizzical, arched eyebrows, and brown, slightly wavy hair, just beginning to recede. His hair was combed straight back without a part, just as it was when he was awake, and was surprisingly neat.

Then, forcing myself, I looked at his body. He had

241

creamy skin that looked like marble, with a slight covering of dark hair on his chest, and though he wasn't fat, there was an overall look of smooth roundness—a complete contrast to Ross's tauter, stringier muscularity.

I tried calling Lee—first softly, then more loudly—but he didn't move. Finally I began to shake him—tentatively at first, then with more determination—and finally he looked up drowsily. His arm reached toward me and my heart pounded.

But he was pointing behind me. "There's a robe on that hook," he said, looking at me with a weariness that I didn't know how to interpret.

Afraid that my expression would give away what had been on my mind, I turned away gratefully, grabbed the robe, and tossed it to him.

"Thanks," he said. Then, without making any apologies for the strange reception—or lack of it—he added, "Well, good morning. You made it past the palace guards, I see."

I nodded.

"Now that you're here, what would you like for breakfast? Would pancakes suit you?"

I smiled at the suggestion. Pancakes seemed to be involved in a lot of my important breakfasts. And in a flash I remembered more of what had eluded me on the second-floor porch, of what had happened the morning my mother complained so bitterly about the underdone pancakes.

It was my father's fifty-second birthday, and we were going to the theater that night to see my first Broadway play, *Sons O' Fun*, with Olsen and Johnson. Gas rationing during the war had precluded trips to the city for such frivolous purposes when I was younger, and quietly stage-struck at twelve, I was thrilled at the prospect. That was the reason I was so concerned with keeping the peace that morning.

I recalled that as we waited for Nancy to bring in the second batch of pancakes, we were all silent. Suddenly my mother looked at me balefully. "And remember, young lady, I want those black shoes polished before we leave for the city tonight," she said, as though challenging me to refuse.

Just as the piano produced friction between my father and me, so were my shoes one of several sources of ongoing conflict between me and my mother. The fact that the sturdy brown Oxfords she made me wear to school were never polished was a constant irritant to her. Nor did I ever bother untying the laces, so the backs of the shoes were always broken and worn, with short, scraggly threads hanging down. But I got a certain satisfaction out of leaving them that way, though it frequently incurred my mother's wrath. It was one means of silent—if subconscious—rebellion against my mother's preoccupation with the appearances of things. In any case, I hated the Oxfords, and longed for a pair of the loafers worn by all the other girls.

We disagreed about "dress-up" shoes, too. Ever since I was little, I'd longed for the shiny patent leather Mary Janes worn by my schoolmates to birthday parties. My mother proclaimed them to be impractical and "in bad taste"—a nebulous but powerful and unanswerable argument. She insisted I get shoes with a dull black finish that I detested. Such were the shoes to be worn to the theater

243

that night—sandals with a little circle of tiny holes around the toes, a feature that repelled me.

But nothing could entirely dampen my spirits. Still ravenous as we waited for the pancakes, but elated at the thought of the evening ahead, I was more than willing to be cooperative.

"Sure, Mom, I'll do them later."

But something had happened about the shoes later—something terrible. What was it? And then, at last, I remembered the rest.

That afternoon, to my surprise, my mother made one of her rare appearances in my room. She almost never came in, except to kiss me good night when we had company downstairs. In years past, the hours till she arrived seemed interminable, since the maid who slept in my room to assuage my nighttime fears was also downstairs helping to serve the guests.

"Darling, it's time to get ready. Did you do those shoes yet? Let me see them." I went to the closet and pulled them out.

"My God, Jo, they're really filthy."

I studied the shoes. They were dull, because of the finish, but as far as I could tell, not dirty, certainly not "filthy." I could tell that this was to be another of my mother's make-work tasks. Though Frank and I were not required or even encouraged to help around the house, my mother occasionally thought up what he and I agreed were superfluous jobs to save us from "taking everything for granted."

Despite myself, I could feel arising within me an acute and unwelcome spirit of rebellion. Frank would have shouted, "I won't do it. Make me," I knew, but, disgusted

244

with myself, I heard my own voice whining, "But, Mom, they're okay. They're not even dirty. I've only worn them twice." Then I added, suddenly inspired, "You don't like shiny shoes anyway." I was shocked at my own effrontery, but she ignored the thrust.

"Are you going to give me an argument, young lady, today of all days? Now look, I want those shoes polished or we're not going to the theater tonight. And that's final. Here. I bought you some new shoe polish while I was out. But you'll have to be careful with it; it's liquid. Do them in the bathroom, not in here."

Filled with resentment, but realizing I'd lost the major battle, I now hoped to win a minor skirmish on another front. "There's no room in the bathroom. Why can't I do them out here where I can spread out?"

"Don't be ridiculous, Jo. The polish could spill all over the rug. Of course there's room in there." She marched into the bathroom and surveyed the area. "Sit on the hamper and do them there, or sit on the floor. There's plenty of room. You're just being stubborn."

The feeling of pleasant anticipation I'd had all day was gone, and in its place was a familiar mixture of anger and helplessness. I hated the shoes, and they didn't need polishing. But to get to the theater I'd have to wear the shoes, and they had to be polished. I was stuck.

Not yet aware of the extent of my own resentment, I went downstairs, got some old newspapers from the storage bin, and came back up. Then, with deliberation, I spread a few sheets in the middle of the rug in my room and put the shoes down. I sat cross-legged next to the paper and opened the shoe polish box. It featured a picture of a happy little girl staring at her own feet, which were shod in shoes whose sparkle was represented by short, straight lines angling out all around them, an artistic technique I had only recently perfected myself. Inside the box was the bottle and a tiny sponge, almost like a doll sponge. I shook the bottle perfunctorily, opened it, and put some polish on the sponge. Then, with great care, I set the bottle down on the newspaper. The rug beneath the newspaper was not a firm base, and the bottle had a narrow bottom. It toppled immediately.

The tiny sponge still in my hand, I watched for a horrified second as the thin black liquid spread into a wide, uneven pattern on the newspaper. Springing up, I grabbed the bottle to stop the flow and put it on the dresser. Then, terrified, I bent over and lifted the section of the newspaper to look underneath. The single sheet of newspaper had been useless; the free-form spot was exactly duplicated on the rug.

I ran to the bathroom, unrolled a handful of toilet paper, and rushed back to rub at the stain. Some of the wetness was absorbed, but the blackness remained. I began to realize, in despair, that I might even be rubbing the dye in more permanently.

In later years, I sometimes wondered why I hadn't simply finished polishing the shoes and taken them in to my mother for inspection. The chances of her re-appearing in my room that afternoon were slim, and I could have left my crime undiscovered till the next day. But that afternoon the thought never occurred to me.

Like a prisoner walking the last mile, I trodded down the long hall toward my parents' room. The beautiful arched window at the landing, halfway down the handsome front staircase outside their room, reflected the same sunny skies as it had when I'd looked out happily on my way up earlier, but the beauty of the weather was lost on me now.

I knocked on the door.

"Who's there?" said my mother gaily.

"It's me," I said, bracing myself for the confrontation to follow.

"Come in, dear. The door's unlocked."

I entered wordlessly and saw my mother picking some earrings from a box in her dresser. Her drawers always smelled pleasantly of sachet and were beautifully organized. She put strips of adhesive tape on all her cardboard jewelry boxes, or even on the fancy velvet or leather ones in which some of her pieces had arrived. Then, in her bold, round hand, and using her "trademark" turquoise ink, she labeled them "pearl earrings," "diamond clip," etc.—an expenditure of time I found both touching and somehow symbolic of too much time on her hands.

She looked up. "Did you do the shoes?" And, not waiting for a reply, "Let me see them."

For a moment, I looked at her mutely. Then I said, "Mom, something awful happened. Come and see."

My mother's face changed. "What do you mean? What happened? Can't you tell me? Really, Jo, it's getting late. We'll be late meeting Dad and Frank."

"I can't tell you. You have to see." I turned back down the hall. My mother followed me into my room.

The black spot looked even worse than I remembered it. It had taken a strange shape, something like the amoeba I had seen in the A volume of Compton's Encyclopedia.

To my amazement, my mother said nothing. She simply looked at me and walked out. I followed her back down the hall.

"Mom, I'm sorry. I really am. Well, say something. What are you going to do? Please, I'm sorry." The ominous silence was new to me, and somehow far worse than one of her familiar outbursts would have been. But she simply walked back into her room and slammed the door.

I stood uncertainly in the middle of the hall for what seemed hours but was probably not more than ten minutes. Then I heard my mother's voice calling down the stairs. "Nancy, please have Al bring the car around." I was relieved. So we were going after all. I rushed back to my room, tore off my skirt and top, and quickly put on a peach-colored dress. I combed my hair hastily, and put on clean white socks that folded down at the ankle. Then I looked uncertainly at the black shoes. To polish them now would almost add insult to injury, I decided. I put them on and walked down the hall.

"Mom, I'm ready. Are we leaving?" There was no answer. "I'll be waiting by the front door, Mom. Okay?" Still, no answer. I walked down the steps and sat on the "banquette"—one of Peter's finds—near the door.

I heard my mother's door slam, and looked up sheepishly to see her coming down the stairs smartly dressed in one of Peter's latest creations—a black suit with wide, padded shoulders—and a wide-brimmed hat with a short veil. A red rose on the jacket of the suit and some red trim on the hat added a striking touch of color. On her feet were the high-heeled, platform shoes she always wore, even when she went to the country, to compensate for her shortness. She didn't look at me.

248

"Are we leaving now, Mom?"

Still my mother didn't answer. Without even glancing at me, she walked by me and out the door, slamming it behind her.

As the awful truth dawned on me, I hurtled to the door and flung it open. Al, his beet-red neck redder than ever, was holding the door of the car open for my mother. "Isn't Jo-Jo coming, too, Mrs. Rosengarten?"

"No. Now let's leave. We'll be late."

I was incredulous. This couldn't be happening. "Mom, please, please. I'm sorry. I'll never do it again. Please let me come, please." Desperately, I grasped for reasons. "Dad and Frank will be disappointed if I don't come. And the ticket will go to waste. Please, please. Let me come." But my mother, now seated in the car, sat staring straight ahead.

The car door slammed and then Al, embarrassed and confused, was at the wheel in front of her. My mother's car window was closed, but I could tell from her leaning position that she was telling Al to start. The Packard, its small blue lantern gleaming, moved slowly out the circular driveway and out past the white gates.

I ran beside the car in frenzied pursuit. "Mom, you can't go without me. You promised. You promised I could see a play." For a moment the memory of a hysterical child chasing her brother down the street came into my head. "Wait for me," the child had cried. "Please wait for me."

But my words were different. Suddenly the play no longer mattered, and from the young child still within me emerged a primal and overpowering need. "Just tell me that you love me," I screamed. "Please, Mom, tell me that you love me." The car was gaining speed. Tears pouring down my face, I raced after it, finally tripping on an uneven piece of sidewalk. The car had disappeared around the corner by the time I could pick myself up. My knee was bleeding, but I didn't notice.

George Chapman, a nasty boy from across the street, who sometimes threw stones at me as I rode my bike, was watching slyly from his yard. "Something wrong, Jo-Jo?"

I stumbled back down the street, into the driveway, and through the front door. Then, like an animal, I lay down on the wood floor and howled—terrible howls that brought Nancy running from the kitchen. "Mom, just tell me that you love me," I cried over and over, indifferent to the fact that my mother could no longer hear my cries.

"What happened, honey? What's wrong?"

"It's the rug . . . the shoe polish . . . it's all because of the rug—the rug in my room."

Nancy disappeared briefly, but then came back. "Now, honey, don't you worry none. I'm gonna work on that rug and get it good as new." She had brought a wet cloth and a bandage. Kneeling down, she applied it to my knee.

Just at that moment, I heard the crunch of car wheels on the gravel. I looked up and saw the Packard coming to a stop in front of the house. My mother waited for Al to come around and open the door for her. She looked at my streaked face and swollen eyes with distaste. "Well, get in. You're probably right. It would upset Frank and Dad if you weren't there. But," she added, her eyes blazing, and looking directly at me for the first time since the accident, "believe me, that's the only reason I'm taking you. You deserve a good lesson, young lady. The nerve of you, doing those shoes on the rug. Just who the *hell* do you think you are?" And as we sped silently toward New York, I realized that I had no answer to the question.

Suddenly, I realized Lee was looking at me, one eyebrow raised. "I can see by your expression that pancakes aren't pleasing to your palate, so forget it. We'll have toast à la Rodman. Now how about going down and mixing up some delicious frozen orange juice while I make my ablutions?"

He'd remained discreetly covered in the bed and, both relieved and disappointed, I descended the stairs with the acquiescence I noticed Lee's authority always inspired in me.

I had never heard of frozen orange juice, a relatively new product at that time, but I didn't want to bother Lee while he was dressing to ask what it was or how one made it. I'd already noted that he often moved with the same deliberation with which he spoke, and I didn't want to distract him. I decided instead to bring all the previous night's leftover dishes, glasses, and ashtrays into the kitchen.

Lee finally descended. "Why, bless you, my child," he said. "And you did all this without even being asked." He seemed amazed.

He explained the wonders of frozen orange juice, and I was happily conscious of what a normal domestic scene we were enacting. I was so relieved at the events of the morning that I'd almost forgotten the time. Then I suddenly noticed a small clock on the counter. "My God, Lee, it's eight forty-five!"

"Not to worry, Jo-Jo," he said calmly and went on buttering the toast he'd made us. As I gulped down the dry half I'd managed to grab before he got to it with the butter, I was vaguely aware that the balance was somehow wrong. *Lee* should have been worried about the time, not me.

Soon it was five to nine. Lee was all set to put the breakfast dishes in the washer before we left but I said, "Come on, I'll help you with them later," and we finally took off in his Chevy. We arrived about ten minutes late. Patients and nurses were hanging around the A, many of the patients grumbling and peering in uneasily.

As I rushed past them to help open the sliding doors, I noticed Babe striding back and forth, dressed in one of the smart but worn tennis outfits she wore summer and winter, an irritated smile on her face. Her short, bushy red hair was tossing as she paced, and she was muttering under her breath. "Of course, it's the goddamn Jews who rule the world and spoil everything, you know. They've gained control of the banks, and now they're taking over all the stores." Since Lee wasn't Jewish, her last barb was clearly directed at me, and I blushed in spite of its unfairness.

Because the doors had opened so late, and the student nurses who had classes coming up had to get their coffee fast, my help was really necessary if all the opening procedures—making the coffee, setting out the small, round tables, filling the cigarette rack—were to be accomplished on time. In the exhilaration of feeling important I squelched the dual realizations that if it weren't for me, Lee might not have been there at all that morning, and that once there, I was really doing half the work he should have arrived early enough to have been able to handle himself.

252

I hung around the A for the rest of Lee's morning shift, even, under Lee's direction, placing an order with the candy salesman, who, obviously unnerved as Dorothy lifted her skirt to masturbate and Mary Acosta croaked her demands for "that other brown one," was only too happy to write the order quickly and bolt.

Between the activity and the steady observation of Lee and the others, I wasn't even tempted to snatch a candy bar or dig into the ice cream with my fingers.

We went to lunch in the main building and I noticed Ellen, depressed and abject, at a table by herself. I hoped Lee would sit with her. Eating with Ellen would divert his attention from me, from my essential dullness and my strange eating habits. Yet it didn't occur to me that I could sit with her on my own. That might risk a separation from Lee or possibly incur his annoyance.

I needn't have worried. It seemed Lee had rid himself of all his resentment the night before. "Recovered from your mysterious malaise?" he asked Ellen, not unkindly, as he sat down opposite her. She looked grateful and nodded, although she didn't say anything.

Bent on scraping the breading from my veal cutlet, I was startled when Fay sat down on my other side. "Where were you this morning?" she asked me. "Evvie wanted to work on your head."

"Really?" said Lee. "Are they doing analysis in the O.T. shop now?"

Fay chuckled and looked at Lee as though reappraising him. "I meant the head Evvie's modeling of Jo-Jo," she said. A few weeks back Evvie had asked me to sit for her.

"Oh, *that* kind of head work," said Lee, looking at me with a half-smile.

I felt my face burning. I was sure he was wondering

why anyone would want to sculpt me. I doubted if he'd have agreed with Evvie that I had "a terrific face—great cheekbones, great eyes, lots of character."

"I—I'll come up to the O.T. shop later if I can," I muttered.

"Never mind. She won't be free then," said Fay. "They're bringing down the fourth-floor brigade to throw clay around, so she'll be busy. As for me, I can live without my ex-floormates, so I'm going home. But why don't all of you come over to my room for a drink when the A closes this afternoon? We can celebrate my eighth week of outpatienthood."

I was amazed. What had happened to Fay's mistrust of Lee?

"Why, that would be delightful," said Lee, also looking surprised.

Then suddenly, unexpectedly, his eyes fixed on my plate where the denuded cutlet lay. "Jo-Jo, what on earth have you done to that pathetic piece of meat?"

I remembered my evasive response to his question—"Are you on a diet?"—just a few weeks back, and the subsequent horror of eating the greasy chicken and the rest of the meal with all eyes, I felt, upon me. I knew I couldn't let that happen again. "I scraped it off because it's less fattening that way. I always do that because I once weighed two hundred twenty-five pounds and I never want that to happen again."

Ellen, Fay, and Lee were all looking at me, astonished—though whether at the fact I'd been so fat or at my statement about it I wasn't sure. Then Lee smiled, turned to Ellen and Fay, and said casually, "Eminently sensible, scraping off all that junk, eh? Maybe we all ought to do it."

254

Happier than I could remember feeling in years, I finished the cutlet in silence.

"I thought you didn't like Lee," I whispered to Fay when we left the dining room a few steps ahead of Lee and Ellen. "How come you asked him over?"

Fay shrugged. "I guess if he's good enough for you, he's good enough for me. Anyway, he's clever. That makes up for a multitude of sins. And who knows, maybe the whole nurse story's a fake anyway."

My God, she was accepting Lee on my say-so, implied or otherwise. To my elation at having told the truth about my weight was added a strange and novel feeling of power.

Lee seemed to assume I'd go back to the A with him, and even though I remembered a half-finished dress waiting in the O.T. shop, I didn't mention it. Troubled again by my docility after the courageous lunchtime announcement, I helped him open up.

The phone rang almost as soon as we got the doors open, and I saw Lee's eyes narrow as he listened. "Art's, quote, too depressed, unquote, to work this afternoon," he said. "I'll have to take his shift." Then he looked at me speculatively. "Well, as long as you're here, we might as well extend the range of your skills, right? Who knows? At this rate you may end up on the payroll of our humble establishment yourself."

I hadn't realized people got paid for working at the A. I'd thought it was some kind of hospital-sponsored O.T. work. But Lee looked too busy to talk about it for the moment.

"Oh, su-sure." Actually I wasn't sure at all, but I didn't dare refuse.

While Lee set up the coffee machine, I refilled the small metal milk pitcher in the icebox. "Nothing—but nothing that pours freely can be left on the counter," Lee had explained that morning. "When Art left the glass sugar dispenser out by mistake yesterday, Mary Acosta grabbed it and started to write 'that other brown one' in sugar on the counter before the aide could stop her."

"Good remembering," Lee said, turning to see what I had done. "We seem to work well together, don't we?"

I was pleased by his casual praise and concentrated on learning to make banana splits and enter charges with the concentration I'd reserved for counterfeiting prescriptions just a few months back. The hours passed quickly until I had to leave for my appointment with Dr. Poole.

Feeling more communicative than usual, I briefly sketched in the previous evening's events, while Poole stretched, grimaced, smoked, and yawned.

But when I got to my morning visit, his activity suddenly stopped. It was the quietest I'd ever seen him, a wary, watchful quiet. I tried to hurry quickly past the bedroom awakening, but he interrupted me. "Now, Jo-Jo, are you tryin' to tell me that Lee didn't even try to touch you?"

"No, he didn't, and I was glad." I was sure the subtleties of my ambivalence would elude him, so there seemed no point in getting into them.

"Glad, hunh? Why would that be?"

Now it was my turn to shift uncomfortably. "Well, I hardly know him, and you remember how I feel about myself—about my body."

"Yeah, ah seem to recall you sayin' somethin' about that. But ah don't understand what's wrong. You have a vagina, don't you?"

256

I was shocked. Words like "vagina" weren't tossed about freely then. "It isn't my—not *that* I'm worried about." I knew my face was scarlet and hated myself for it.

"Well then, what is it? You look okay to me." He gave me what in high school we had called the "once-over." "Ah surely wouldn't kick you out of bed."

I decided that Poole would never cease to surprise me. But I was angry that he thought my fears so groundless and, stung, I blurted out, "Well, if you must know exactly what it is, it's my breasts. Mostly my breasts, anyway."

Poole stared at my chest. "They look pretty good to me."

I was too outraged to be embarrassed now. "Well, they may *look* pretty good. In fact, I know they look pretty good when I'm dressed. But the reality is that they're *not* pretty good. They're not good at all. Do you have any idea what it does to your body to gain a hundred pounds and then lose it again? It stretches your skin—horribly. *Horribly.*" I felt tears forming at the back of my eyes.

"Uh-huh," said Poole calmly, still staring at me. "Now ah want you to tell me, just how bad are they? Down to your waist? Your hips? Down to your knees?"

Speechless with rage, I couldn't reply and felt the tears begin to drip down my face.

Perhaps aware that he might have gone too far, Poole at last averted his eyes, and handed me a Kleenex.

"Jo-Jo," he said as I struggled for composure, "now ah want to tell you somethin'. No fella worth his salt is gonna give a damn about your breasts. Not if he really likes you. Believe me, ah know men, and that's the truth."

I thought fleetingly of Ross and his seeming indifference to my bodily flaws. And of course I'd never dared to test Mike or Alan, so how they'd have reacted I couldn't say. But though I realized Poole's remarks were well meant—even kind—I didn't believe him.

Uncomfortably aware that my eyes were still red and my nose runny, I returned to the A just in time to help Lee with closing up.

"Something wrong?" he said, "or do those watery eyes mean you've had the big breakthrough, the Revelation That Makes It All Clear to You?"

"Just the opposite. Poole keeps upsetting me because he's so damn dumb. I mean, he isn't really dumb, I guess. He couldn't be and have his job. But he says dumb things." I stopped suddenly, realizing that I couldn't possibly tell Lee what Poole and I had been discussing.

To my relief, he didn't ask. "Well, then, maybe you can elevate the level of his discourse."

I looked up to see if he was kidding but I could see he wasn't, and wondered how he could have been so sarcastic just a minute before and so helpful now. "Well, maybe," I said, "but I don't think so."

"Anyway, what do you say we wend our way over to Fay's?"

I'd forgotten her invitation. "God, I don't know, Lee. I managed to get away this morning, but I don't think I can leave the grounds again without special permission or a student nurse."

"I don't think there'll be a problem. I called Mrs. Johnson while you were baring your soul to the barbarian, and what she told me was surprising indeed. It seems that when she first reported you'd gone out to see me again, Cunningham was furious. But an hour later his

258

secretary called and said they were granting you unaccompanied town privileges. Odd, isn't it?" He seemed genuinely puzzled. "Usually patients have to bow and scrape to the almighty Cunningham before they get them."

"Maybe not so odd," I said grimly. I sensed Poole's fine hand in all this. What was his game? Would he get a vicarious thrill from my being seduced, willingly or otherwise? Or did he feel me truly able to cope with more freedom?

I headed silently down the path with Lee toward Main Street just as Harry Horner, honking loudly, came rattling up the drive. It was time for his evening litany. "How are ya now? How are ya now, sonny?" But I realized with a thrill that I would no longer need to be up on Two, or on the Small Oaks porch, or anywhere within earshot to hear it.

CHAPTER 17

"What! You got unaccompanied town privileges without even asking?" Fay was incredulous. "When I think what I had to go through to get them! And now I can't even get permission from Cunningham to go home and see my kids for the weekend."

Fay's furnished room on the first floor of Mrs. Callahan's, three blocks toward town, was small and cosy—just big enough for an old-fashioned armoire, a rocking chair, a heavy oak dressing table, and a huge bed with a shiny lavender bedspread.

Lee and I sat on the bed, and Ellen, who had come earlier, sat in the one chair while Fay went down to the hall to the icebox Mrs. Callahan kept for her unusual boarders. She came back and handed us each a malt liquor. "Well," said Lee, "as we all know, and as I've said before, Cunningham works in mysterious ways . . ."

I sipped my malt liquor slowly and noticed uneasily that Lee downed four in rapid succession. He looked all right, but I was relieved when Fay returned from her fifth trip down the hall and said, "Well, I'm all out. Worse

260

luck. Guess we'd better head back to Ye Olde Oaks Dining Room if we're going to catch dinner."

We trooped back to the hospital cafeteria and after dinner, just as I was beginning to realize I'd been with Lee for ten hours straight, he took my elbow and steered me away from the others outside the main building. "You did say you'd come out to my place and help with the breakfast dishes, didn't you?" He looked, again, apprehensive, and I could see beads of sweat on his forehead. Thrilled at the invitation, but again somewhat frightened about the powerlessness I felt about refusing to go, I agreed.

My new privileges meant I only had to report my destination, though I still had to be back by ten. I drove off with Lee.

"I just want to make one stop—at the package store, if you don't mind," Lee said. We left the grounds, turned right on Main Street, and drove to the store, where Lee bought a fifth of bourbon and one of Smirnoff vodka.

The dishes, I saw clearly, were a pretext for Lee's inviting me back, but one which it was obviously important for him to have in order to rationalize the invitation. When they were done, I wiped off the stove and Lee wiped the counters. I noticed that he did this with the crisp thoroughness he used on the counters at the A, holding a hand underneath to catch the crumbs.

As soon as we had finished wiping up, Lee put down his sponge and took out two large tumblers. "Want to join me?" he said, waving the bottle of Jack Daniels he'd bought in front of me.

Till then, unless I was at a party, it would never have occurred to me to have a drink after dinner. But now, afraid to seem unsophisticated and too naive, I complied.

"I do have to be back by ten," I reminded him nervously. Maybe this would be it—the moment Lee had been aiming for. He'd ply me with drinks . . . and then? Furthermore, there was time—time for anything. It was only 7:30.

"Where's Kip?" I asked.

"He has late classes tonight. You're not really going to spoil this excellent bourbon with ginger ale, are you?"

"Well—I, I just don't like the taste plain."

"My dear child, you've got a lot to learn." Did the remark have a double meaning? A lot to learn about what? About drinking? About sex?

I realized Lee was staring at me. "You've ghosted off again, Jo-Jo. You do that quite often. Did you realize that?"

"No, not really."

"Now all you've got to do is make one simple decision. If you're sure you want to contaminate the Jack Daniels, nod."

I nodded, and to my relief he poured in the ginger ale. He added ice to both our drinks and then filled the space left in his glass with more bourbon. We headed back to the living room, and sat down on the couch. I looked around the room nervously. What subject should I broach? Surely he was bored with me. Now the truth about my terrible dullness would come out. But Lee just sat there, seemingly content. He finished his drink quickly, returned to the kitchen, and came back with another. And suddenly, without my asking, he began to tell me about himself.

His father ranked high in the Mormon hierarchy ("I guess I drink and smoke so much just because they're all such self-righteous, self-satisfied bastards") and he had three brothers, all of whom were model citizens and who, along with his parents, prayed for him constantly. Lee announced this with a degree of bitterness I found it hard to comprehend. He had been a child prodigy on the piano but was discouraged by his parents from pursuing it as a career and so had gone into medicine. But then, just as he was completing his residency, he had developed "symptoms." Besides the sweaty palms brought on by the slightest stress, which he'd had for years, a new and baffling lethargy had developed. He couldn't get up, often felt exhausted all day.

While he talked, I, too, had been sipping my drink, and somewhat less nervous, I found myself saying, "Won't you please play for me? I know you still play. I saw the music on the piano."

Lee's eyes were somewhat glazed, and I could see sweat breaking out on his forehead. "All right. I haven't played for anyone in years, but I'll try."

We walked into the parlor and he sat down, a towel next to him. He paused a few times to wipe his hands at the start, but soon the dampness must have vanished since he didn't stop again. His technique—firm and sure—and his subtle, sensitive interpretation of Debussy's "Dr. Gradus ad Parnassum" were extraordinary.

When he was finished, he sat staring at the keyboard. Then he looked up. "You know, that piece is about a little girl practicing. I was thinking about you as a child as I played."

"It was wonderful," I said, too moved to say more.

He looked up with a tortured smile. "Now it's your turn."

"I'm out of practice," I started to say. But in view of Lee's courage, I stopped in mid-sentence. I would have to play. But what?

How different I'd been from Debussy's dreamy, diligent girl. Though I was playing difficult sonatas by eight or nine, I was never quite up to my father's standards. Invariably, he would hear the smallest error. "Can't you play anything through without making a mistake?" he asked, even if it was at a musicale with my relatives present.

The piano was our battleground and I never won, but early on I resorted to all the passive resistance tactics of the defeated. I drew large X's on my music, banged the keyboard, and scratched and nicked the wood above it with my fingernails. Yet I was always drawn back, always hopeful that the next time my father would say, "Yes, yes, that's good," as he did to my older cousin Florence, who never complained about practicing and never, it seemed to me, made mistakes.

Now I had to decide what to play. "It sounds silly," I said, "but I think I'll play a sonatina I know from Schirmer's *Sonatina Album*." The simple ABACAD structures, the rippling runs and melodious rondos—all charmed me.

"Would you like to use the music? That book's an old favorite of mine, too," said Lee. And from the dusty music box I had noticed on my first visit, he took out the familiar yellow book, which looked almost as dog-eared as mine had grown over the years.

I played the first sonatina in the book, a Kuhlau. "Go on," Lee said when I'd finished, so I played another sonatina, then two of the Chopin waltzes I'd perfected at

Dovecote Hill. Amazingly, after the first few measures, I lost my nervousness.

"You play nicely. You have a nice touch," Lee said when I stopped.

I felt myself flushing with pleasure. I realized that Lee's good opinion—of my playing, and by extension of me—had assumed enormous importance.

Then I looked up. I saw his eyes, still glazed and unreadable, staring at me. At me, and yet, I saw with intense disappointment, through me, past me. He wasn't really thinking of me at all. Some private torment, a secret sadness more profound than I had ever seen, was taking up the space I might have occupied.

What are you thinking about? Tell me. Maybe I can help, the sympathetic adult in me wanted to say, while the needy child in me protested, Look at *me,* think about *me.* Would I ever matter to him as I knew he already mattered to me?

In fact, as I closed the piano I said nothing but, "Thanks. The tone is wonderful."

Lee smiled, his demons in temporary abeyance. "Good. Glad you like it. You must come out and practice anytime you want."

And I did, mostly in the evenings. In one night and a day the broad outlines of our relationship had been drawn, and with only a few changes, they remained essentially the same. Lee came to rely heavily on me in many ways, but at the same time sometimes resented his dependence; I in turn relied on him for emotional support, entertainment, and probably most important, for the first time in my life, a feeling of being truly needed by someone. Within days, with great trepidation, I worked a shift at the A, though this time it was Lee, not Art, who failed to show up, and I who had to substitute. And a week later, I took on a regular shift of my own, then two, and eventually three.

At first the idea of being in charge, even for a few hours, was terrifying. It was one thing to be a patron, or Lee's helper at the A, another to be behind the counter surrounded on every side by the weapons of my destruction—Hershey bars, Peanut Chews, and Little Chunkies.

But after my initial panic, I developed ways of coping. Before the start of every shift, I made myself iced coffee, and as the hours passed, I would steadily and methodically chew the ice, replacing it at regular intervals. Between the ice and my new allies, Viceroy cigarettes, my mouth was never empty.

It was Lee who taught me to smoke. He regularly offered me cigarettes, and I always accepted them. In the absence of my long-term crutch, Dexedrine, they made me feel more at ease with him, more like an equal. Soon, every time I felt the least bit uncomfortable, or felt I might eat something I shouldn't, I smoked instead. Soon I was smoking one, then two, and eventually three packs a day.

A few weeks later, Lee was finally elected manager of the A by a committee of Evvie, Martin, Dr. Cunningham, who had finally agreed to try one more patient-manager, and himself. It had slowly dawned upon me that just as in the outer world Lee would have sought to be Chief-of-Staff, here, too, he was acting out the conditioning of a lifetime and wanted the pathetic status that he felt managing the A would bestow.

I, at his insistence, was made assistant manager and also a member of the A Committee. I felt the title undeserved at the time, but Lee was adamant. "Never underestimate the importance of a title. If you've got the game, you might as well have the name."

I increasingly had the game, since Lee, I quickly discovered, was incapable of arriving anywhere on time, and because, as an inpatient, I could be located much more easily than he. Ellen, still a frequent A patron, though she and Lee were more distant since the dinner party debacle, dubbed us the Bobbsey twins, and soon, if someone was looking for Lee—and someone frequently was—I'd automatically be summoned to explain his whereabouts or to handle problems at the A.

And there were plenty of problems. One of Lee's first innovations as manager was an evening shift, but staffing three shifts a day from the unreliable patient pool proved to be almost impossible. No-shows were frequent, and in addition to my own shifts, I found myself filling in more and more, particularly for Lee himself.

We never discussed his drinking and what part it might be playing in his problems. Though I felt he drank too much—and in fact was soon following his lead and drinking more myself to keep up—he never became incoherent and always seemed able to drive me home. Nor was it at all clear that his drinking was causing the lethargy that made it so difficult for him to get up or be on time. Even when he was sober, he was often tired and inexplicably listless. So that when Mrs. Johnson would call up the stairs in the morning, "Jo-Jo, no one's there to open the A," I swiftly—even gladly—dashed over with my key. Aside from my personal sense of responsibility, I was motivated by a desire to keep Lee from facing the consequences of his own frequent derelictions from duty.

Yet, though I revelled in feeling important, I could never quite get over being awestruck by Lee, and paid for it by the repression of a lot of my own spontaneity. I dreaded being on the receiving end of his sardonic humor to such an extent that I'd often remain silent when questioned rather than risk expressing the "wrong" opinion or making a mistake about a fact.

Lee decided to launch an extensive advertising campaign. We wracked our brains trying to think of clever slogans, and quarreled—as much as I dared—over matters of style and wording. Lee's bold, brash, and direct approach (a poster stating in big, black letters that "A-Frame Coffee Is Better Coffee") vied with my attempt at a more witty approach:

> "Know your A B C's: *A*-Frame Coffee is
> *B*etter
> *C*offee."

A large and crudely drawn but recognizable cup of steaming coffee was central to both. The absurdity of the fact that there was no other coffee around for it to be better *than*—just as there was no other source of "special" Cokes—escaped us at the time. We also ran an "I prefer A-Frame coffee because . . ." contest. Answers were to be the traditional "twenty-five words or less." The response was minimal, and Lee's enthusiasm for the ad game, and in fact for the job of manager, began to wane.

As our association went on, and my early-morning visits to Lee's house continued, there was a certain amount of talk. Poole in particular was way ahead of everyone else in his suspicions. One day soon after Lee and I had begun to "go together," he said abruptly, "Now, Johanna, ah feel it my bounden duty to advise you to get a diaphragm."

I was too shocked to reply. "All ah can say," he went on, "is that ah sure never heard of a nice young fella like Lee and a pretty girl like you bein' out there in the country without somethin' happenin'. Ah mean, unless both of 'em's got some kind of problem about sex."

I was outraged at his implicit assumption that all man-woman combinations would quickly end in bed, ignoring the fact that not long before I'd thought along similar lines myself, and offended that he would suggest this about Lee and me at a point when I was having trouble just trying to make conversation with him. When I huffily tried to explain, Poole laughingly, and I felt rather insultingly, added, "Well, if you all cain't talk together, what else *is* there to do? Ah always say there's no problem that a good screw won't make you feel better about."

Such gratuitous and, to my way of thinking at the time, vulgar remarks hardened in my mind the already-established conviction that Dr. Poole was totally wrong for me, and that he had no grasp of what I was really like.

But at the same time, I felt more and more that it didn't matter, that I could change on my own; that, in fact, I was already improving on my own. Without the pills to befuddle my mind, I knew I was thinking more clearly. And remembering—remembering incidents that, while none alone could explain why my life had followed such a disastrous course, when put together seemed to offer clues, perhaps starting with the effects of Hennen's

269

departure and the second-grade setback, on an already troubled and lonely child.

Though he never included the subject of sex in his speculations, Lee liked to theorize about our relationship. "Do we have a *sick* dependency, Jo-Jo?" he'd ask intently—a "sick dependency," he explained, being one in which people's neuroses fit snugly together to the mutual detriment of both parties.

I always found the question threatening. I didn't know if ours was a "sick" dependency or a "healthy" one, if in fact such a thing were possible in a place like the Oaks. Certainly I was dependent on Lee for company, transportation, and entertainment—but was that bad? I was afraid to tell him that his question made me feel nervous, and tried to change the subject as soon as possible. All I knew was that I was having the most exciting time I'd had in years, and that I was having it without the aid of Dexedrine.

The A, and in fact the whole Oaks environment, began to have an almost hypnotic attraction for me. I was regarded enviously by Fay, Ellen, and many of the other patients as being "in good shape"—an accolade in Oaks jargon that meant, roughly, "not acting out and able to function on some very minimal level." Almost high with relief at staying free of drugs and being able to work at the A without gorging myself, I realized that I at least appeared to meet those criteria. Secretly, however, I reasoned that, while of course I could function here, where there was virtually no one to challenge me in any role, in the "real" world I would surely be driven back to drugs or obesity.

Ross wrote every few weeks from Harvard—"What's happening to you? Why don't you write to me? I must know what's going on"—but I didn't respond. He was part of another existence, and I wanted no connection with it.

My parents, with whom I had re-established telephone contact—cordial, polite calls in which we verbally tiptoed around each other—were, with Fay, Ellen, and some of the other patients, equally (and falsely, I felt) impressed by my progress. They began to suggest that I was ready to return home, even, perhaps, to get a regular job or go back to school. I panicked and for once was grateful for Cunningham. "You just tell your folks you are far from ready to leave heah, far from ready." Relieved, I repeated what he had said and they were silent again.

I clung more and more tightly to the security of the Oaks and of Lee and the other patients. The feeling of superiority and control in what I tried to forget was both a bizarre and a highly protected environment was giddy, irresistible, and almost dangerously attractive. In fact, I was developing yet another and more insidious addiction. Slowly but surely I was becoming hooked on Great Oaks.

CHAPTER 18

"The Center is finished at last!" cried Margot Swift, as she flew into the A, the heavily embroidered shawl she was wearing to protect her from the cold of late November flying behind her. Margot was a part-time dance therapist at the Oaks, an aging nymph who dressed in attire that was often at least as outlandish as that of the patients she urged to become "flowers" or "statues come to life."

Lee and I were stacking empty Coke bottles in wooden crates. Art, on duty at last after a long bout with melancholia, was behind the counter pouring a Coke for Roy Vanderman, a fourth-floor patient prone to urinating on the floor when he was feeling particularly hostile.

"Well, that's wonderful, wonderful," said Lee.

Margot's eyes brightened. "And now that we've got the space, we're going to have our first psychodrama session. Tonight. I expect all of you—Art, Jo, Lee—to be there."

Lee smiled. "I'll come if you'll tell me what psychodrama is." I was glad he had asked.

"It's marvelous—a wonderful way to draw the patients out. I may even prefer it to dance therapy."

"Yes, but what is it?"

"You re-enact your problems—your traumas—practice for a difficult situation: rehearse it, if you will. Let's say you had a fight with Jo-Jo here"—I blushed, embarrassed to suddenly be center stage—"and you wanted to make up. You could practice what you'd say with someone else, someone who'd stand in for Jo-Jo. Or, even more to the point, if you wanted to get to the source of the problem, you could re-enact the original scene and figure out what had gone wrong. Anyway, I've got to go. See you all at eight, all right?"

I waited for Lee to answer. "Sure, Margot, your every wish is our command."

A cold fluorescent glare lit the stark modernism of the Center as Lee, Fay, Art, Ellen, and I entered. I waved to Addie. She was there with a few other patients and Dorothy, who hovered near the bridge chairs, her hand under her skirt. Rosemary, her almost bald head reflecting the light, sat quietly nearby. Accompanied by an aide, Roy too, his fly open as usual, had put in an appearance.

Margot had cleared one end of the room as a stage and was busily arranging chairs. "All right, who'll start?"

Nobody said anything, and I heard Dorothy giggle in the silence. Undaunted, Margot looked out at her "audience," her hand shading her eyes. "All right, you—Lee and Art—up here pronto." She beckoned coquettishly. Relieved that she hadn't called on me, I watched as Lee and Art, smiling uncomfortably, went forward.

"All right, Art, you set the scene. This is your stage, your scene, your life."

Art was stroking his pitted face, and I noticed a haunted look in his soft, almond-shaped eyes.

"How about a scene from home," Margot said. "Let's try to work out some of those problems at home."

I winced at her simplistic approach, but then I caught myself. After all, what did I know? Margot was a pro.

"All right," Art said suddenly. "Lee, you could be my father, okay?"

"You know, you can do role reversal, too," Margot interjected. "You, Art, could be the father, and Lee could be you, if you like."

"No," said Art intensely. "Let's leave it as it was. I'll be myself."

"Whatever you say," said Lee. "But what's the situation?"

Art explained that he and his father had had a quarrel just before he had come to the Oaks about whether he should return to Cornell. "In fact, that's what got me here," he said grimly. "Just argue with me. That's all. Whatever I say, disagree with me."

I had never seen Art so involved or so animated. Maybe I had underestimated the effectiveness of Margot's new technique.

The scene began, Art stating that he was going back to school, his father suggesting a term off, mocking him for his recent poor grades. Lee was doing a good job, I thought. But then, sarcasm was his forte. As the scene went on, my attention wandered for a moment to Roy, who was ambling near me, muttering softly. Where was his aide? I wondered nervously. Then I heard a terrible scream. I looked at the stage and saw Art undergoing a transformation, a leprechaun becoming a devil in front of our very eyes. His usually pensive and thoughtful eyes grew wild and he leaped toward Lee.

Totally unprepared, Lee crashed backwards, hitting his head on a chair as he fell to the ground. Art's hands were at his throat.

Addie flew to the wall phone to call for extra help. Margot stood helplessly at the side of her makeshift stage, saying, "Art, stop that. Oh, please stop."

For a moment, I, too, sat paralyzed, stunned by a sudden memory of Jasper, Nancy's husband and our occasional butler. He had seemed quiet and pleasant enough until one night, after he and Nancy had had a fight, when he waited for her with an ax in their dimly lit room off our kitchen. He missed his target only because of the gloom, and in a minute, Nancy's piercing screams had roused everyone in the house.

As I waited at the top of the back stairs, frozen with fear, sure that Nancy—and then by a logical progression, me, whose room was closest—would be systematically murdered, my mother suddenly appeared. Undaunted by Jasper and his ax, she swept by me in her silk robe and curlers, as I stood cowering and weeping on the steps. She had marched to Nancy and Jasper's room like a Valkyrie. "Stop that nonsense at once and give me that ax. How dare you cause this racket and wake us all up in the middle of the night. You ought to be ashamed of yourself."

"Mom, he'll kill you," I'd sobbed, terrified.

But Jasper had looked up shamefacedly and, meekly lowering the ax, handed it to my mother.

Now Lee was lying half-conscious on the floor and I could see Art reaching for a chair. He was going to hit Lee with it—could possibly kill him with it—and I dashed forward and put my hand on his shoulder. "Art, stop that. Put the chair down. Stop that now." I could hear in my own voice my mother's commanding tones.

Art did not comply at once, but he hesitated for a moment, just long enough so that the group of aides who had come running from the main building in response to Addie's frantic call could reach the stage, pin him down, and tie him into a straitjacket.

Lee, looking dazed, sat up, rubbing his head. "You may have saved my life. Do you realize that?"

Fay, who'd come up behind us, nodded in agreement. "God, I admire you for what you did. Violence terrifies me. Where did you get the nerve?"

"I don't know," I said. "Maybe it runs in my family."

Art was confined to the third floor for several weeks, and then, as he remained calm, made the transition back to the Cottage. He began to reappear at the A as before, though he wasn't yet permitted to work there.

Lee, with the objectivity of the former psychiatrist, bore him no malice. "Art's an interesting case," he told me, and they resumed their conversations at the A—but minus my participation.

In spite of my act of bravery, I now found Art's visits frightening. My awareness of the violence underlying his soft, kindly exterior made me speechless in his presence. Who knew what chance remark on my part might set him off?

And the episode had still another effect. It forced me to confront what I'd been trying to avoid: that some of my charming companions at the Oaks were truly insane, insane in ways that I—for all my years of anorexia, compulsive eating, and drug dependence—couldn't possibly fathom.

For the first time, the idea of putting myself at one tiny remove from the hospital began to have a certain appeal. So that when Fay, who had at last obtained permission to visit home, suggested I take over her room at Mrs. Callahan's, I was far less reluctant than I'd have been only a few weeks before. After all, though I'd be freer to come and go, I'd still be under the protective wing of the Oaks, for I knew the Oaks remained very much *in loco parentis* for outpatients. Decisions on jobs, school, trips—all had to be discussed with the administration before one took action. It was a kind of "honor system" with which I and many of the others—still dependent whether we lived "in" or "out"—were only too happy to comply.

"If you hadn't suggested movin' out, why, ah would have," Dr. Cunningham said when, having obtained Poole's enthusiastic okay, I nervously requested his permission to become an outpatient. "You'll have no trouble at all. None, ah'm sure. But don't be a stranger, heah."

I wasn't so sure I'd have no trouble. Even the three blocks seemed an enormous and terrifying distance from the hospital. Nor did I have any intentions of "being a stranger," and immediately resolved to keep no food in Mrs. Callahan's icebox, to continue eating my meals in the Oaks cafeteria, and to spend all my days at the A or the O.T. shop.

The next day I packed my bags, and Lee drove me to Mrs. Callahan's—to the cozy room with the lavender bedspread and the old oak armoire. Art's explosion and what it revealed about the turmoil beneath his seeming composure had succeeded where pressure or persuasion might have failed, and almost six months to the day from my arrival, I became an outpatient at Great Oaks.

"You must be truly mad," Lee said one day about a month later. We were in the A, but he wasn't talking to one of the patients. He was talking to Sally Porter, a peppy brunette theater major from Catholic University who had been hastily hired by the O.T. department to fill the theatrical void left by Margot's disastrous venture into psychodrama.

Sally's approach to drama therapy and its uses was far more conventional than that of Margot, who, glad to have escaped firing, was sticking strictly to *la danse*. Sally, too, believed in "improvisations," but "I'm a pragmatist, and I leave psyches to the psychiatrists." The "warm-ups" we did with her involved such prosaic exercises as pretending to open and shut imaginary doors, setting imaginary alarm clocks, and looking as though we were walking or running when we were actually still in place. As for "scenes" and "role playing," we did excerpts from O'Neill and other recognized playwrights rather than creating our own.

But as was so usual at the Oaks, where the patients' attention span was short, a pall soon began to fall on Sally's biweekly drama group. I remained a regular, but general attendance began to drop off.

Now Sally was proposing something new—a wild, seemingly impossible inspiration—a full-scale musical with sets, costumes, fancy lighting, the works. "I've thought it all through. We'll do it 'in the round,' at the Center!"

Her enthusiasm, I felt, was almost irresistible. Still, I waited for Lee to respond. He tapped the ash from his cigarette into an ashtray with a graceful forefinger. "The

278

very idea of undertaking a project like that with a notoriously irresponsible group like us is more than brave, my dear; it borders on the quixotic," he said. "But I guess if you really want to try it, I'll go along."

I couldn't believe that Lee, who had undergone such tortures before playing even one piece for me, was now agreeing to provide the piano accompaniment for whatever show we picked. And there was now a piano to do it on. Through some magic, Sally had wheedled the funds for one from Cunningham.

For the next few days, we feverishly discussed and discarded possibilities with Sally, Evvie, Ellen—when she was on her customary stool at the A—and occasionally Fay, who took the bus out almost daily.

Finally, we agreed on *Guys and Dolls*. I was thrilled. I'd seen the original Broadway version, had listened to the record so often that I already knew all the words by heart, and desperately coveted the part of Adelaide.

At the *Guys and Dolls* "tryouts," I realized with a kind of wonder that there was really no one else around who could play Adelaide. I got the part.

Most of the casting was done in this way: by using anyone who showed any interest in whatever role best suited him or her. Dave Benjamin, a former artist, was a natural for Nathan—painfully skinny, with deep-set, soulful, dark blue eyes, a built-in New York accent, and a sharp sense of humor. The stammer and nervous tic that were two of the torments of his existence miraculously disappeared when he became Nathan, even in rehearsals.

Chuck Carter, a stout, ruddy, silent outpatient of about twenty-five, with a magnificent mane of wavy red hair, surprised us by volunteering to do Nicely-Nicely Johnson.

And Archie Harrison, a Cottage resident who was a trainee at the A, offered to play Sky Masterson, the gambler. Archie qualified in the two most important ways: He was male and he was not psychotic. Too, he was good-looking. Only later did Sally discover that his quaint absentmindedness affected his recall of lines, and that his ability to keep a tune was minimal. We decided to adopt the working philosophy that "nobody's perfect."

Within a few days, all the parts were cast—all but Sarah, the mission doll. No one had asked for it. Sally suggested we try to recruit Ellen, whom I'd learned had sung in musicals in college before her breakdown. "Ellen's your friend. You'd better do the talking," she said.

We found her fixing a sandwich in the Small Oaks kitchen. "Oh no," she said. "I couldn't possibly do that. Don't you understand? I'm not well enough. And since they won't let me go to England to see Ernest Jones, I probably never will be."

Try, Ellen, why won't you even try? I wanted to shout, surprised to find myself, for the first time, impatient with her seeming determination to remain sick. Stop talking about Ernest Jones and try—here, now, with us, with Dr. Block. But a look at her impassive face convinced me it would be useless.

Resolved to make it an all-patient cast, Sally decided to approach Pat Dalrymple, who had arrived as a new patient on Two just a month before and had quickly graduated to Small Oaks. She was a hard-looking, thirtyish blonde who always dressed as though she were ready to go to 21. Waylaid in the A by Sally, she was startled but cooperative. "Why not?" she said, taking her hand mirror from her purse to check her makeup.

With the cast complete, rehearsals began at once. The problems inherent in using a cast of patients were exactly as Lee had predicted: failure to appear for rehearsals, and to accept criticism or direction, all interspersed with frequent threats of quitting the show. But these were off-set by the fact that, since most of the cast weren't permitted to leave the grounds, they were always available and could be assembled on an impromptu basis.

Because of the show, Lee and I were seeing less of each other. I made sure the A was running while he practiced his part on the piano; he, less depressed than I'd seen him since we met, became somewhat more reliable, and made sure the A was staffed while I rehearsed my scenes without music with Dave. When Lee came to accompany us we rarely talked, each preoccupied with our own roles in the production.

I was, briefly, euphoric. Unlike the others, I knew my lines within days and was always on time for rehearsals. Also, like the many Hollywood actresses I'd worshipped all my life, I developed a quiet passion for my leading man, Dave, which made the heady excitement of starring in a show—even in this peculiar environment—even headier. We spent hours—more than necessary, really—blocking "Sue Me," and I suspected he reciprocated my feelings, since I noticed him surreptitiously doing sketches of me on the pad he always carried in his pocket. But he never said a word—nor did I.

A few days before the performance, a student nurse appeared at the rehearsal. "Jo-Jo, there's a call for you." I went to the main building filled with a vague sense of alarm.

It was my mother. "Darling, isn't it wonderful? We've spoken to Dr. Cunningham and he's assured us you're

281

ready for a visit. And, of course we want to see you in the play, so we'll be there Saturday."

I was speechless, filled with dread and fear. I'd seen no one from my life as the Other Me yet. What would my parents think of me, of my curious assortment of friends, most importantly, of the new person I was becoming?

My mother was still talking. "We'll stay in Washington the night before and come out to take you to breakfast."

I knew I'd be busy all day Saturday and that their visit might unnerve me completely, but unable to bring myself to say so, I agreed. "Fine, Mom," I said, my stomach churning. "I'll see you that morning."

They were on time! I could see them coming up the front path, and, feeling a rush of the same joyous elation I'd felt when I did, at last, see the Packard rounding the corner all those years ago, I hurtled out the door toward them. To my own surprise, as well as theirs, I threw my arms first around my mother, then my father.

"Well, well, quite a greeting," said my father, looking flustered but pleased.

"You look marvelous, Jo," said my mother. "You've certainly managed to keep your weight down."

"Yes." I didn't want to talk about my weight. I nervously showed them my room at Mrs. Callahan's. Then we drove to Jack's Diner, the only restaurant in town.

I hoped my mother wouldn't insist on warm rolls, a demand she made at almost every restaurant we went to. "Excuse me, dear, could you please bring me some warm rolls?" she'd say sweetly to the waiter or waitress. I knew the sweetness would fade if she didn't get her way, and she'd insist upon leaving, or complain for the rest of the meal. But for once she didn't ask for the rolls. "I'll just have coffee," she said.

"What are you wearing as a costume, Jo? I suppose for Adelaide you'll have to wear something loud and a little vulgar," my mother said. I nodded. "And what about shoes? This should give you a chance to wear some of those shiny shoes you always liked."

God, here we go again. The concern about how I looked, what I wore; the terrible memory of the spilled shoe polish. My stomach began to knot, and unconsciously, I felt for my ponytail. As a child, I'd often sucked strands of my hair when I was nervous—a habit my mother despised. But the ponytail wasn't quite long enough to reach my mouth, and I let it fall back. Instead, I lit a cigarette.

"You're smoking an awful lot, aren't you, Jo?" said my father, but since we all knew my mother was a pack-and-a-half-a-day smoker herself, he dropped the subject.

"Yes, the shoes are shiny," I said. My mother looked surprised at my return to the topic. "And you're right, I always did like them. They didn't need polishing as often as the dull ones." Would she remember, too? Or had the incident been important only to me?

I saw tears in my mother's eyes, and for the first time I could ever recall, she looked away, embarrassed. "Darling, I don't give a damn anymore what kind of shoes you wear. Or even whether they're polished. I don't know why it ever seemed so important."

So she did remember. And she was sorry. I felt momentarily triumphant—and then, almost simultaneously, enormously sad for her. How often in recent years she must have reproached herself for that and other incidents.

And as I looked at her, suddenly I, too, felt like apologizing. Why had I been so intractable on that long-ago

283

day? Seen from her point of view, what I'd done was outrageous, however understandable my subconscious motivations.

"I don't know either. Why it was so important to me *not* to polish them, I mean."

As our eyes met over the coffee cup, I knew that we had reached some kind of a turning point in our relationship. She flashed a hesitant smile at me, and I tried to smile back. But above the smile I could see that her eyes were filled with tears. And so were mine.

CHAPTER 19

The performance went smoothly, interrupted only by Mariel Schwartz, a second-floor patient who kept lifting up her skirt, giggling, and whooping happily, "Oh my God, I can't stand it! I can't stand it!"

But nothing could have rattled me that night. At the last minute Ellen had agreed to prompt, but I didn't need her. I felt confident, sure of my lines, sure of my voice. "Sue Me" was such a hit that Dave and I had to do it twice, and "Adelaide's Lament" got a standing ovation.

The place was jammed. Doctors, aides, student nurses, and administrators were there, and patients from all the floors—remarkably well-behaved. From "backstage"—a makeshift curtain a few feet from the back wall—I'd seen Dr. Poole sitting with Dr. Cunningham, and a few rows back, my parents, early for the performance for once. Ordinarily, the presence of any one of them would have rattled me completely, but, sustained by excitement and my satisfaction at the unexpected moment of unity with my mother that morning, I felt invincible.

"You were wonderful, darling," my mother said after the performance. "I never realized you had a voice."

Evvie, who had designed the sets and costumes, had obtained permission for a cast party at her house. "First time they've allowed social intercourse between staff and patients off the grounds as far as I know," said Lee to my parents, who were studying him warily. I'd stressed that Lee and I were "just friends"—trying to think why it felt like a lie when it wasn't, and wishing he hadn't used the word "intercourse."

"Well, you won't want us there," said my mother decisively. "We'll come back to say good-bye tomorrow morning." I didn't argue.

Cheese, crackers, and huge bottles of Gallo red and white were out on Evvie's checkered tablecloth. There was candlelight, a fire, and a record of *Guys and Dolls* playing in the background.

Lee went to the phonograph. "I don't know about anyone else, but I've had enough of that. Anyway, they're not half as good as we were."

"Not as good as Jo, anyway," said Dave. I hadn't seen him come in, but he was right at my elbow. The attraction between us had grown stronger during the weeks of rehearsal, perhaps even more so for remaining unspoken.

I stood silently as Lee changed the record. "Hey there, you with the stars in your eyes." I felt the words were meant for me tonight. I had stars in my eyes, and I wanted something to happen, was even determined to *make* something happen.

I took out a cigarette. Dave had a lit one in his hand. Amazed at myself, I moved closer to him, took his hand with the cigarette, and guided it toward me, so I could get a light. Could this be me? In charge, and actually— yes, actually flirting?

"Let's sit down," I said, and with Lee's eyes still on us, Dave and I sat down on the daybed next to each other. I was conscious of his thigh against mine, but mostly of his dark blue, deep-set, penetrating eyes.

"I have something for you," he said.

"Oh?" I realized I was trembling.

"Bu-but it's out in Evvie's car. She b-brought it from the O.T. shop. I'd like to give it to you. I could get it from the car."

"No," I said. Dave looked surprised. "No, I mean, 'no, you shouldn't bring it in.' Let's go out and get it together."

Our eyes met and he looked away uneasily. "Won't Lee mind?"

"Forget Lee." In that moment I *wanted* to forget him—forget our careful, platonic, "working" relationship, of which he spoke with such pride.

Silently, we put on our coats and walked outside to Evvie's car, which was unlocked and parked by the curb.

"Let's sit inside. It's cold out," I said boldly.

"All—all right."

The inside of the car was frigid, and I moved closer to Dave. He reached behind him into the back seat.

"I've been working on this for weeks," he said, and handed me a large, framed, pastel portrait—the head and shoulders of a striking, dark-haired girl with the same eyes as the Other Me.

I was stunned. How could it be that Dave had seen me as that other person, a person I had seen as a complete fake; a person I'd thought gone forever?

"But I don't really look like that—not anymore," was all I could stammer.

Dave looked crushed. "What do you mean?" he said. "D-don't you like it?"

I could see that he had taken my comment as a criticism of his skill. In my self-absorption, I'd momentarily forgotten his feelings, forgotten the enormous time and effort it must have taken to produce such a finished work, ignored the admiration he must have felt to make that effort. So this is what the furtive sketches had been about. Dave had a crush on me. On *me!* Not the Other Me, not the fake one—the *real* me.

"Forgive me, Dave. It's wonderful—a wonderful picture," I said. "Did you sign it?"

He brightened. "Turn it over," he said.

I turned it over and saw an inscription. "To Jo. Sue me, sue me, what can you do me? I love you. Dave."

"Dave," I said and turned toward him. "Dave, I want to kiss you."

"But what about Lee? Won't Lee be jealous?"

"Maybe," I said calmly. "But he shouldn't be. He's never even tried to kiss me himself."

"Bu—but I thought . . ."

"I know. Everyone thinks. But let's not talk about Lee. Let's . . . not talk at all."

Our lips met, and I could feel his slender arms around me. We kissed again, our tongues now touching. His trembling hand moved tentatively toward my breast. I steeled myself.

Suddenly there was a blinding shaft of light as the front door of Evvie's house swung open, and I saw Lee, coatless, coming unsteadily down the path toward the car.

Dave looked stricken. "Oh my God," he said. He began to tremble violently. "I—I've got to leave. We should

288

never have done this." He leaped from the car and, almost running, headed back toward the Oaks grounds.

Lee moved in beside me and looked at me with a slightly unfocused gaze. I could tell he'd already had too much to drink.

"Terrific lover you picked," he said, "a neurotic mess of a human being who's scared of his own shadow."

I was fuming. And what are you? I wanted to shout.

"Well, was it fun? Did you enjoy your faint-hearted lover's kisses? 'Why so pale and wan, fair lover, why so pale and wan?'"

Ignoring the sarcasm, I thought about the question. Had I enjoyed it? And realized the answer was yes.

As Lee sat brooding beside me—tiny beads of sweat on his forehead, his underarms damp despite the cold—I saw, to my astonishment, that quite inadvertently, I'd accomplished something else. Without even trying, I'd made Lee jealous—sexually jealous in a way I wouldn't have dreamed possible and couldn't possibly have planned. I sensed a subtle shift in our "working" relationship, and I was elated, for in that moment I realized that Dave had been, at least in part, a substitute for Lee, that for a long time what I'd really been yearning for was to touch Lee and to have him touch me back.

The next morning my parents reappeared and we returned to Jack's Diner. I showed them the picture Dave had done. "Very good. Looks just like you," said my father. "Now what's a talented fellow like that doing in the hospital, I'd like to know? What's his problem?"

"It isn't that simple," I said. "I guess if he knew exactly what his problem was and it was just one thing, it wouldn't be so hard to figure out or cure. I mean, these things are complex."

I realized they were listening carefully and that they were aware—as I was—that I was really talking about myself as well as Dave.

"I've got to know—and I want you to tell me the truth," I said. "Do I seem different to you now?"

"Different? In what way? What do you mean?" my father asked.

"I mean, different from the way I was last summer, and for the last few years. Do I seem quieter?" I wanted to say "duller, less interesting," but stopped myself.

My parents looked at each other. "Jo, I don't know what you're talking about," my mother said. "You seem a little calmer maybe, but otherwise you're just the same."

"The same as what, though?" I persisted. "The same as I was before I started to really, unh, lose weight"—I didn't want to remind them of the Dexedrine—"or the same as I was in high school?"

My mother stirred her coffee. "That's a funny question. I guess now that you mention it, you did change a lot since you started college."

Yes, yes, I thought, but I have to know—who am I? The old me? The Other Me? Some amalgam of the two?

My mother brightened. "Speaking of college, that lovely Ross from Wisconsin called the other day to see how you were. He says he's been writing you regularly, but that you've only written back once."

"Ross is a case in point. I guess I feel I was such a different person when I knew him that he'd hardly know me if we met again. I mean, you did say just now that I'd changed a lot since college."

"Well, not *that* much. I suppose I'd have to say that the main difference is that you seem happier. Calmer. Less nervous. Don't you agree, Herb?"

I looked quickly at my father, who was glancing at his watch. Conversations like this made him uncomfortable. "Sure, sure. I don't understand all this, but I don't see any difference from the way you were before you came here. I certainly hope you're beginning to *feel* different, though." He sighed. "Anyway, from what I can see, you're just the same."

I was just the same. Could that be right? And if I was, or appeared to be, what did that mean? Could it be that the real me wasn't so different from the Other Me after all?

Yet how could that be? How could the frightened, fat seventeen-year-old have changed into the poised, slender twenty-two-year-old? How had the metamorphosis come about? Could it be that while I was taking the drug for so long, I was also learning new ways of behaving, new ways of being with people, new ways of dealing with food, that had stuck with me even afterward; that the drug had, in fact, given me a chance to practice and perfect those new ways over a period of four and a half years? And if so, could it be that the four and a half years hadn't been totally wasted?

It was all very confusing. Yet perhaps my parents were wrong. I had, after all, succeeded in keeping the truth about myself and the pills and the Other Me from them for years. Perhaps now, too, they were deceived by appearances. I couldn't be as much like the Other Me as they claimed. As we left the diner, I concluded that they were, in fact, mistaken.

Our good-byes were brief, but I felt tears come to my eyes as we stood on the curb. "Jo, you're doing fine. We're proud of you," my father said, "but I just wanted to say one thing before we go. Now I know they're all still cautious at the hospital—overly cautious, maybe—but I think it's time for you to think about going back to school, or getting a real job someplace else. It's morbid at the hospital. It can't be good for you."

My mother glared at him. "Herb, leave her alone. You know what Dr. Cunningham said." They had had a conference with Dr. Cunningham the day before, but we hadn't discussed it.

Morbid? The hospital was morbid? For a moment I saw it as my father did, as I had the day I arrived. But I couldn't hold the image. For me, it had been transformed into a place of magic where wonderful things were happening.

"I *am* thinking about it," I said. "I think about it a lot." But what I was really thinking about just then was getting back to my seat behind the counter at the A.

It was two months later—April. A furnished third-floor walkup apartment in a large rambling house directly across the street from the entrance to the Oaks was available, and Dr. Poole was urging me to take it. "You're a big girl now, ain'tcha? It's just a few dollars more than Mrs. Callahan's, and you'd have more freedom there—and a lot more privacy. You could throw parties there. You could live a little."

How strange to hear Dr. Weinstock's favorite phrase again. Could it be a bad omen? Far more frightened at the prospect of an apartment than I'd been of moving to

Mrs. Callahan's, I was ready to believe in bad omens. Though I'd often protested to Lee about the curfew at Mrs. Callahan's—she locked her door at midnight—I was secretly glad of it. It afforded me a kind of protection. But what scared me most was that an apartment meant a kitchen of my own; a kitchen, as it happened, that you had to walk through to get to the bathroom, so it could hardly be shut off and ignored. Who could protect me from that?

Poole ridiculed my fears. "Ah thought you told me you hadn't gone haywire over food in more than four years."

I nodded uncomfortably. "But I've never had my own apartment, either."

"Now, Jo-Jo, ah think you owe it to yourself to give yourself a chance to live like a normal human bein'. But ah know you don't listen to me. Ah mean, you nevah even got that diaphragm, did you?"

I ignored the remark and he went on. "Far as the food goes, ah'm bettin' you'll be okay."

"I'm just scared," I said weakly.

"Jo-Jo, ah'm disappointed in you. Ah thought you had guts, but ah guess ah had you wrong."

I could see straight through his reverse psychology, but I rose to the bait anyway. "Okay. You win. I'll try it. But if I come back here blown up like a balloon, it'll be on your conscience."

Poole grinned. "Whatevah you say."

Lee took me shopping, and bravely I bought a few groceries and put them on the shelves and in the icebox. Unsweetened grapefruit juice, tuna fish, a small loaf of bread and a stick of butter. There was a toaster, and on my second day I made a piece of toast for breakfast. My own toast in my own toaster. And the miracle recurred: I stopped at one slice.

More confident after a week of breakfasts at home, I decided to follow Poole's advice. I'd have a party—a housewarming party, the first party I'd ever given. I'd have the entire cast and crew of *Guys and Dolls*, the workers at the A, Kip, Ellen, Fay. I set the time for the very next Saturday. "You hardly need worry about booking far ahead with this guest list," said Lee.

Then, two days before the party, I found a letter from Ross in my box. I was carrying paper bags and almost forgot about it till I climbed upstairs and unpacked the groceries. Then, as I was about to leave for my shift at the A, I noticed the long envelope with the familiar handwriting on the table where I'd dropped it. Hurriedly, I ripped it open. His letters were almost always the same: some of his own news—the letter in December told me he'd been inducted into the Army and had had to take a leave from Harvard—and the inevitable, "Why don't I hear from you?"

Now I felt suddenly weak. This letter was different. Ross was driving down from Fort Dix to see me on Saturday. "No ifs, ands, or buts about it. This nonsense has gone on long enough. I spoke to your parents and they told me you have your own apartment and that you were also in *Guys and Dolls* a few months ago. I'm terribly hurt that you didn't tell me, so that I could have come to see you in it. But we can talk about that when I arrive. I'll be there around seven. Perhaps we can go out to dinner. Please don't try to stop me from coming. I must see you."

I thought of cancelling the party, escaping to Lee's, hiding out—but then it occurred to me that having a lot of people around might make our meeting easier, would in fact expose Ross in one shocking dose of reality to my new life.

Ross called that night at 7:00. "I had a flat tire and got delayed. I can be there in an hour or so. Hope it didn't inconvenience you."

It seemed incredible to be hearing his voice after so long. He sounded just the same. But of course he would, I thought. It was I who might sound different.

"No, but it happens I'm having a party in a little while." I was actually relieved at the delay. At least now I'd have no chance at all to be alone with him before the party.

"Am I invited?" He sounded hurt, and I felt a pang of guilt.

"Of course. I just wanted to warn you about what to expect."

There was a pause. "I had hoped to see you alone."

"Sorry, it was planned a long time ago." Then I weakened. "After everyone leaves, we can talk."

"Well, okay, I'll be there as soon as I can. I can't wait to see you."

By 7:30, almost everyone was there. I'd had to start the party early, since the inpatients had to be back by 10:00. To my relief, Lee, too, had managed to arrive on time to set up the bar. I tried not to think about how Ross might interpret Lee's role as unofficial host. As for Lee, all I'd told him about Ross was that an old college friend was visiting.

At 8:00, there was a knock on the door. I knew it had to be Ross. Strangely calm, I opened the door and saw the familiar bony face and the rangy frame, but thinner than I remembered him. "You got a haircut," I said stupidly.

"And you didn't. Your ponytail is longer." He smiled his broad smile. "But then, you're not in the Army, are you? Anyway, I like your hair that length."

I was, as ever, impressed with how observant he was about me. Even my parents hadn't noticed the few extra inches.

"I'm glad you like it. I actually just haven't had time to get it cut." God, I must be sounding dull already. And why were we talking about haircuts? "Come in. I'll introduce you around." I quickly introduced him to Archie, Ellen, Chuck, Fay—and finally, to Lee.

"Can I get you a drink?" asked Lee suavely, looking at Ross with the penetrating look I privately thought of as his X-ray vision.

Ross's eyes moved swiftly from Lee to me; I could almost see his mind at work. But I didn't want to explain. Let him think what he liked. It had been his idea to come.

Ross followed me into the kitchen where I had gone for more cheese and crackers. "Who's that?" he asked.

"Who?"

"That guy who offered me the drink."

"He's an outpatient, and we work together. We're co-managers of a store on the grounds of the hospital."

"Is that all?"

"God, Ross, you just got here and you're hitting me with all these questions. He's just a friend, okay?"

"Are you sleeping with him?"

"Wow—you don't beat around the bush," I said. "It's really none of your business, you know, but the fact is, I'm not." And as I said it, I realized how much the total

296

lack of physical contact between Lee and me continued to rankle. The longing I'd first noticed the night I kissed Dave had turned into an ongoing ache that was gaining in intensity.

At the same time, it struck me as curious that Lee, so recently jealous of Dave, appeared untroubled by Ross. Could he sense there was no danger?

I remembered the one sexual encounter Ross and I had had at Wisconsin. It had been good—the only satisfying sexual experience I'd ever had, however affected by the Dexedrine. Yet for some reason, I hadn't burned with desire for him since then as I had with Mike, or Alan, even with Dave.

Ross seemed relieved at my assurance. He went back to the living room with me, and began to talk to Ellen and Archie and then Fay. How kind he was, I thought guiltily. Here he had come to see me, and he was having to make conversation with a group of strangers. And what a group!

Finally, everyone but Lee and Ross had gone. "Want me to help clear up?" said Lee. I was aware that he had drunk too much, but surmised that Ross probably couldn't tell. Lee's voice and gait were steady. Only his eyes were a giveaway.

"No, I'll do them. Thanks, Lee. Thanks for all your help." I knew I couldn't put off being alone with Ross any longer.

"My pleasure. But before I take my leave, I have to tell you it was a wonderful party. Did you know that? And you were a superlative hostess."

"God, thanks, Lee. It seemed easy."

"Lots of people would find it terrifying to throw a party for thirty people," Lee persisted. "I would."

His compliments were so rare that I knew I should be thrilled, but this one irked me, both because I felt it was largely inspired by liquor, and also because it was for something I hadn't felt was even an effort. Why didn't he compliment me on my efforts to understand and talk to him when we were alone? On my not gorging myself at the A? On my learning to cope with Babe, and Roy, and Art? But I knew he had no grasp of those things and for a scary moment, I realized how different we were—how different our problems.

Ross was watching and waiting.

"Thanks, Lee," I said again, and then, decisive with him for once, "I'll see you tomorrow."

Lee got the hint. "Certainly. It's been a pleasure meeting you," he said to Ross as he left.

Ross and I were, at last, alone. "Jo-Jo, I have to get back to Washington soon, and to camp tomorrow."

"I'm sorry," I said, but I really wasn't.

"I have a few things I want to say—that I have to say—before I go." I waited as he paused, seeming to struggle for words.

"First of all, you know you don't belong with those people, don't you?"

"How do you know?" I said defensively. "You don't really know anything about me now, any more than you knew what I was hiding from you for years."

"I realize that, and I'll always regret it," he said quietly. "But just watching you this evening—I mean, you seem fine compared to them. You don't shake, or stutter, or have chronic headaches, do you?"

"You sound just like my father! I assure you, you don't land at Great Oaks for nothing. You'll have to take my word for it. Even if I look okay now, I have a long way to go."

Why were we arguing about this? I had my own agenda for our talk, though it was one I hadn't been aware of till then. I looked at him as I had at my parents two months earlier. "Ross, I have to know the truth. Do I seem very different than I was at Wisconsin?"

"How do you mean, 'different'? Oh, you mean that stuff about the Dexedrine you wrote me? Now listen, I've said it before and I can say it again with even more conviction now that I've seen you. You're different, all right"—my heart stopped for a moment—"you're better. Not so frantic and upset, I mean."

Ross, then, was confirming what my parents had said. Could there possibly be some truth to it, or were they all just being kind, trying to assuage my anxiety with reassuring lies? I sat for a moment, thinking again about the Dexedrine and how it might have made gradual but permanent changes in me during the course of my four-and-a-half-year addiction.

But Ross was clearly impatient with the turn the conversation had taken. "What I really want to talk about is us."

"Us?"

"Jo, you must know how much I care for you—how much I love you."

I looked down, embarrassed, wishing he'd stop. "Now, I know what I'm saying is a little nervy, but after seeing you tonight, I think you can leave this place. Leave tomorrow and you'll be fine. Then you could move back to

299

New York and I could come to see you from Fort Dix or wherever I may be stationed, and maybe, eventually, we could—well . . ."

He was asking me to marry him—if not now, then someday. And for a minute I was tempted. Here it was, my chance to fulfill the dream of every girl of my era: marriage, a home, the love of a good man. And Ross was a good man, I knew that. Ross would validate Poole's prediction that "If someone really cares for you, he won't give a damn about your breasts." Then why was I only wondering how to handle the conversation tactfully, instead of falling into his arms?

"Ross, you're crazier than anyone in this room was. Don't you understand what I'm saying, what I wrote you? Sure, I stopped taking the medicine, but what made me so desperate to take it, what made me eat so much before that—I'm just beginning to understand why those things happened, or what might make them happen again. I couldn't possibly leave. I don't even want to. And there's another thing. It isn't me you're in love with anyway—or think you are. It's the person I used to be. Because I look the same, you think I am the same. But I'm not. In spite of what you said, I'm not."

Ross was shaking his head. "It's Lee, isn't it? He's a big part of it, too, isn't he?"

"I like Lee," I admitted. "But that's not what's keeping me here."

"Yes, it's Lee and this place," he repeated. "I'm telling you, Jo-Jo, they're both no good for you." He leaped up, and I realized he was in genuine pain. What had I done to cause it? What damage had the Other Me wrought?

"Now listen to me, Jo. I'm going to leave. And if I walk

out that door and you don't stop me, you'll never see me again." How pseudo-dramatic it all sounded—like a thirties movie, I thought. But this was no movie, and Ross was obviously sincere. "I can't stand it. While I know you're alive and single, I can't seem to get involved with anyone else. I just can't forget you. But I'll tell you one thing, I'm going to try. I can see just by looking at you that you don't feel the same way I do, so I'm going to have to try."

I was mute, frightened at the strength of his feelings and saddened by his bitterness, but unable to say the words I knew would make him feel better.

Ross studied my face for a minute, then turned swiftly on his heel and went to get his coat. "Do you have anything to say?"

I followed him meekly, wishing he wasn't so adamant, wanting him to forgive me for not loving him as he loved me, yet desperately wanting him not to be angry with me because of it. "Only that I'm sorry. Terribly sorry. I'd like to be your friend. Your friendship has meant a lot to me in the past, but if you don't want to—"

"No. No friendship," he interrupted. "Not anymore. I just can't handle it." And without a word, he turned away and slammed the door behind him.

I stayed where I was, staring at the door, and for a moment I had a wrenching sense of loss. Always, in the back of my mind, I'd known I could turn to Ross, that he wouldn't abandon me. Now he was saying he would do just that. And I had brought it on myself. Why? What craziness made me prefer the company of Lee, an unstable and unreliable neurotic, and a life with a bunch of patients in a mental hospital, to what Ross was suggesting?

The answer, I knew, was that I still felt safe here, and only here. Ross, with his personal demands, his connection with my past and potentially with a future far away from Great Oaks, was trying to pull me away from that security. And I wasn't ready. Too soon, I told myself. Too soon.

CHAPTER 20

Not long after my party, just when things had re-turned to "abnormal," as Lee put it, a new group of mostly "in-contact" patients began to arrive at the hospital who were to alter the status quo and my own life at the Oaks in some radical and very unexpected ways.

Justin Levine came first. He ambled into the A one somnolent summer afternoon almost a year to the day from my own arrival with an awkward, pigeon-toed gait, and in the deep, cultivated tones of a Shakespearean ac-tor, said, "I say there, bridge, anybody?" Then he added, "I'm a 'life master,' don'tcha know. Love the game, but haven't played since college." I didn't know what a "life master" was, but sensed that it was a rank in the world of bridge that was not easily come by.

I found the combination of Justin's skinny body and awkward carriage, his surprisingly theatrical voice, and his quite ugly face—yellow, pimply skin; narrow, slanted, heavy-lidded eyes which were disconcertingly focused on the ceiling rather than on me as he spoke—so astonishing that it was a moment before I could reply.

"I don't know how," I said finally.

Dave, who had slowly begun to reappear at the A since bolting from the car the night of *Guys and Dolls,* didn't know how to play either, so, though Art and Lee were agreeable, the idea was temporarily shelved.

Not for long, however. One of the student nurses had overheard Justin's remark and took it upon herself to round up some partners for him. The next day a dynamo burst into the A, breathless with excitement. "Who wanted to play bridge here? My God, I'm going crazy up on Two with that bunch of nuts. I love bridge! Let's start right now!"

This whirlwind was Jill Steele, also newly arrived just that week. Her boyishly cut, wiry, strawberry-blond hair bristled, her green eyes snapped. When forced to sit still, she seemed tormented, and bit her nails to bloody pulps; while playing bridge, she never stopped pulling nervously at the short strands of her hair.

Soon a game was underway, with Justin and Jill pitted against Lee and Art. Lee was actually on duty, but he took a deck of cards off a shelf, removed one of the small round tables from circulation for the game, and sat down to play with the others. He clearly assumed I'd cover for him, and I did.

I watched enviously from behind the counter, wishing desperately that I knew how to play. Between customers, I came over to watch, but even after Justin's sporadic explanations, I found it impossible to follow the drift of the game. I ended up doing all the closing chores myself, since the quartet at the table was clearly not going to stir unless driven out.

After dinner, during the evening shift, I covered for

Lee once again, so he could be Justin's partner. I felt resentful and excluded, yet vaguely guilty about feeling that way. After all, Lee knew how to play and I didn't. Why shouldn't he—especially when there was such a shortage of players?

When the A closed, Lee said, "Let's all go down to Quinn's for a nightcap." Quinn's was a bar in town that was a frequent nighttime hangout for outpatients and patients with town privileges.

In the past, I'd often wanted to go to Quinn's with Fay and Ellen, but Lee had preferred to drink at home. Now he wanted to go, but I didn't—at least, not with his new bridge cronies. But I reluctantly went along—with Justin, and, to my amazement, with Jill, who, while still a patient on Two, had managed to get an okay to go, though of course a student nurse had to accompany her.

I was more and more impressed by Jill, but there was something vaguely menacing to me about the piercing looks she darted at me and others.

In Quinn's, attempting to be friendly despite my uneasiness, I began to ask her where she came from, how many brothers and sisters she had, and similar non-probing and impersonal questions. Suddenly, in the middle of one of them, her eyes narrowed, she jumped up, knocking over her chair, and simultaneously grasping her beer glass in her hand, she threw its contents into my astonished face. "It's none of your goddamn business!" she snarled, and followed by the horrified nurse, she stalked out of the tavern.

It was a fitting conclusion to what had been one of the worst days I'd yet spent at the Oaks.

Jill arrived early at the A the next morning, full of apologies—but also checking to see if she could put together a bridge game. "I don't know what gets into me," she said with a puzzled smile, for all the world as though she'd done nothing more unusual than stamp her foot. I mutely accepted the apology. But, as with Art, I knew I'd never really trust her again.

For the next few days, Jill and Justin continued their daily pursuit of a foursome, but often Art wasn't "in the mood," or preferred to talk with Dave. Lee had A obligations he couldn't always ignore or turn over to me. Then, just as I'd begun to hope the whole bridge fad would blow over, another new arrival turned up on the doorstep of the A to fill the void.

From my first view of Tessa Farrell, I wouldn't have expected her to be a very likely "fourth." She walked gracefully into the A on black patent-leather high heels—a beautiful girl of about twenty-five with a knock-out figure encased in a plunging black sheath dress. She had white, powdered skin, dimples, a small, perfectly placed "beauty mark" on her upper cheek, and large, near-sighted hazel eyes behind horn-rimmed glasses. In this case the glasses only enhanced her charms by offering a scholarly contrast to her otherwise almost too voluptuous appearance. Her dark hair was, like Jill's, cut as short as a boy's and lay close to her head; but any masculine resemblance was more than counterbalanced by two spit-curls, one of which lay below each tiny ear, and by her long, dangling earrings and dark lipstick.

But it was not her appearance that made her seem an unlikely bridge partner that afternoon. No sooner had she entered the A than, for no apparent reason, she suddenly froze and remained absolutely immobile. I had seen a few catatonic patients before—Mary Acosta was one—but they had all looked and acted peculiar in other ways as well, and I had pretty much secretly identified them as lost causes. Tessa was the first person I'd seen enter the door as a vivacious and lively girl only to change incomprehensibly into a statue.

After giving the nurse some time to try to bring her back to reality, Lee asked what the new patient's name was. He approached her gently. "Tessa, why don't you sit down and let us get you a Coke?" he suggested with a touch of gallantry. I suddenly was reminded of the fact that Lee was a trained psychiatrist and well equipped to handle this kind of crisis.

Almost like a princess delivered from a magic spell, Tessa began to revive. Her eyes slowly focused on Lee, her tense body relaxed, and she was again the charming creature she'd been when she walked in. "Why not?" she said, and without any reference to the past five minutes, walked over and sat on a stool at the counter, where she tapped out an accompaniment to the song on the jukebox with her long, beautifully manicured fingers.

Noting Lee's keen interest, I felt a stab of jealousy. It would be hard to ignore those hands, any more than one would be likely not to notice the beautiful legs she crossed and recrossed at regular intervals.

Jill, too, had been studying Tessa, and when, after about ten minutes, Tessa showed no signs of reverting to her catatonic state, lost no time in finding out if she could play bridge. When she said yes, Jill was delighted, and immediately set up a game for that afternoon, with Lee and Justin as their partners. "But let's play on the Small Oaks porch instead of here. These tables are too tiny, and it's too crowded."

I was to be on duty at the A that afternoon, and this change of locale for the game disturbed me. If it was to take place at Small Oaks, I'd be completely left out.

Lee was silent, watching Tessa, clearly unaware of, or indifferent to, my discomfort.

"Sure, why not?" said Tessa.

That afternoon as I sat alone in the A, glumly chewing ice, I could hear occasional laughter floating over from Small Oaks, and I felt worse and worse. I was painfully conscious of feeling deserted, "used," and trapped at the A, yet realized I'd been only too happy to volunteer for martyrdom when Lee and others I admired were around to appreciate my self-sacrifice.

Furthermore, I saw everything that had seemed so secure just a few days before—my relationship with Lee, my status as co-manager of the A, my whole role center stage at Great Oaks—slipping away. The foundations of my present existence that I'd thought so solid and unshakable were proving as treacherous as quicksand.

My eyes moved to the metal chest where we stored the ice cream. At my suggestion, we had just begun to carry coffee, my favorite flavor. Slowly I got down from my stool and took the metal scoop out of the milkshake container where it sat in water to keep it slippery. I opened the top of the ice cream chest, took a large hot drink cup from the pile, and began to methodically fill the cup with ice cream. When it could hold no more, I closed the chest and took a flat wood spoon from the bunch held together with a rubber band.

Then, just as I was about to plunge the spoon into the ice cream, I stopped, my hand frozen in midair. I felt as though I were waking from a dream. What was my hand doing holding this tiny wooden paddle over twice the normal portion of ice cream? I could feel sweat breaking out all over me, and, shaking, I quickly ran hot water over the ice cream to dissolve it.

I wasn't invited to Lee's house for breakfast the following day, or the next. And then, only three mornings after Tessa had joined the bridge group, as I was on my way to open the A, I saw her leaving Small Oaks in a taxi.

I knew her destination, and felt as though I'd been slapped. There was no question in my mind that Lee wouldn't have asked Tessa out if he hadn't intended to make some kind of formal break with me. Trembling, I braced myself and waited for a repetition of the searing pain I'd experienced at the breakup of my relationship with Mike in college, for the feelings I'd come to know and expect in response to rejection—the unstoppable tears, the despair, and, worst of all, the renewed temptation to seek solace in food and pills.

I examined my feelings cautiously, probing the extent of the damage with a tentative touch. But somehow I remained relatively calm. And I was curious—more curious than hurt, I realized. Would Tessa, with her almost blatant femininity, stir sexual passion in Lee? I was able to pose the question with a detachment that amazed me.

Immensely pleased at my own reaction—or lack of it—I began to see possibilities opening up. My relationship with Lee had become confining and inhibiting; in fact, if I were honest, it had actually been so almost from the start. And if Lee's opinion was no longer to be the standard by which I measured myself, then I would no longer have to worry about making a fool of myself in front of him.

The solution to my recent feelings of misery and exclusion came to me with the clarity of a revelation, and that very morning, when Justin came in for a cup of coffee, I got him to start teaching me the basic principles of bridge.

Justin was a good teacher, and he took a half-paternal, half-professorial pride in my rapid progress. Halfway through the first lesson, he soothed my recently bruised ego by saying to Jill and Art, "Jo's a natural. We'll all have to look out for her soon. I never saw anyone pick up the game so fast."

I wanted to keep going in the afternoon, but Justin had a date to play at Small Oaks. Noticing my disappointment, he said, "I know what! Come on over and watch. If you watch carefully, you'll be able to pick up all the finer points in no time."

Never having played out a hand, aside from a few Justin had dealt and explained to me in the first lesson, I was suddenly drafted into being a fourth. Lee, off somewhere with Tessa, had failed to turn up on time, and so I was to replace him as Justin's partner against Jill and Ellen.

Terrified, I sat down to play. The first few hands went well enough; I could count my high card points, I could follow suit, the right bids were fairly obvious.

Then it happened. "Do you know what you did, Jo-Jo," Justin cried. "You trumped my good ace! What the hell were you thinking of?"

"Well, you see . . ."

"No, I don't see," said Justin. "Of all the idiotic, bonehead plays I've ever seen, that was the worst! How could you do it? The only way to set that hand was for you to hold onto that trump!"

Horrified by what I'd done, and at the force of Justin's attack, I burst into tears. I was stupid, an outsider, just as I'd been all my life. What had ever made me think I could belong? Without a word, I fled back to my apartment, the literal and figurative house of cards I'd been constructing during the past few days collapsing around me.

In the week that followed, I realized I had a decision to make: to give up bridge or not to. In spite of my recent folly, I had to admit to myself that I was fascinated by the game. It had begun to take on a mystical importance to me that went beyond the intellectual challenge, or its current dominance at Great Oaks, or even the simple pleasure of playing. It had somehow become symbolic of all the life skills I'd never learned. I'd have to try.

But where? I didn't dare ask Justin to continue my lessons.

The answer came, unexpectedly, from Fay. She knew of "a gal in Alexandria who'll teach you to outdo Goren in no time."

Still, I hesitated. I hadn't been involved in any activity outside the Oaks in two years. Could I fit in with normal people?

Finally, gathering my nerve, I called the number Fay had given me. My voice shaking, I arranged to start lessons the next week.

My father, pleased at even this tiny and tentative step

away from Somerset, sent me money for a small secondhand blue-and-white Ford, since he knew public transportation from the town was poor. (When I'd asked Lee how much he thought such a car would cost me, he'd quipped, "Less than ten cents, if you call collect.")

Having the car gave me an enormous sense of power and freedom, and I felt exhilarated as I headed for my first solo excursion beyond the town limits. But then, a few miles outside Alexandria, all the fears I'd been repressing in the past few days began to assault me. By the time I found the garden apartment where the lessons were held, I was in such a panic that I almost turned around and headed back. I forced myself to keep going—then to park, open the door, and get out. Feeling faint, I walked up the flagstone path, and pressed the button.

I needn't have worried. The fashionable suburban matrons in the group were too absorbed with themselves and their friends to pay much attention to me. As for the teacher, Connie Sherman, she had a one-track, religious devotion to her teaching that didn't include involvement in the personal lives of her students. I relaxed and began to pay close attention to what she was saying.

Six weeks later, when the course ended, I felt ready to try playing at the Oaks again, and I soon got the chance. That very night, at dinner, Justin came into the Oaks cafeteria grumbling that he couldn't find a fourth.

"I'll play," I said.

Justin looked startled. "Are you sure? I think it only fair to tell you that you'll have to be my partner. Art backed out, and Jill and Ellen want to play together."

"Yes, I'm sure. I can take it if you can."

Justin grinned. "Sold American."

After dinner we walked to Small Oaks, and almost ill with anxiety, I began to play. The game went relatively well. Justin and I were the winners, and I knew it wasn't all because of him. At the end, Justin told me I had learned a lot in a short time. A blessing from the Pope couldn't have meant more.

At about the same time as I joined the bridge scene, Lee and Tessa rejoined it. They were suddenly available to play much more than they had been since first taking up with each other. Tessa's trips to Lee's place seemed to have ended, and she began to spend more and more time on the phone talking to "Daddy," the father in California who I'd heard was paying her Oaks bills. She also began to cast somewhat contemptuous looks at Lee as she sat and whispered with Jill in a corner of the A. Her possible engagement to Brad, an airline pilot back home with whom she'd had an on-again, off-again engagement, surfaced once more as a prime topic of her conversation.

Lee was preoccupied and distant, and I noticed, almost with disbelief, that he was now treating Tessa with some of the same polite indifference with which he'd treated me when he was pulling out of our close daily association. He began to pay more attention to matters at the A again—and as an inevitable consequence, to me as well. What was going on?

It dawned on me that Lee wanted to pick up our relationship pretty much where we'd left off. Six weeks before—even a month before—I'd have been thrilled. Now, to my amazement, I realized I wasn't at all sure I was interested.

Despite my reservations, I found myself slowly succumbing to Lee's charm and attention once more. But I was determined to try to hold on to my own identity and not become submerged. When Lee first invited me to his house again I drew back, steeled myself, and said, "Sorry, Lee. Not tonight. I promised Ellen I'd be her partner."

Obviously surprised, he raised his eyebrow in the worldly fashion I'd tried with no success to emulate. "Very well, Jo-Jo. Maybe I'll hang around and try to get into a game, too."

A surge of relief and confidence in my own ability to have some control over the situation swept over me. At the same time, I made up my mind that if we did resume our relationship, I was going to satisfy my curiosity about Lee's sexual hang-ups, which had for so long dovetailed so neatly with mine. Was it because of me, or him, that nothing had happened between us? Almost mischievously, as I had the night with Dave, I decided I'd "make" something happen—just as soon as an opportunity occurred.

One morning a few weeks later I arrived early to open up the A and saw a patient in a straitjacket being hustled by some aides and nurses onto the side elevator in the main building—the usual means of transporting hard-to-handle patients to the third and fourth floors. I wondered idly what news the grapevine would bring about the latest addition to our motley crew.

The grapevine brought news soon enough—but it was not about a newcomer. The straitjacketed figure was Tessa. She had become completely psychotic, her psychosis triggered by her final call to Daddy, in which she'd heard the news of her boyfriend Brad's sudden death in an auto accident.

314

With Jill suddenly and mysteriously transferred to another hospital by her parents (did they know something mine didn't?), Justin working more and more shifts at the A, and Tessa so tragically removed from the scene, the bridge craze lost some of its momentum. I was ready for what was to be, for me, the last of those all-consuming diversions that temporarily managed to delude a few of us into thinking that we were part of the real world, and not just patients in a mental hospital, doing our best to keep going hour by hour, day by day, year by year.

CHAPTER 21

"Ah've been ruminatin' long and hard about it, and ah've decided you both need some shakin' up," Kip said to me and Lee one evening when we were all sipping malt liquor on the porch of their house. "How come y'all are always sittin' around here talkin' and smokin' and drinkin'? And when you're not sittin' around here, you're virtually fixtures at the A. It isn't right. Lee, you're too soft, and you've got Jo-Jo here gettin' the same way. Now I think that what you both need is to stop talkin' so darn much and to start *doin'* somethin' with your bodies."

For the first time since I could remember, I saw Lee blush.

I waited, hardly believing Kip was saying these things, but he went on, seemingly unaware of his shaft. "Now what ah propose to do is to get Ellen out here with y'all and ah'll give the three of you dancin' lessons, free of charge." Lee was so relieved to find that that was all Kip had in mind that he burst out laughing.

"Well, how about it?" Kip said earnestly.

316

"I've never been much of one for the light fantastic, but I guess I'd give it a try. Okay with you, Jo-Jo?" Lee said.

How things had changed, I thought. Only a few months back, my acceptance would have been assumed, once he agreed. Now he and Kip were waiting patiently for my answer. "Oh, sure," I said. Maybe the ballroom dancing would be the thing that would literally throw Lee and me together.

From the first moment of Lesson 1, it was clear to me, if not to Kip, that neither of our goals would be achieved easily. Lee looked as anxious as I'd ever seen him and was obviously having second thoughts. "Let's have a drink before we start," he said edgily.

Finally, he put down his glass and we all mounted the steps to the sparsely furnished second-floor bedrooms where Kip had carefully waxed and polished the floor and set up his phonograph.

The first record he put on was Xavier Cugat's "Green Eyes," a forties hit that evoked memories of movies featuring Carmen Miranda, and of adolescent afternoons in Mitzi's "finished" basement trying to master the rhumba, a dance we considered the height of sexy sophistication.

Kip began to show us the simple basic steps of the dance, and I became so engrossed in following his movements that I didn't really look at Lee until Kip said, "Now you two, go practice in that other room and ah'll work out with Ellen here." Ellen had been plodding along behind Kip—her feet in step, but with none of the other bodily movements, the sinuous hips and steady shoulders, necessary.

I reached out casually for Lee's hand and then quickly withdrew it. His palms were pouring with sweat, and when my glance traveled upward I could see that his shirt was soaked, his face glistening.

I tried to pretend not to notice, since he seemed to want to go through with it, and we followed Kip's instructions and went into the other room. Here, another phenomenon occurred. Lee, whose musical perceptions were so fine that he could play the most intricate rhythms by ear, was so crippled by his panic that he couldn't even grasp the basic rhythmic pattern of the dance. His legs were almost rigid, and when he did move, it was ponderously and on the wrong beat. "I don't know what's wrong, Jo-Jo. I'm sorry. I just can't do it."

As we stood there uncertainly, I thought for a horrified moment he might cry, but Kip bounded in and demanded to see what progress we'd made. Now two neuroses met head-on; Kip's urgent need to succeed as a teacher was in direct conflict with Lee's inability to learn, but Kip could see this inability only as a reflection on himself and his burgeoning efforts. The more he urged Lee to "just do what ah do, damn it," the more immobile Lee became. Kip's face grew redder and angrier, and finally, in frustration, he said, "Christ, get the hell downstairs—both of you. Ah don't even want to look at you anymore. You all are the most disgusting, uncoordinated pair of jackasses ah've ever seen. So just go downstairs and *talk* some more, hear? And have a few drinks while you're at it."

Since I actually hadn't been doing badly myself, and had only had a drink to keep Lee company, I felt unjustly condemned, but clearly Kip had linked Lee and me together in his mind, as had so many others. I saw my first real opportunity to draw physically closer to Lee fading fast.

We descended the stairs in silence, and I heard Kip saying to Ellen, "Lift your feet up, damn it." Apparently, Ellen wasn't faring too well either—and small wonder, since in her present depressive state she'd lost even the remnants of her former grace.

Lee poured himself still another bourbon. I heard the record being stopped in the middle. Then there was a period of silence, followed by Ellen's and Kip's descent—Kip with a set, angry look on his face, Ellen with a resigned, unhappy one on hers.

Wordlessly, Kip stormed out, followed by a defeated-looking Ellen. Not for the first time, I was reminded of how sick these, my friends and constant companions, were. And I was right there with them, I had to remember that. Good-bye, Carmen Miranda. Good-bye, Xavier Cugat, I thought sadly. The ballroom dancing lessons were over.

During the next few days, neither Lee nor I discussed the fiasco at his house, but I noticed that not only did he seem unusually enervated, but also more preoccupied and distant than before.

I, too, was preoccupied. Lee's reaction to the dancing had been my first real indication of the kind of difficulty that led to his being at the Oaks. I could see now how such extreme anxiety could interfere with his functioning—both as a doctor and as a man—and my determination to try to become more physically intimate with him was shaken.

Also, encouraged by my success with the bridge lessons, I'd begun to think about taking some courses at George Washington or American University in the fall, and was busy perusing catalogs.

So I had a lot on my mind when Lee came into the A with a broad smile. "Let's have dances at the Center every Saturday night! We'll let all the patients from all the floors—every misbegotten soul from Small Oaks to Four—come down for them, if they want to. Morale-wise, it would be great for them, and selfishly speaking, it would be fun for us. I'm sure I can round up a committee of volunteers to help out, and you and I can run them. Well, what do you think?"

What I really thought was that it was a pretty clear-cut case of Lee's sublimation of his own inability to dance. I decided to keep this opinion to myself, however, since he seemed so pleased with the idea.

Staff approval was obtained, even to the greatest innovation of all: beer for those patients with an okay from their doctors. I knew that Lee's sponsorship of this angle was not entirely altruistic either. If he was to be in charge, he didn't want to spend his Saturday evenings "dry."

Justin, Dave, and Chuck joined our committee readily, and we were in business. Music was provided by Evvie's ubiquitous phonograph and some hastily purchased records. We borrowed large institutional garbage cans from the kitchen to keep the beer and sodas in, and arranged with them to supply ice to keep them cold. Scrip was issued through the A, so the more seriously disturbed patients could have the novel experience of paying for their drinks, as opposed to the usual charging. A list of patients with "beer privileges" was hastily gotten together for the first dance.

It was a sensation. Everyone who wasn't under virtual lock and key came, and I realized with sadness that Tessa's continued absence must mean she was still in this category.

I was very popular as a partner, dancing most often with burly, fiftyish Dr. Schulman, a patient from the third floor. He had been a successful ob./gyn. before his breakdown, and had the sex appeal and gentleness that men who deal with women in such a way often have. Aside from the dances, he came down very rarely, and I liked to think that he came to be with me, though nothing he ever said or did could directly confirm that. Our relationship was, in fact, totally nonverbal. When I danced with Dr. Schulman, I often saw Lee's eyes enviously following me about the floor.

It was after just such a Saturday night—in the January of '55, my second January at the Oaks—that, keyed up, yearning, and slightly high on several beers, I decided to try at last to break the curious and frustrating "hands-off" policy Lee and I seemed trapped in.

I was in a reckless, now-or-never mood. After the dance, when we had toted up the scrip and returned the garbage cans and the unused beer to the kitchen, I invited Lee to come to my apartment for a nightcap. It was quiet and moonlit that night, and as we left the kitchen and I looked up at the lone figure of Addie silhouetted in the lighted window of the second-floor office, I was aware of how far I'd come since arriving, to be walking about freely on the Oaks grounds with my own keys to the Oaks kitchen and the A, and no one to answer to in terms of where I was or what I was doing.

We mounted the steps and entered the living room. We'd been here alone together many times before, but I knew—and I think Lee sensed—that this was different. I was shivering with nervousness.

I got us bourbons. Lee sat on the couch with his drink and a cigarette, inscrutable and distant, as he so often was. I, too, lit a cigarette and sat next to him. "Lee, you do like me, don't you?"

Lee seemed uneasy at the question. "You know I do, Jo-Jo. You shouldn't have to ask."

I hesitated. Then, taking a huge swallow of bourbon, I went on. "Then what's wrong? Why don't you ever try to kiss me—or, or anything? I mean, maybe it's me. Maybe I've been discouraging you without meaning to. I mean—" I hesitated but then rushed on—"I know you were interested in Tessa that way, or at least I thought you were. And maybe that's because she was so much more—so confident about herself—physically, I mean. I'm not. I'm sure you've sensed that. But I care about you so much, and I feel there's something wrong, something missing between us."

I avoided his eyes as I waited for his reply, fully expecting him to say, half-mockingly, as he so often had in the past, "Now, Jo-Jo, that feeling has everything to do with you and nothing to do with me." But he didn't.

"Yes," he said slowly, still studying his drink, "something is missing. And yes, I knew you were frightened. But that wasn't the problem."

So he was at least acknowledging that there was a problem. Thank God!

"Then why . . . I mean," I said, almost afraid to voice my fears. "Maybe you're just not attracted to me."

Lee put his drink down and with a gentle hand he turned my face toward him so that he was looking directly at me. His expression was tormented, and there was sweat on his forehead. "No, Jo-Jo. Never think that. As a matter of fact, I'm enormously attracted to you; if anything, more than I was to Tessa. I can't tell you how many times when you came to the house to get me up in the mornings—right from the first time—I wanted to make love to you. And not just because I was physically attracted to you. I care about you a lot—probably more than you can realize."

I felt wildly, unreasonably happy. But instead of being relieved to have everything out in the open, Lee looked, if possible, even worse than he had before.

I searched my mind for answers.

"Then what's wrong? I mean, I know about the nurse and everything."

"The nurse. Betty Jane, you mean?"

"Well, Fay did say . . . I mean, was there anything to that story?"

"Yes, there was. But that was just after I'd come to the hospital. I guess I was scared by my symptoms—scared by . . . this terrible feeling of weakness." Again, he was staring at his half-empty glass as though mesmerized by it. "I wanted to prove I could still—that I could still perform, I guess." There was a long pause and then he added miserably, "It wasn't easy, even then."

Suddenly he put his head in his hands and began to sob. "I don't know, Jo-Jo. I just don't know what's wrong. I'm so tired all the time. I have no strength, no energy."

I was incredulous. "And Tessa?" I said. "Was it the same with her?"

"Worse," he said. Then he began to sob again. I waited as he fought for control. "Jo-Jo," he said, tears streaming down his face. "Jo-Jo, I'm impotent. I'm twenty-eight years old and I'm impotent."

I was speechless. The moment of pure happiness I'd experienced only a few minutes before was replaced with a sense of enormous pity for this tragic figure—a failed psychiatrist, a frustrated musician, and now cursed with what he clearly felt was the worst affliction of all.

So this was it, what was behind the opaque expression, the flip, brittle shell. I felt a stab of pain and stubbed out the cigarette that had begun to burn my fingers.

I wanted to put my arms around him, to say something to ease his anguish. But just as I turned awkwardly toward him, he began to speak again. "I wasn't going to tell you this yet, but now I think perhaps it's best. My parents want me to come home for a while. They don't feel I'm getting anywhere here, and the truth is, they may be right. I've been feeling sicker and sicker. I don't seem to have any energy left at all. They think maybe some medical tests should be done."

I was dumbfounded. The thought of Lee's leaving—temporarily, or possibly even permanently—was shocking. My own eyes filled with tears. I would do something to prove my love—something that would help restore his faith in himself. "Then all the more reason to kiss goodbye," I heard myself saying.

Wordlessly, we stood up and embraced and then, more than a year and a half from the time we'd met, we kissed, a long and passionate kiss filled with sadness and already a kind of nostalgia.

Instinctively I knew what I had to do next. I didn't care where it would, or wouldn't lead, I had to be close to him. I took Lee's hand and led him into the bedroom, which was lit only by the lamp at the far end of the living room. He followed without protest.

I was grateful for the darkness as I began to undress in front of him. I hadn't forgotten about my breasts; unfortified with pills or enough alcohol to achieve oblivion, total forgetfulness was beyond me. But somehow, between my faith in Lee and the magnitude of what he'd told me, my own difficulties seemed unimportant.

I walked toward Lee, who was standing there immobilized, and began to unbutton his shirt. Sweat was glistening on his forehead. "But you know . . ." Then his voice trailed off.

"It doesn't matter. I just want to be near you," I said, and silently Lee finished undressing and got into the bed next to me. It was warm in the apartment and we could lie without covers. Lee's body was gleaming white and beautiful in the moonlight from the window.

For a few minutes we remained without touching. Then, as he lay motionless next to me, I turned my head toward him. He, too, turned toward me and we kissed again, now moving our bodies so that they, too, were close, but not yet in actual contact.

Our kiss in the living room had begun with a soft brushing of our lips, then a more intense pressure, and finally, a gentle touching and intertwining of tongues that I had found enormously exciting. Now I felt the same excitement. My body felt warm, and though Lee's hand on my stomach was actually cool, it felt like a brand.

But his kiss was no longer passionate. Somewhere between the living room and the bedroom he had changed. Now he was unresponsive, and I noticed the same clamminess about his face, his hands, and his body as I had at Kip's dancing lesson.

Oddly enough, at just that moment he repeated the very words he'd used that night. Pulling away, he stroked my face gently and said, "I don't know what's wrong, Jo-Jo. I'm sorry. I just don't know what's wrong. But maybe at home, with the right doctors, I can find out." He looked at me with unaccustomed tenderness. "It isn't your fault. I know how your mind works, so I want to be sure you understand that. And I want you to know and remember how much I care for you."

I knew that even this small emotional concession cost Lee a great deal, and I was enormously moved.

We lay comfortably and sadly in each other's arms till morning. Within a week he was gone.

CHAPTER 22

With Lee off so swiftly, unexpectedly, and for an unknown and indefinite period, I found myself in full charge of the A and the Saturday-night dances. I thought of him every day, but the extra work was an excellent distraction from his absence. I was also now traveling to D.C. twice a week for a logic class at George Washington.

I'd chosen logic because I'd found it intriguing but completely baffling at Wisconsin during the height of my Dexedrine consumption, and had soon dropped it from my program. At G.W., with nothing to lose, I felt I could risk trying again. And as the term went on, I began to enjoy the realization that not only was I going to pass the course, I was going to do well in it.

Elated, I decided to write for my transcripts from Barnard and Wisconsin and find out if G.W. would accept my credits for the fall.

Almost four months passed with no word from Lee. He stayed on my mind, but something told me not to try to contact him. He'd let me know when he was ready, I was sure. Yet I could hardly believe it when, one day in late

327

June, I looked into my mailbox and saw an airmail envelope addressed in Lee's neat, efficient combination of script and print.

The letter was short. He'd had a series of tests that showed something "slightly off" with his white blood count. Further tests were to be run to pinpoint the problem. Would I like to come and visit him in San Francisco? His parents had agreed to have me. Above his signature was written "Much love."

I read and reread the letter. I was looking for emotional reassurance, some word to indicate I was missed. But I had to draw what solace there was from the esteem implicit in the invitation, and the affectionate closing.

I made up my mind to go, if I could get my parents' permission and financial backing, administrative approval, and someone to run the A and the dances.

The arrangements were surprisingly easy. Though they might have preferred me to visit someone else, my parents were only too happy to see me venture out, and Dr. Poole raised no objections, saying as I left his office, "But ah'm still in favor of that contraceptive."

I was amazed at his persistence in the face of everything I'd told him about Lee. "Well, ah don't know, ah've seen those things change *overnight*," he went on. "Ah'll tell you one thing, ah sure wouldn't have laid there next to you like a dead fish." Used to his vulgarity by now, I ignored the remark.

As for Cunningham, he was surprisingly cooperative, and clarified a point I'd been unsure about. "You know, young lady, just between the two of us, once you've been an outpatient as long as you have—and have proven yourself as trustworthy as you have—you can really decide fo' yourself when you want to take a trip. But don't tell that to the others," he said with a conspiratorial smile. "Let's just say that every case is different."

Justin volunteered to manage the A, and Chuck and Archie the dances. I was free to go!

In the plane, I tried to suppress my nervousness at the prospect of seeing Lee again. How would it be to meet him in a different setting? In order to invite me, he must have had to discuss me with his family. What had he said? That I was a friend? A girlfriend?

I could see Lee waiting at the gate, and I was shocked by his appearance. He weighed at least twenty pounds less than he had when I'd last seen him. As I drew closer, I noted that the slight puffiness that had formerly blurred his aristocratic features was gone, but he looked pale and haggard next to the three tan and hardy young men standing by his side. "A reception committee," Lee said wanly, as he kissed me on the cheek and introduced me to his brothers.

I assumed that Lee's wasted appearance was due to the strain of living at home with his family again. I knew that his ambivalent feelings toward them and toward the Mormon beliefs that were central to their lives would make life together—even temporarily—very difficult.

We were in the car before I had a chance to say anything to him about his appearance. "My God, Lee, you're so *thin*. Have you been dieting?"

"No, not dieting. Not dieting at all."

The sudden silence in the car confirmed that I had stumbled onto something. Only then was I forced to admit to myself that his weight loss probably had something to do with the "slightly off" white blood count he'd mentioned in his letter. I questioned no more, fear suddenly touching my heart.

What I remember most from that visit are the winding roads curving around the hills near San Francisco, and at long last meeting Lee's parents: Marjorie—prim, pretty, devoted to Lee, but at a total loss to understand his behavior; and Wayne—bluff, hearty, inscrutable.

Lee had decided to address them by their first names in what I knew to be an attempt to grow closer to them and establish an easy familiarity, but they looked startled every time he did it. And it was clear to me, though apparently not to Lee, that they had inevitably and tragically interpreted the attempt as an insulting overboldness on his part.

The tension created by Lee's iconoclastic behavior—smoking, drinking, and occasionally swearing—and beliefs, or lack of them, reached a climax in the nightly crisis about cocktails. As the dinner hour approached, and I attempted to help Marjorie in the kitchen, Lee would enter and, fixing me with a tortured stare, ask, in a voice icy with fear as well as a certain false bravado, "Well, Jo-Jo, it's about 'that time.' How about a little pre-dinner cocktail?" I could see Marjorie stiffen, but she said nothing. Apparently, Lee had fought out the battle for the right to a pre-dinner cocktail or two before my arrival.

The first night this occurred I was thoroughly rattled. I knew Lee was testing his parents, but in a way I felt that I, too, was being tested. Though I would have liked the drink, under the circumstances I'd have gladly given it up for the sake of peace.

But more importantly, I had a real desire to please Marjorie and Wayne. Since Lee's admission that he cared for me, I'd begun, in some girlish and thoroughly unrealistic fantasy, to hope he and I might eventually marry, his illness and sexual problems miraculously cured. And if that were so, I didn't want to start off the very first day of my visit by flaunting my defiance of everything his parents lived by, though I doubted they'd ever completely accept anyone who wasn't a Mormon.

I also harbored some wild notion of reconciling Lee with his parents. If I accepted the drink, I knew I'd be allying myself with him against them, and could probably write off any chance at effecting such a reconciliation.

All of these thoughts flashed through my mind in a second as Lee stood there—proud, hurt, hopeful, desperately wanting me to back him. I saw my hopes for the future in direct confrontation with my loyalty to Lee, and I knew there was only one answer. "Sure, Lee, I'll have one." Then, unable to stop myself, I added, "That is, if it's all right with your mother."

Unwittingly, I'd given Lee an opportunity to be even more outrageous. "Of course it's all right, isn't it, Marjorie? Perhaps you'll even join us in a libation. I'm offering martinis or Manhattans."

Marjorie managed a grim smile. "No thank you. You know I don't drink."

"Ah yes, of course. How stupid of me."

Since it was a family dinner, I'd also felt jeopardized in my incipient relationships with Lee's brothers—Gene, Darryl, and Teddy—and a beautiful girl named Linda, Teddy's fiancée. Ironically, even as Lee continued to sip the martini he'd insisted on bringing to the table, the talk was all of missions past and planned (young Mormons in good standing were expected to do a period of missionary work) and other church matters.

As I watched Linda and Teddy, Darryl, and Gene, all full of energy, clear-eyed, drinking V-8 juice, not smoking, I couldn't help but wonder about Lee—the prodigal son returned, but prodigal still—who smoked and drank defiantly and unhappily at the table. Why hadn't he fit into the life pattern that seemed so perfectly suited to his brothers?

Despite my outer show of loyalty, I realized I was still angry at him when we went out later on for a nightcap. "God, Lee, why do you have to be so damned perverse?" I cried.

When he didn't answer, I maintained a stony silence until we got to the bar where there was a pianist he'd long admired. In the middle of some dazzling variations on "Penthouse Serenade," Lee suddenly turned to me. "I just have to do those things, Jo-Jo. Somehow I've got to keep proving they can't run my life."

Then, to my astonishment, for the second time since I'd known him, tears began to pour down his face. My crankiness melted. What right did I have to come into his home and try to make him conform to the standards that he felt had made a psychological wreck of him? What extraordinary effrontery on my part!

"Forget it," I said awkwardly. "I had no right to interfere."

The rest of the visit was uneventful and pleasant, the nightly cocktails an uncomfortable but accepted ritual. I carefully avoided discussing anything serious. I could see that Lee was too involved with his parents to think beyond them. And I knew now that, consciously or unconsciously, he had asked me out to back him in that struggle. It was a tremendous sign of his confidence in me, of a trust I sensed he had rarely given before. For now, it would have to be enough.

He was calm and cheerful when I left. It was late July, and he told me his parents had finally been convinced he'd be best off back at the Oaks once his tests were completed. "I'll be there by the end of August," he promised, "and then maybe we can have a serious talk about *us*— and where we're heading."

When Ross had wanted to talk about "us" only six months before, I'd been nervous and reluctant. With Lee, I was looking forward to it.

I interrupted my trip back with a short stop in Chicago to see Toni, who had moved there with her husband and two children. We picked up as though the six years between had never existed, and I thanked God that at least with Toni I didn't have to worry about living up to the Other Me. She'd never known me in that persona.

Then I returned to my apartment, but barely long enough to be sure all was well with the A and the dances. In the mail that had accumulated was a letter from G.W. All my credits had been accepted and I could matriculate in the fall if I wanted to.

My parents were delighted at the news and assumed I'd do just that, though I was far from sure of it myself. Eager to drive the wedge deeper between me and my life at the Oaks, they suggested still another trip. They offered to send me to see my brother Frank, who was working on a Ph.D. in Italian in Florence and living there with Beth.

I'd missed Frank. He had written encouraging letters

and we'd occasionally talked on the phone, but I felt we'd lost touch since his marriage four years ago. I decided to go. I figured that my eventual return to the Oaks would jibe nicely with Lee's. Justin had worked out well as A manager, and there was really nothing to prevent me from leaving.

Almost from the first, the trip was a melancholy one. As soon as I arrived in Florence, I could see that something was terribly wrong between Frank and Beth. I sat helplessly in the uncomfortable back seat of their Volkswagen as they shouted at each other, bickering constantly as we made a hasty week's tour up to the Dolomites and then down to Venice. It was clear that while I needed support and solace, so did Frank, floundering in the bitter remnants of what he now saw as his too-youthful marriage.

Once, I knew, I'd have been secretly pleased that Frank and Beth weren't getting along—in the days when I felt his marriage was a rejection of me. Now, my own life had changed so much that I could view what was happening between them without feeling that I had something to gain from their failure.

I was relieved when we got back to Florence, but there was no letter from Lee. Two weeks of my trip remained—weeks in which I knew I'd have to stay on as an unwilling witness to Frank and Beth's deteriorating relationship. But I had to. Though I secretly longed to go home and find out what was happening, I couldn't. My ticket was for a three-week stay and couldn't be changed.

When at last I was able to fly home, my parents met me at the airport. My immediate impulse was to ask if there'd been any mail from Lee, but some sense of delicacy prevented me from doing so right away. My parents had met Lee after *Guys and Dolls,* and on a few brief visits to Great Oaks, they'd invited him to dinner with us. Still, I knew their feelings toward him were mixed. They could hardly ignore his status as "mental patient"—not exactly the kind of boyfriend one would actively endorse for one's daughter. They were also aware of his Mormon background, so different from ours, and his proclivity for alcohol.

When Lee had come out to dinner with us, he hadn't felt at all compelled to restrain himself from his habit of drinking three or four cocktails before dinner, and an equal number of "nightcaps" before leaving my apartment later. Though both of my parents themselves drank, and my mother smoked, and though I'd never been actively discouraged from doing either, I knew they strongly disapproved of excess.

By contrast, they were, in my opinion, overweeningly fond of Ross, whom they'd also met a number of times over the years. My mother never tired of telling about "the time we met Ross at Tanglewood with a group of lovely young people. He ran over and said, 'Oh, Mrs. Rosengarten, how is Jo-Jo? When will she be home again?' He seems to be so fond of you, Jo. I don't know why you don't see more of him. Anyway, we invited him to join our picnic that night, and he did."

"Sure," I muttered, after hearing the story for the third time, "it was a free meal."

I hadn't liked being reminded of Ross, and perversely enough, their enthusiastic endorsement of him only served to irritate me and set me against him. I was still sad at how we'd parted and felt something in my life was missing—something I'd counted on for years. Yet even though I had a sense that I'd done something wrong, that I'd been unkind, even unwise, I didn't really want to see him again if it would mean a repetition of our last unhappy scene together.

But it wasn't Ross I was worried about as we waited for my luggage that afternoon.

I said nothing about what was really on my mind until we were settled in the car and I'd finished regaling my parents with an edited version of my visit. We were almost home by then and I couldn't wait any longer. "By the way, has there been any mail from Lee?"

My mother didn't look directly at me. "Yes, we've had news—some bad news. Let's discuss it when we get home."

What news? What bad news? My mind was working feverishly. Why would my parents have received direct news, and who would have delivered it to them? Was it Lee? Someone at the Oaks? His parents? Perhaps Lee was very ill after all. "Do you know if he's back in Somerset yet?"

"Yes, he went back to Somerset; he went back a few weeks ago—in the middle of August," my mother said. We were rounding the bend in our circular driveway. "We'll tell you about it inside."

I rushed into the house, not even bothering to say my usual hellos to Nancy in the kitchen, and hurried into the library. My parents followed and we all sat down. My father spoke.

"Jo, we have terrible news. Tragic news—and I hate to have to tell you about it on your first day home, but since you asked, there's no putting it off. Lee is dead. Dr. Poole called to tell us just yesterday."

The room reeled and I felt faint.

"We don't quite understand all the details. Apparently they found him slumped over his desk at his house. He was alone. He'd been writing a letter and seems to have just keeled over and collapsed at the desk."

Wildly, irrelevantly, I wondered who the letter was for, what it contained.

"They're not sure of the cause yet; it might have been a heart attack—or, Dr. Poole said, it might have been a result of his low blood count. He seems to have had a kind of blood disease—not leukemia, but something like it. They really just don't know."

The words, "He was alone," echoed over and over through my mind. The thought of him sitting in his house, in the very room where he'd played the piano for me, at the desk I had dusted—often resentfully—during what Lee had called our "clean-up parties," was unbearably poignant. Why hadn't I been there for him?

Automatically, I reached for a cigarette, lit it, stared at it blankly, put it out. A cigarette wouldn't soothe the dull ache in my chest. Nothing would. Nothing would, because nothing would bring Lee back. He was gone now, really gone. Not to San Francisco. Gone forever. I felt frozen, numb, comprehending yet not really believing.

As though reading my thoughts, my father went on. "His parents are having the body shipped home for the funeral. Jo, we're sorry—really sorry. We know how much you cared for him."

"Cared for him," I echoed dully. Such a cautious phrase. How tactful my parents were trying to be. And how cautious Lee and I had been with each other, only tentatively admitting toward the end how much we meant to each other. Now we'd never have the talk he'd promised.

And then suddenly, I felt the numbness within me dissolve, and in its place a stab of intense pain. "I didn't just 'care for' Lee. I loved him," I said, almost shouting now. "Oh my God. And he's gone."

Startled, my father got up and walked to the window, where he stood looking out.

My mother reached toward me helplessly. "I wish I knew what to say."

At these sympathetic words, I collapsed entirely, and began to weep. I couldn't get the picture of Lee in that final moment out of my mind: the upright piano on the wall behind him, his pen poised in midair; and then the look of shock—a glazed look, something like his "third-drink" look—and a body crumpled at the desk. Why had I gone on that crazy trip to Italy? What error in judgment had kept me 3000 miles away as Lee lay dying? I realized I was swaying back and forth as I cried, tormented now by a gnawing sense of guilt that turned my grief inwards. I had to find out more.

"He'd been there at least a day when Kip found him," I heard from Dr. Poole when, fighting for control, I phoned him at his home later. Poole was still on vacation, but due to return to the Oaks in a few weeks, as was I. "Kip was out of town, and at first he thought Lee had just fallen asleep at the desk. Ah'm real sorry, Jo-Jo. I thought Lee was a real fine fella." This posthumous accolade, a rare one from Dr. Poole, moved me deeply, and once again I began to cry—helpless, despairing tears that brought no sense of release.

The next three days were dazed and almost dreamlike,

rendered even more intolerable because there was nothing for me to "do"; there was no funeral for me to attend, and aside from my parents, no one who'd known Lee for me to commiserate with. I wanted to call Marjorie and Wayne, but feared a rebuff and held off. Perhaps in some obscure way they connected Lee's return to the Oaks, and his ultimate death, with me.

I woke in the middle of the night and wrote them a long letter instead, one I hoped would make them proud of him—would make them able to see what a good person Lee had been in spite of his illness, and what they considered his vices. I wanted to erase the shame I knew they felt at their "failure" and replace it with pride. I wept as I wrote, and memories flooded back—of Lee laughing at the A as we wrote our "ads," of his playing the piano for *Guys and Dolls,* of our watching the McCarthy hearings at his house together with Kip and Ellen on cool spring mornings.

Hoping to cheer me, my parents took me to their club with friends for dinner. Suddenly, unexpectedly, even to myself, I burst into tears and fled from the table.

My mother found me in the ladies' room. "Jo, you can't go on like this. Why don't I call Fred and have him prescribe some Phenobarbitol?"

"Yes, yes—anything," I sobbed. "Oh God, I feel so awful. It hurts, Mom. My heart actually hurts."

But then, as she went to the pay phone on the wall, I suddenly heard an echo of the time years before when I'd forced her to call Fred, the time I'd also thought I couldn't live another day, another hour, without some medicine. I got up slowly, wiping my eyes, and touched

339

her sleeve. "No, Mom. No Phenobarb. I think I'd better try to do without it."

Even though I wasn't due back for another week, I felt an increasing compulsion to return to the Oaks, to find out more. There must be more, I was convinced. What about the letter? And why had Lee gone back so early?

Most of all, I wondered if there weren't something for me—something in his papers that might have been a farewell. I knew that by even thinking this way I was admitting to myself some element of intent and self-destructiveness in Lee's death, but I couldn't get the thought of a message out of my mind.

I returned to Somerset, expecting to see some visible change—something to show that Lee was gone—but of course there was none, and surprisingly little shock or grief, even among those closest to Lee. Deaths, disappearances, and suicides were so commonplace at the Oaks that the news of still another—even of someone as central to the life of the hospital as Lee had been—was received with what I felt to be an almost maddening apathy by all but a few.

Fay, who was living halfway between D.C. and the Oaks, drove out for the day with me. She was sympathetic but realistic. "What a goddamn shame," she said. "But you know, Jo-Jo, it would never have worked—the two of you, I mean. Lee was a great guy, but he was too screwed up for you. He'd just have dragged you down with him."

Though in some rational part of my mind I recognized the truth in her words, they were small consolation.

When I walked into the A, Justin came over and awkwardly put his arms around my shoulders. "I'm so sorry, so very sorry," he began.

Roy Vanderman, who was standing nearby, suddenly interrupted. Roy was a lot calmer since he'd been taking a new drug called Thorazine, but his abrasive personality hadn't changed much.

"Where's Lee? Where's the great Dr. Rodman?" he asked sarcastically. "I never see him around here anymore. These guys," he whined, making a sweeping gesture to include all the A patrons as well as Justin, "don't know how to run this place. Where the hell is Lee, Jo-Jo?"

"He's dead, Roy; he died two weeks ago," Justin said, since I couldn't speak.

"Dead? Whaddaya mean 'dead'? How'd he die?" His whine was plaintive and incredulous. Then, suddenly withdrawing into himself again, he shuffled off without waiting for an answer.

But my own questions remained, and I wanted answers. None of the patients seemed to know the full story, and if the staff knew, they wouldn't tell. Kip had returned to his home in Louisiana, so he was unavailable for questioning, and somehow I didn't have the heart to track him down.

I arranged an appointment with Dr. Cunningham. "Miz Rosengarten, ah swear ah don't know any more than you do already," he said. "Ah can assure you ah'd tell you if ah did." Would he? I wondered. "Ah believe the letter he was writing was just to an old friend. But that letter and all his other things—all his papers and puh-sonal effects—were shipped back to California weeks ago."

At these words, I knew the door was closed. There was no way for me to find out any more than I'd known the first day I had returned from Italy. I'd have to live with the ambiguities that remained, and in a moment of self-awareness, I realized that perhaps it was just as well. Did I want to know that Lee had been deathly ill all along and that I had blithely ignored it? Did I want to know that possibly his death was self-willed, maybe even self-induced, and that my love for him hadn't been enough to make him want to live?

But the tragedy of Lee's death did, in the end, precipitate what I had never been able to imagine: a final separation from Great Oaks hospital.

CHAPTER 23

I made a sudden decision to give up the Somerset apartment and move to Washington. I would be studying at G.W.; it seemed the sensible thing to do.

My mother came down to help me look for a place in D.C., delighted at what appeared to be part of an orderly progression of steps away from the Oaks. My grief over Lee had gone underground, the tears frozen into a cube of dry ice that burned no less steadily for being invisible.

But none of the apartments felt right to me. We visited quaint basements in Georgetown townhouses, modern efficiencies in high-rises along Connecticut Avenue, garden apartments in new developments, and apartments carved from converted mansions near Dupont Circle. Nothing was right.

I knew why. Deep down, I didn't really want to move. I was terrified—terrified of being left alone in Washington; terrified of leaving the structure of my life at the Oaks; terrified at leaving my old friends, sick as they may have been, for the struggle to make new ones. Most of all, I was terrified at the thought of testing myself in the real world. Still, I had promised Ellen the Somerset apartment, and I felt a compulsion to keep that promise. Though Ellen was still bloated, depressed, still complaining that she couldn't breathe, Dr. Block was urging her to move out of the hospital to a room or an apartment nearby. Perhaps, I speculated, he hoped to break the stalemate she was in.

For no special reason, I took the last place we looked at, a second-floor walk-up in a relatively new building on the outskirts of Georgetown. My mother was about to leave, worried and frustrated by my indecision, and I suddenly felt that any decision was better than none.

It was a mistake. With my mother gone, desolation and futility overwhelmed me. I felt isolated in the apartment, cut off from human contact. And there were still two weeks left until school began at George Washington.

I went down to register the next day, and again experienced a paralyzing indecision, but this time it was about which courses to take. Suddenly, it seemed as if whether or not I took Victorian Poetry would affect the rest of my life. I left it off my course list, panicked, signed up for it, dropped it, then signed up for it again—each change requiring the signature of Dean Tweed, a cold, antiseptic, totally bald man with an icy expression.

On my first and second trips to his office, he was relatively cordial. On the third, he stated flatly, "Miss Rosengarten, if you come into this room one more time, you will be taking no courses here at all in the fall." I crept out, irrevocably stuck with Victorian Poetry and absolutely convinced, now that it *was* irrevocable, that I couldn't possibly handle it, and that as a result I'd fail it and all my other courses as well.

344

Three G-2 secretaries shared an apartment down the hall from me. Late that evening, I knocked on their door asking to borrow some coffee—a desperate pretext for making contact. They were friendly, sitting around in flowered bathrobes and curlers, doing their nails. They invited me in, but after five minutes of their chatter I had such an intense and painful feeling of disorientation that I rushed back to my own apartment.

I couldn't sleep, and drove to an all-night drugstore to buy a bottle of Nytol. The next day it left me feeling as though I'd been struck a heavy blow on the head.

I called Dr. Poole in the morning—truly anxious, even desperate, to see him for the first time I could remember. Poole had long since given up the role of enigmatic analyst. Ten months before, he had suddenly married at the age of thirty-nine, and he had been having terrible marital problems ever since. One day the previous winter Fay came into the A and told me the news. "They say Tom Poole had a fight with his wife last night. He was drunk, I guess, and he smashed up all the furniture in the house. I hear she walked out on him."

Dr. Poole hadn't appeared for my "hours" for weeks after that, and there were rumors he had been fired from the Oaks. Finally, he'd reappeared, but a subtle change took place in our relationship from then on. It was as though, since I knew the worst about him, there was no longer any need to maintain an analytic distance. In a curious role reversal, he'd begun to tell me all his troubles. His wife, Alice, had returned, but "Ah tell you, Jo-Jo, marriage is damned difficult."

I'd been finding our new and very unconventional patient-doctor relationship strangely comforting. But now, once again, our roles had flipflopped and I needed support, help, advice. Sounding hung over, he agreed to meet me in his Washington office at two that afternoon. He arrived sleepy and irritable.

"Let's go to the bar downstairs," he suggested, immediately putting our altered relationship on a kind of official basis. "Mah back's killin' me, Jo-Jo." I was flattered, but somewhat worried about the change of location. Was he intending to get drunk again?

In the bar, I tried to describe my despair—my sense of loss, of alienation from my new surroundings.

"Hell, Jo-Jo, ah'd try to stick it out here if ah were you. Just relax. You have the damnedest habit of always tryin' to *make* somethin' happen. What would be so wrong with just stayin' in the apartment and readin' and enjoyin' yourself?"

For once I was impressed by his observation. Was it true? Mabe he was right. Maybe I *was* always trying to "make something happen." Wasn't that what I'd really been up to when I got so terribly thin, then so fat, then so addicted? And all those phases had been successful distractions from the real business of life.

I wasn't ready to acknowledge the point. "There'd be nothing wrong with just staying in the apartment—if I had a few friends, and if Lee hadn't just died," I snapped, annoyed at his failure to give that crucial factor sufficient weight.

"Well, that was tough, ah'm not denyin' it. But you know, you're a damned attractive gal. Ah've told you ah don't imagine any guy you'd be likely to meet would kick you out of bed. Ah know ah wouldn't."

He'd done it again—maddeningly, frustratingly, reducing all my current problems to what I saw as a purely animal level. I had learned to understand his somewhat cryptic messages by now, and knew he was trying to tell me, in his own way, that he felt I needed someone to be close to, a new life with new people, but his suggested solution was so unlikely, so impossible under the circumstances, that I was speechless.

For a moment, I had the wild notion that perhaps he was hinting that he himself might be my partner in this proposed surcease from sorrow, but I dismissed that fantasy as the feverish product of my current loneliness.

I left the bar without a word—sick with disappointment at our useless meeting and wondering, on another level, if he'd send my father a bill for it.

Without calling ahead, I headed straight back to Somerset and my old apartment. Ellen was sitting there, despondent amid unopened cartons. A few books were scattered on the floor. Some of the furniture had been shoved around in what I took to have been a feeble attempt at redecoration, but the tables and cartons were covered with unwashed coffee cups and the dried crusts of peanut butter and jelly sandwiches. The windows were all closed and the air was stale. I grasped the situation at once. Ellen wasn't going to be able to handle the apartment; she was too depressed. She looked at me with lackluster eyes, registering only slight surprise at my sudden appearance.

"I want to come back, Ellen," I blurted out. "I should never have moved. I can't *stand* it in Washington. I'm lonely. We could share the apartment and I could help you get it organized." The vision of myself as a savior for Ellen as an outpatient was an appealing one, and off the kitchen was a good-sized extra room that I'd never used but that would make a fine separate bedroom. "I'll work some shifts at the A and commute to D.C. for my classes," I went on. "That way I can still be in touch with you—with everybody. And I could go on seeing Poole at the Oaks."

Ellen's expression was guarded, and there was an edge in her voice. "If that's the way you want it, Jo-Jo. But of course you'll have to pay half the rent." I was shocked by her cutting tone.

"But of course; that goes without saying. Anyway, let's try to get the place straight."

I began collecting cups and saucers, but Ellen didn't stir. Her glance was now clearly hostile.

Suddenly she began to speak. "You were queen of the walk around here when Lee was alive, weren't you, Jo-Jo? You had Lee as a boyfriend, you ran the A, had the best part in *Guys and Dolls,* were in charge of everything. And you had this apartment, too. Well, now you gave it up and I've got it. And I don't intend to get out."

There was so much malevolence in her voice that I didn't even bother to remind her that I'd intended to share it with her, not take it away.

"Okay, Ellen, I'll leave," I said. "You can have the apartment." She didn't answer me. I put the cup I'd been holding in my hand down and for the last time descended the steps I'd climbed so often.

I ran across the street to tell a surprised Mrs. Johnson what had happened, and to suggest they send someone to check on Ellen. I didn't stay to chat.

It was to be two more years before I made another—and final—visit to the Oaks.

CHAPTER 24

I rushed back to New York to fill the week and a half until school began, then returned, reluctantly, to the Washington apartment. Classes began; I couldn't concentrate. I still felt rootless and lost, out of touch with the world. All of my emotional energy was taken up with a search for something to connect to; I had none left for the life of the mind.

One day I was walking to class when far ahead of me I saw the back of a tall, familiar figure. It was Ross, talking and laughing with a boy and a pretty girl as he strode rapidly along. How well I remembered the difficulty of keeping up with him.

But what was he doing here in Washington? Could he really be working or going to school here and not have called me? I couldn't believe it. At some elemental level, despite his angry words, his ultimatum, and the long silence that had followed, I—who ordinarily hadn't the slightest belief in the mystical—continued to feel a strange, almost psychic connection with him.

Suddenly I realized I wanted to talk with him, to tell

him everything that had happened, to find out what had happened to him; at least, to be friends again. I began to run toward him. "Ross, Ross!" I shouted, almost knocking the books out of the arms of a student who had turned unexpectedly to see where the shouting was coming from. But Ross ignored me, even as I drew closer.

Then finally, responding to a tap on his shoulder, he turned. And I saw, with intense disappointment, that it wasn't Ross at all, that it was instead a man who bore a striking resemblance to him. He paused and looked at me curiously, but not unkindly. "I think you had me mixed up with someone else."

Too disappointed even to feel embarrassed, I nodded, surprised at the tremendous letdown I was feeling. "I'm sorry. It's just that the resemblance is really amazing."

The incident brought Ross back into the forefront of my mind, and for the next few days I found myself thinking about him obsessively. It was a year and a half since he'd come to the apartment and left so angrily. What had happened to him? Perhaps he'd found someone who loved him in the way he wanted to be loved—respectfully, romantically, with no reservations. I found I didn't like the idea.

I remembered his phone number in Forest Hills, and one evening I picked up the phone and dialed it. His mother answered. She was warm and friendly, though she didn't know who I was, nor did I identify myself.

"Yes, dear, Ross is back home now. He's out of the Army."

Is he going out with anyone special? I wanted to ask, but of course I didn't. And I wondered about the M.A. in Chinese studies, but I didn't want to seem too nosy.

Suddenly I was embarrassed at my call. How selfish of me to barge into Ross's life again just because my own seemed so empty and meaningless.

"Do you want to leave your number?" his mother was asking.

"No, never mind."

"But whom shall I say called?"

"Nobody. Never mind. It wasn't important." I abruptly hung up.

A half hour later the phone rang. "Why didn't you leave your name?" said Ross.

I was astounded. "How did you ever figure out it was me?"

"I don't know. I just knew you'd call someday and that I'd know about it when you did."

So Ross had known I'd call, just as, for so long, I'd known he'd be there when I did. How comfortable—and comforting—it felt. Why did I never feel the constraints with Ross that I felt with other men; the need to perform, to be "on"? And why, instead of rejoicing in that ease, did I still have a nagging hunch that his acceptance was wrong, misplaced, misguided?

We talked for an hour.

"My God, that's terrible," he said when I told him about Lee. "He was so young."

"Yes," was all I could manage as my eyes began to smart.

Ross, hearing the catch in my voice, changed the topic quickly. "Guess you don't know I was stationed in Germany for a year." Part of the year and a half we hadn't spoken, I thought. "Then I finished the M.A. in Chinese.

351

But I've decided I'm not cut out to be an intellectual. I'm trying business—real estate—and it's going all right."

Since he'd always been modest, I knew that "going all right" meant he was doing well.

Suddenly, now that we were all caught up, there was an awkward pause. The unanswered questions, the really important ones, remained to be asked.

"So. I gather you're still single," I said nervously.

"You know what I said. As long as you're alive and unmarried, I'll probably stay that way."

I stubbed out the cigarette I'd been smoking and reached for another. Here we hadn't seen each other for more than a year, and within an hour we were right back where we'd left off. Or were we? Was I really the same? Was Ross?

"My God, Ross, I've said it before and I guess I'll say it again, but you certainly don't beat around the bush."

"Well, are you ready yet?" he said insistently, almost impatiently.

Was I ready? How much more tempting even than last year it would be to get married now, to have everything settled, to be cared for; more than cared for—adored. I wavered. "I don't know. Maybe."

"I'll be down to see you this weekend."

He came on Friday and I welcomed him with frenzied eagerness. How foolish it would be to turn down Ross's offer now, I thought. There was nothing else in my life. Ross would be a safe haven. I would have no decisions to make; no worries about Victorian poetry, about being alone, about what to do with my life.

We were engaged for a day—a day in which I tried to ignore the sinking feeling in my stomach, in which I uneasily held off calling my parents to tell them the news, and asked Ross not to call his. Was this how you were supposed to feel when you were engaged?

"I think I should talk it over with Poole first," I said, when Ross—initially overjoyed at my acceptance, but increasingly skeptical as the day wore on—asked why I didn't want to tell anyone. "And since when have you considered what Poole has to say so important anyway?" he asked. I'd told him my reservations about Poole in the past.

"He's helped me sometimes," I said weakly. "I mean, I just feel I should talk it over with someone."

"It's up to you," said Ross curtly.

"Jo-Jo, you're doin' this for all the wrong reasons," said Poole, confirming what I knew to be true when he returned my call late that afternoon. "I'm sure Ross is a nice guy, but you wouldn't be doin' either one of you a favor if you got hitched up now. Ah'm afraid you're just goin' to have to get your life straightened out alone before you tie in with anyone else. You know ah've told you that marriage is damned difficult under the best of circumstances. Can't you see what you're up to? Fact is, you're just tryin' to make somethin' happen again."

I knew he was right. My reasons for marrying were all wrong, and this time even Ross agreed. "I can wait," he said.

"Don't, Ross. Don't wait. I don't want to feel I'm holding you back, and I don't want to feel held back myself."

Ross looked at me, then turned away, his face tense. "I don't know about you, but I haven't got any choice," he said.

Still unable to concentrate, I dropped all my courses,

answered an ad, and got a job as a file clerk with an insurance agency. I found the work soothing, pleasant, and the people in the office were kind. It was warm and cozy there—company, at last. I threw myself into the monotonous work and was soon "promoted" to typing policies.

One day I saw an ad: "Hartnett Hall. Room and board. $18 a week and up. Transients welcome. Maid svs. incl." The place sounded right, felt right. I wouldn't have to face the kitchen and living room in the apartment, with all they implied about a circle of friends, and a full and satisfying life.

The place was filled with students and young people in various government jobs. The day I moved in, the girl down the hall knocked on my door. "Hi. My name's Julie Anne and I'm a writer, or hope to be. What's yours?" She was a bluff, extremely gregarious girl from the Midwest who'd had her share of troubles. I had a friend now, and through her I made others.

In late summer, I was offered a bigger job and a big raise if I'd commit myself to staying with the agency. "We think you have a real future here," my cherubic, cigar-smoking boss said, twisting the diamond ring on his pudgy finger. I almost said yes, then thanked him, gave my notice, and re-enrolled at G.W.

This time I made it. I had friends now, a life away from school as well as at it, a life further and further removed from the Oaks. I saw Dr. Poole once a week in Washington. Otherwise, aside from occasional visits with Fay, the door seemed shut on my Oaks existence. But I thought of it often, dreamed of it, and sometimes longed to return for a visit. How would it feel? And what had happened to all my old friends?

Graduation came in June of '57—and with it a sense of loss, of anticlimax. My parents urged me to come back to New York, but I couldn't, wouldn't, though I had no clear plan, no ideas for my future. I had enough money saved from my job to get along on for a while, and the summer months floated by. I stayed up late with my friends, and began to sleep till twelve, one, two o'clock; turning day into night, and finally waking with a sense of waste and futility. I had no energy, no direction.

At my parents' insistence, I went to a new female doctor, a friend of a friend from New York, for a general check-up. She was white-haired, wise, kindly, interested, and I liked her for not asking a lot of questions about my breasts.

As I turned to leave after the examination she said, "Wait a minute, young lady. I don't know you very well, but I don't have to know you very well to see something's wrong. No," she added hurriedly, "nothing's wrong with you physically, but something is definitely wrong. What do you do? What are you doing with your life?" I turned back, sat down, and we talked for almost an hour. At the end of our talk, she took out a prescription pad and wrote a name on it. "Here, take this. I think what you need more than anything else right now is some order in your life. A job will give you that." She handed me a piece of paper. "This lady is a friend of mine at the Maryland Board of Education. They need teachers badly there. Why don't you give her a ring? I'll tell her to expect your call."

I was offered a job teaching fifth grade at once, and given three days in which to decide whether I wanted it. The idea of teaching was incredible, impossible. Even in my childhood fantasies I had never imagined myself a teacher. A nurse, yes; an actress, yes; a teacher, never. But I knew I had to do something. I took the job.

There were orientation meetings. At one of them a man said, only half kidding, "One nice thing about teaching is that you'll never have to wake up in the morning ever again and wonder what you're going to do today." The statement was true. The languorous days of summer were suddenly part of another life. I was catapulted into working days that began at 6 A.M. (the school was far out in Maryland) and ended with my collapsing on the sofabed at four. There was little time for introspection; little time for anything. I began to resent the weekly visits to Poole. So this is what most people did; what their lives were like, I thought. At twenty-seven, I was finally facing reality.

I marched into Poole's office one day in early January, sat down upright on his narrow couch—the Washington office had no chair—and announced that I felt I'd had enough; that I wanted to quit therapy; that I didn't need it anymore, and in any case didn't have time to come.

"Maybe you're right, Jo-Jo, maybe you're right," he said uncertainly and, I felt, somewhat wistfully.

"'Maybe you're right,'" I mimicked cruelly. "Is that all you have to say after almost four years of being my so-called analyst?" I was suddenly overcome with anger at his lassitude, and with a paralyzing sense of sadness that this might really be the end. Why didn't he say something, do something, try to stop me?

"What should I say? You seem pretty determined."

"Well, what do you really think?" I persisted.

"Ah always said you were a damned attractive girl, Jo-Jo, and ah still think so."

356

"So what?" I said, becoming impatient again. "What's that got to do with anything?"

"Ah never could understand why you thought so little of yourself."

"No, and you never did succeed in finding out why either, did you?"

"All ah mean is that ah like you. Ah really do."

I was touched, and completely taken aback. He was blushing deeply.

"Well," I stammered, "even though you've made me furious at times, I guess I like you, too." Then, to break the sudden silence that followed, I said, "Good Lord, we sound like the kids in my class."

"Well, how about it?" he said, still blushing deeply.

I thought I grasped his meaning, but I couldn't believe my ears.

"How about what?"

"How about a good-bye kiss to begin with?"

My God—I was being given a chance to break the prohibition against physical contact between patient and therapist. And I knew in that moment that I'd always wanted to; that I'd never before admitted my attraction to Poole to myself simply because of the mind's convenient trick of dealing with impossible wishes by not admitting that they exist.

I lay motionless on the couch, unable to speak, as he came over and sat down next to me. The distance in actual space was only a few feet; it was a continent in terms of the two of us.

He leaned down and we kissed, gently at first, then with more passion. He put his arms around me, then lay down beside me. And it all seemed perfectly natural—the

357

perfect culmination of all our discussions about di-
aphragms, about my breasts, my body, my self-image.

I felt his arms around me and his hand reaching toward my breasts, still sheathed, as always, in their heavy
cotton casing. Then I felt his hands moving toward my
back, toward the hooks on my bra.

Acutely embarrassed at the width of the bra's back, in
spite of all our conversations about my "problem," I
moved his hands away and reached for the hooks myself,
hoping to block out my anxieties and to sink once again
into the voluptuous pleasure of just a few seconds before.

But before I had a chance to unfasten them, he suddenly turned away, and I could see that something was
troubling him, too.

"You never did get that diaphragm, did you?" he
asked.

"No," I said, relieved that it wasn't something about my
body that was holding him back.

"Ah always said the day would come when you'd regret
it," he said with a half-smile, "but that's not what's stop-
pin' me now. Ah have what they generally call 'protection'
available myself. No. It isn't the diaphragm, though ah
still say you should get one."

"I will," I said, thinking how far we'd come together for
me to be able to say that, but still wondering what the
problem was.

"The fact is that, damn it all, ah just cain't bring myself
to go through with it. Ah want to, but ah cain't. It feels
okay to me raht now, but there's no gettin' around the
fact that it's damned unethical. Ah know it, and you know
it, too. And even if it seems okay to both of us today, it
may not tomorrow, or next week, or next year." He

paused, more reflective than I could ever recall, then added sheepishly, "Guess this time *ah* was tryin' to make somethin' happen."

Though I was surprised at his sudden attack of morality, I was enormously relieved at his words. I had found our kisses infinitely moving, tender, and comforting, but I suspected that the pressure on both of us to succeed under these unusual circumstances would have been almost unbearable. At the same time, I had a sudden sensation of *déjà vu;* the scene bore an eerie resemblance to Lee's and my abortive attempts at lovemaking. "I don't know," I said, only half joking, "it seems as if, aside from a few people I don't even care much about, my score with lovers I really *love* is pretty low these days."

He laughed softly. "Don't worry, Jo-Jo. You're okay. You just gotta find the right fella. Ah wish to God it could have been me." And I knew he meant it.

I have always been grateful for those delightful, bittersweet, completely unexpected, and thoroughly unprofessional moments, which were the last I ever spent with Calvin S. Poole.

CHAPTER 25

Brief and unthreatening as my surprising final encounter with Poole had turned out to be, it nonetheless reawakened all the doubts about my body and my sexuality that the new job and my new independence had kept in check for months. What would have happened if we'd gone ahead with it? I shuddered as I thought of how humiliating it would have been if he'd touched my bare breasts. Easy for him to say they didn't matter. Despite all my recent successes, I knew now that they still did—at least to me. After all, if I couldn't even feel comfortable with Poole, who knew my feelings so well, with whom would I feel at ease?

One day after school had ended in June, when I was trying to decide whether to work at the insurance agency for the summer, I was leafing through a copy of Julie Anne's *Time* magazine when I saw two pictures that riveted my attention. On the left was a photo of the chest of a girl with drooping, unattractive breasts; on the right, the same girl after plastic surgery. Her breasts were uplifted and shapely, the scars almost imperceptible.

360

I read the accompanying article over and over, incredulous not only at what it said, but that I'd come upon it. I didn't usually read *Time*. The fact that I had read it today, and that the article was in that particular issue must, I felt, have been brought about by a benign and directive fate.

That evening I called my parents. I'd never mentioned my feelings about my breasts to them, but now I knew I had to. "My God, Jo, that's terrible. Why didn't you tell us how you felt before? I've been hearing about that operation for several years now," said my mother. "I'll get the name of a good doctor and make an appointment for next week."

Dr. Terry Chase was blunt and enthusiastic. "You're a perfect candidate," he said. "Young. Slim. We should get a beautiful result. But how'd you ever get into this mess? You must have been enormous to do this much damage."

I liked his honesty. "I was," I said. "Two hundred and twenty-five pounds."

"Um-hm. Now listen to me, Jo-Jo. I can do a lot for you, though I always start out by warning my patients that they may lose all or some sensation in their nipples and may not be able to nurse; probably won't be able to, in fact."

"I don't care," I said.

"Okay. But I have to tell you that if you have any idea that you'll ever get really fat again, we might as well stop right now. The operation would be ruined, and you'd be left with stretched breasts and scar tissue to boot." He looked at me keenly. "So what do you say? Think you can keep your weight down?"

I paused before I answered. It was, after all, an all-encompassing question, one that touched on the matter of my faith in myself, in the changes that had taken place in me, and in my future.

"I—I don't know," I said, suddenly frightened at the idea of making such a long-range commitment. "I think I'd better think it over."

"Good idea. Just call the office when you decide."

I left his office almost in a daze and walked for block after block in the hot, humid June afternoon. Was I able to promise that I could keep my weight down? To say, at last, I'm all right and I'm going to stay that way?

Finally, I realized that my dress was sticking to my back; strands of my hair, which had come loose from my ponytail, were damp on my neck. I walked into an air-conditioned coffee shop, sat down at a table, lit a cigarette, and ordered a coffee ice cream soda.

Could it happen again? As I sat there, I tried to go back and remember how it had all begun—the helpless anger and frustration that, during my long years of therapy and even more of self-analysis, I'd gradually come to admit to myself must have lain behind the anorexia, the weight gain, and the addiction; to recall the obsessive need always to be best (thinnest? fattest?) bred in me by the second-grade trauma, and fueled by my father's albeit unspoken perfectionism; to relive my bitter resentment at my mother's self-absorption, her indifference to my needs, the chronic lateness that perfectly reflected that indifference.

Of course, I hadn't realized then that I was angry, wouldn't acknowledge it to my parents, to Schmidt, most of all to myself. Or that the helplessness I'd felt instead had masked the fires of an unexpressed rage. I'd felt then that I had no rational justification for that rage; insufficient evidence. After all, was I beaten or abused? Hadn't I had what the teachers at Woodmere Academy always called "all the advantages"?

Unable to justify my fury on strictly rational grounds, I'd therefore denied it, forgetting that the mind and heart of a child have their own relentless logic. And the energy I'd spent denying it had left me powerless to control my body or my life.

Preoccupied, I finished the coffee soda in front of me, from which I'd automatically removed most of the whipped cream and half the ice cream to a separate saucer. And suddenly, as I looked at the uneaten, melting ice cream and the empty glass, I knew that the answer to Dr. Chase's question lay there, just as surely as though there were tea leaves spelling out my fortune at the bottom of the glass.

What had happened with the ice cream soda had been happening over and over for several years now. I had actually gained control over my eating to such an extent that I didn't have to think about it anymore. And in so doing, I'd gained control over the rest of my life as well.

I went to the pay phone at the front of the store, took out the doctor's card, and dialed the number. "Is Dr. Chase there?" I said.

"Sorry. He's with a patient. Would you like him to call you back later?"

"That's not really necessary. Just tell him Jo Rosengarten called, and I can make that promise he wanted."

The operation was set for late July, the earliest date the doctor had available, and enough time for me to settle things in Washington. I told Julie Anne and a few teacher friends that I was having surgery for a cyst and they didn't ask for details.

The day before I was to enter the hospital, the phone rang in the cool white library of our house on Long Island. "Is Mrs. Rosengarten there?" said a familiar voice—one I hadn't heard in six months. I was suddenly, inexplicably happy—suffused with an extraordinary calm, a "God's in his heaven, all's right with the world" feeling as I said, "No, she's not, Ross. Will her daughter do?"

Brief pause. Then, "My God, Jo. I can't believe it's you. I was just calling to see how you were, and if you were at the same address in Washington."

"You always were psychic about me."

"I guess so."

"Still mad at me?"

"I was never really mad. More sad that you're such a dope about what you're doing with your life."

I held the phone between my shoulder and my ear as I lit a cigarette. "Sorry you feel that way. But I'm about to do something that I think will help me straighten it out a little." And I told him about the planned operation.

"Okay, okay. But I just want you to know that as far as I'm concerned, you're perfectly all right as you are. You're . . . beautiful," he said.

"Thanks, Ross. But I'm going to do it."

When I woke up, Dr. Chase was looking at me, smiling. "You're fine. Really fine. And you're going to love the results."

He was right. I was thrilled, even that first day. Under

the bandages, I felt weightless, transformed, as though a miracle had occurred. But still, the bandages had to come off, the stitches be removed before I could really tell.

I left the hospital a few days later. In two weeks, the bandages came off, and three weeks after that, the stitches were removed. When I got home that afternoon, I stood naked in front of the mirror, examining myself carefully from every angle, holding a hand mirror up so I could see the shape of my body's profile. Was it really me? Once, feeling silly, I shut my eyes for a moment, and then, frightened, opened them quickly to see if I was still the same. Yes, miraculously, I was, and I felt dizzy with joy.

As I stood there, turning and twisting, I suddenly remembered a dress. Years before, on a visit home from Wisconsin, I'd seen it in the window of a local shop—a beautiful cotton dress with exotic dark blue, light blue, and purple flowers on a white background. It had a shirred midriff and shoestring shoulder straps, a style I knew then I couldn't possibly wear. Nonetheless, I had bought it, and kept it for years at the back of my closet. I figured it was still there.

I moved to my closet and searched among the clothes. Sure enough, there it was, as beautiful as I remembered it, though slightly crushed. Trembling, I slipped it on over my bare body and turned to look in the mirror once again.

"Mom, Mom, look," I cried, as I raced down the hall toward my parents' room.

"What is it?" she said, alarmed. Then, seeing me, she stopped short and gasped. "Oh Jo. Oh darling, I'm so happy for you."

Just then, the phone rang, and turning away, my mother picked it up. "For you, Jo," she said.

It was Ross. He'd visited several times in the hospital and had called or come to see me every day since I'd been home.

"Well, who do you look more like—the Venus de Milo or Helen of Troy?"

I laughed. "Venus is too small." Then, embarrassed, I said, "I just mean I don't really look so different when I'm dressed. Oh God, no matter what I say it doesn't seem to be coming out right."

"Sounds all right to me," he said. "In fact, it sounds pretty interesting." I was glad he couldn't see me blush as he went on. "How about going out with me tonight to celebrate?"

"Fine. That would be great."

That afternoon, I found I couldn't get the thought of Ross, of his kindness, his devotion over the years—eight by now, impossible as it seemed—out of my mind. And his teasing about the results of the operation ("Sounds pretty interesting") had suddenly reminded me of the passion we'd both felt that cold night in Madison so long ago. Would it still be there if we tried again? I'd put him off so often, I wondered if he'd ever again even make another attempt. And how I'd respond if he did.

"Pretty nice," Ross said with a smile when he looked at my flowered dress that evening. But I could see that he had actually only glanced at me. For a moment, I was hurt, then suddenly thought: I should be grateful. Much as Ross admired my looks and often noticed little things about me, the details of my appearance had never been important to him. It was the overall person he cared about.

At dinner, we talked about Jerry, who was working in an art gallery in Boston, but was to come down for a reunion dinner with us in a few days. "We'll *parler en français seulement*," said Ross, with an exaggeratedly Gallic toss of the head and a touch of the manic humor I'd loved in college.

Later, we parked near a small duck pond where I could hear the occasional plop of a duck submerging. There was a sudden silence between us, and then Ross leaned over, took my face in his hands, and kissed me—a gentler kiss than I remembered from Madison. My eyes were closed, but through the soft cotton of my dress, I could feel his hand move from my back to my breast. In the reflex reaction of years past, I pulled back violently, then remembered the operation. This was what it was all about, a good part of why I'd gone through the whole thing. "Sorry," I said. "Guess I'm not used to being normal yet. This is the first time I've had a chance to—to try them out."

"Then is it all right if I begin again?" said Ross. I took his hand and put it back on my breast. With his middle finger, he began to stroke my nipple. I felt a delicious, dizzying sensation, unlike anything I'd ever felt before, and on some far-off, cerebral level, rejoiced that at least one of Dr. Chase's "possibilities"—the loss of sensation—hadn't come to pass.

"Feels awfully good to me," he said.

"To me, too."

"Want to give me a chance to see if you look as good as you feel?" he said.

"All right," I said. Yet I couldn't move.

"Here. I'll help you." He slowly lowered the skinny straps of my dress and pulled it down. And leaning forward, he again touched my nipple, now bare in the faint moonlight.

Without my dress on, the feeling was electrifying, and as he moved closer to me, I could hear his rapid breathing. Then I, too, felt my heart pounding, my breath quickening.

There, in the car, eight years later, we recaptured the strange ecstasy of that night in Madison. And as I suppose I'd known all afternoon he would, and even before that, Ross asked me to marry him again.

For a fleeting moment, I thought about my plans to sample what for so long I'd thought of as the life of a Real Girl—to me, one with a normal body. In my Real Girl fantasy—aside from sports I could try unencumbered, and exciting clothes I could wear—there were romances with new men toward whom I at last wouldn't have to feel guilty or deceptive when they were attracted to me, love scenes that flowed spontaneously from kisses to bed, a world of experimentation in silky bras, or, like tonight, in none at all. Could I give up all that? Should I? And might I regret it someday in years to come?

But then I thought of another fantasy, one that had nothing to do with the physical details of my body—a fantasy of peace and security at last, of long-standing, long-tested love, of the children that had begun to people my thoughts since I started to teach.

If I agreed to marry Ross, the irony of my having had the operation only to proceed to marry the one person to whom it was completely unimportant was not lost on me. And yet, I knew now that it was right; that it felt right beyond question. "Yes," I said. "Yes, Ross. Of course I'll marry you."

EPILOGUE

A balmy breeze blew through the window of my second-floor room at Hartnett Hall as I began to pack for the return to New York. In the alley outside a child was crying, "I want to see my mother; I want to go home and see my mother." I put down the blouse I was folding, and time was suspended. It was eight months since I'd seen Dr. Poole, almost two years since I'd been near the Oaks and fled from Ellen, exactly two years from the last time I'd seen Lee alive.

But just as in later years the occasional mention of "Westchester County," the occasional "other brown one" overheard on the street, in my home, in a restaurant, could bring memories flooding back, so, in that moment, did the sudden vision of Mary Acosta, her skinny arms reaching out to grasp my arm, her voice croaking, "I want to get well and see my mother," appear before me in poignant detail. I knew what I had to do. I dropped everything and headed for Somerset.

The route, once bucolic, was falling victim to urban sprawl, but as I drove into the center of the small town, I saw it had changed little. Here was the theater where movies never played, the dusty main street, Quinn's tavern, the broken sidewalks down which I had walked with a nurse in charge the first day I had "town privileges." I drove out the other end of the "business area" and past the large, comfortable houses with their wide porches, set back from the street, past Mrs. Callahan's rundown rooming house, past the well-kept house with my third-floor apartment where Ellen and I had enacted our final scene, and into the drive of Great Oaks.

A few patients were wandering aimlessly on the grounds near the entrance, and I eagerly scrutinized their faces. But I realized, with what I knew to be an absurd sense of disappointment, that none was familiar to me.

I parked the car behind Small Oaks and walked slowly through the grounds—by the O.T. shop on the right and the A on the left, and by the Center with its memories of *Guys and Dolls,* of the dances, of Margot's psychodrama session. I went as far as the Cottage and then turned back again toward Small Oaks. Nothing had changed—but something was decidedly different: I still recognized none of the patients I passed; not the tiny man walking along at a rapid pace muttering to himself; not the pretty girl standing in a trance near the Center, sucking on long strands of her long, dark hair; not anyone. And when I got up my courage and walked into the A, the lethargic girl behind the counter only glanced at me curiously, probably wondering, as I used to, about whether the strange face was that of a new patient or a new member of the staff. A group of young patients were sitting idly at a table talking in a desultory fashion, but none of them looked familiar either. I wanted to ask them if they had ever heard of me—or of Lee Jessie Rodman—but decided not to. What difference would we make to them? Why should they care?

I crossed to the rear entrance of Small Oaks and walked through the back door into the kitchen. There was Mrs. Johnson in her starched white uniform, wetting the tip of her pencil with her tongue as she wrote up her reports. For a moment she didn't look up.

"Hi, Mrs. J.," I said.

"Who's there? Who's that?" she asked, peering over the top of her half-moon glasses, her friendly round face with its pale blue eyes ever so slightly more drooping, her bun grayer than I'd remembered.

"Why I declare—Jo-Jo! Come here and let me have a look at you, honey." She embraced me warmly. "You look jus' wunnerful, jus' *wunnerful*. Oh, just wait until I tell Addie you were here. She'll be green with envy. Well, whatcha been doin', honey?"

I filled her in briefly and then said, "But Mrs. Johnson, where is everyone? I didn't even recognize anyone I knew around the gounds."

"Well, honey, some of 'em have gone on. Some went home, some to other hospitals, and some . . ." She hesitated. "Some died. You know, they don't tell us nurses everything. But a lot of 'em here are jus' thrivin' on these new wonder drugs they're givin' 'em. Oh, and we got a lot of new doctors here—a lot. But let's see now. What can I tell ya? Why, Jo-Jo, quite a few of 'em you knew are still here; you just must've missed 'em. Dorothy and Mary— they're still here, and so's ol' Nina and Babe. And Mariel Schwartz, and that funny Dr. Schulman you used to be so fond of. And poor Rosemary! They had her on Two for quite a while, but she started havin' her fits again, so they had to put her back on Four. And now she's back up there jus' a-wavin' her arms around worse than ever. Tria's still there, too." Tria, the beautiful pianist, whom I'd never seen, and now never would. "But Ellen—her parents came and took her back to Des Moines, and I don't know what's become of her."

"What about Tessa, Mrs. Johnson?"

Mrs. Johnson's face changed and she shook her head. "Oh, poor Tess. Her daddy came in a limousine and they drove her back to California. Had to put her in a strait-jacket to take her, I heard. But listen, honey, I've got to finish these reports now or I'm gonna be in a lot of hot water. Why don't you go on and take a walk around again and come and see me later. You're sure to see someone you know. You shoulda let us know you were comin'. We'd of had a party."

I had to smile at the thought of the guest list for the "party"—Roy with his fly open, Dorothy masturbating and giggling, Nina pacing back and forth wordlessly. Perhaps Dr. Schulman and I could have danced once again.

"Never mind, Mrs. Johnson, it was wonderful to see just you." And suddenly I didn't want to stay anymore, didn't want to know who was on Four, or back on Two, or "in," or "out," of the hospital again. I didn't want to see the A with unfamiliar faces, the O.T. shop with someone besides Evvie in charge. I wanted to keep the Oaks in my mind's eye peopled with my own ghosts, my own memories.

And I had to face it—in some remarkable, paradoxical way, they were some of the happiest memories I had. In this place of broken lives, crippled personalities, hopelessness and despair, I had found a new life, had been able to break with the past; had, in effect, been given the chance to create a new person—a synthesis of the old and the new, of the two "me's." I had lived that life intensely here; we all did. And here I had found love, lived out my childhood fantasies of stardom, learned to deal with rejection, cope with envy, face death—and survive.

I still felt pain at the thought of Lee, but the dry ice had finally dissolved. As he'd been in life, he remained a daily companion—a companion of my thoughts now; his humor part of my humor, his phrases part of my lexicon; his attitudes part of my thinking. I knew I'd never forget him. Nor did I want to.

It was almost twilight when I got back into the car. I sat there for a while as the sun began to fade and watched the nurses as they led or followed their charges back to their wards, saw the unknown girl close the A door after the afternoon shift, and—responding to an old habit— watched nervously to be sure she put on the long lock and clicked it shut.

Then I started the car and began to drive out. As I rounded the corner and headed for the main building, I thought for a minute I was having a delusion, for clattering up the driveway in the other direction came Harry Horner—cigar in mouth, shirt collar open, convertible top bouncing up and down as he sped over the bumps and screeched to a halt beneath the fenced-in porches of the locked wards. But he was no delusion. Nearly sideswiping me as he passed, he waved as I went by, for all the world as though he had seen me just yesterday. And through the open window of the car, as I drove away for the last time, I heard him calling out softly, to the patients behind their crossed-wire fences, "How are ya *now,* sonny? How are ya now?"